Presented to

baby Rhodes

by

Nana + Papa Murray

on ♡

Feb. 14, 2015

Discovering Jesus in the Old and New Testaments

the Gospel Story Bible

Marty Machowski

Illustrated by A.E. Macha

New Growth Press

New Growth Press, Greensboro, NC 27404

www.newgrowthpress.com

Text Copyright © 2011 by Covenant Fellowship Church

Illustration Copyright © 2011 by New Growth Press

Art Direction: Matt Nowicki

Cover Design: Tandem Creative, Tom Temple, tandemcreative.net

ISBN 13: 978-1-936768-12-7

ISBN 10: 1-936768-12-7

Library of Congress Cataloging-in-Publication Data

Machowski, Martin, 1963-
  The Gospel story Bible : discovering Jesus in the Old and New Testaments / Martin Machowski ; [illustrations by A.E. Macha]
     p. cm.
  Includes bibliographical references and index.
  ISBN-13: 978-1-936768-12-7 (alk. paper)
  ISBN-10: 1-936768-12-7 (alk. paper)
  1. Bible stories, English. I. Macha, A. E. (Anne E.), 1979- II. Title.
  BS551.3.M245 2011
  220.9'505--dc23

                          2011028987

Printed in Canada

20 19 18 17 16 15 14 13   4 5 6 7 8

Dedication

This book would not be possible without
the love and support of my wife Lois.

Together we would like to dedicate this book to our
six children—the most wonderful kids in the world.

To: Emma, Nathan, Martha, Noah, Anna, and Amelia.

May the gospel story, rich in these pages, transform your lives
and then be passed on to the next generation through you.

Acknowledgments

Producing this book would simply not have been possible without the influence and hard work of many. I would like to thank Dave Harvey for his support and encouragement to develop and publish this material, as well as the pastors of Covenant Fellowship Church for their example, which taught me how to live out the gospel in ministry and life. I am grateful to C. J. Mahaney for his anointed preaching on keeping the gospel central in all we do. His challenge to always "keep the main thing the main thing" was the inspiration behind the creation of this children's story Bible.

I owe a debt of gratitude to my wife Lois and to Jared Mellinger, who read through each story and offered their critique, and to my editor, Sue Lutz, for the careful, patient, transforming effort she put into this project.

As is the case with any children's book, the illustrations form a critical component. I would like to thank Anne Macha for the wonderful illustrations she created.

I love Anne's use of line work to create textures and patterns that are showcased in the stars over Abraham, the steam flowing from Jacob's pot of stew, and the sky spiraling around the crucifixion. A huge thank you to our veteran art director, Matt Nowicki, who helped Anne on this project, transforming the look of this book with his creative infusion of color.

I am also indebted to the New Growth Press team: Karen Jacklin Teears for her artistic eye and commitment to excellence and Barbara Miller Juliani for her valuable management of this project. The retelling of these wonderful Bible stories just would not be possible without these folks.

Introduction

Welcome to *The Gospel Story Bible*. We hope this book opens up the stories of the Bible in a way that captures your children's attention and fosters a love for God's Word that will remain with them for the rest of their lives. This Bible storybook focuses on the same Scripture passages used in the *Gospel Story* children's ministry curriculum. Thus it serves as a storybook Bible for parents at home and a book of Bible stories in the classroom as well.

Most Bible stories unfold over multiple chapters. The ten plagues of Egypt, for instance, are described in the course of five chapters of Exodus. That's too long to read to a younger child in one sitting. Other stories are told in more than one book of the Bible. Each one tells the story from a different perspective and often includes unique details. Read about the birth of Jesus only from the book of Luke and you will miss the wise men; read it only from Matthew and your children won't hear about the shepherds in the fields. Combining these details into one story gives you the complete picture.

It is possible to simplify Bible stories so much that you edit out important gospel connections to God's larger plan of salvation. In *The Gospel Story Bible*, we've set out to preserve this theological detail by ending each story with a short commentary, designed to connect events in the story to God's larger redemptive plan. Old Testament stories point forward to Jesus. New Testament stories point to the cross. The goal is to thread each of the 156 Bible stories like beads on the silk thread of the gospel, creating one picture with them all.

To fill out this larger picture of God's redemption, Bible stories were included from the New Testament Epistles. By combining events as described in the book of Acts with the teaching from the New Testament letters, the history of the early church comes alive.

As is true in any Bible storybook, we had to skip over "good" portions of a Bible story to get to the "best" parts, so reading the Bible itself with your children is still very important. If you read a Bible story from this book first, it will help your child understand the story more easily. Then, if you wish, you can follow up another day and read a portion of the same story directly from Scripture. To help you, we've included the Bible references within the stories and each one lists the larger passages of Scripture on which the story is based.

We hope that this storybook introduces the Bible to your children in a way that creates a hunger and thirst for God's eternal Word.

Using the Gospel Story Bible

A resource like *The Gospel Story Bible* can be used in many ways for a wide variety of audiences. Here are a few suggestions.

AS A STORYBOOK FOR YOUR PRESCHOOLER

Read the story, and then ask simple questions as you point to the illustrations. For example, point to a character and ask, "Who is this?" When your children guess correctly, celebrate their answer and follow up to see if they remember what the character did.

AS A DEVOTIONAL FOR YOUR YOUNG GRADE SCHOOL STUDENT

Start on Monday by reading the next story in *The Gospel Story Bible* to your children. Then, on each following day, Tuesday through Friday, read your children a portion of the story from the Bible itself. In the case of a New Testament letter, you might read portions of the letter each day.

IN THE CLASSROOM

The *Gospel Story* children's ministry curriculum indicates when to read the appropriate story from *The Gospel Story Bible*. Sit down on a chair and invite the children to gather around you so they can see the illustrations as you read. When you finish the story, go over the listed questions with your children and invite their comments on the illustrations by asking them who they see or what is happening in the picture.

By combining these tips with your own creativity, you'll foster a love for the gospel story in your family or classroom. No matter how you use *The Gospel Story Bible*, we hope it will draw you and your children more closely to God and his Word.

USING THE ILLUSTRATIONS AND QUESTIONS

Each illustration is designed to bring the story to life, and the questions, in the "Let's Talk About It" section, are there to help you interact with your child about the gospel. The human figures are intentionally left without color, so that all children can imagine themselves in the story. In the last illustration, a picture of people from every tribe and nation worshiping around God's throne, the human figures are filled in with different colors to illustrate the diversity of God's family.

Table of Contents

THE STORIES OF THE NEW TESTAMENT

The Stories
of the
Old and New
Testaments

Let's Talk About It!

What was the first thing God made?

What did God make the world out of?

What is your favorite part of God's creation?

STORY 1

God Creates the World

GENESIS 1:1—25

God's gospel story starts at the very beginning, when there was nothing at all. Nothing at all is hard for us to understand because we have to start with something when we create. But God didn't start with light, or the clay of the earth, or even invisible air. God started with absolutely nothing at all. God spoke into the nothingness and created the heavens and the earth. Then he spoke out and commanded, "'Let there be light,' and there was light. And God saw that the light was good" (Genesis 1:3–4). God made the daytime and God made the nighttime on that first day.

On the second day God created the sky and the heavens above. When God spoke, it happened, just as he wanted. One second it wasn't there, and the next second it was!

On the third day God created the dry land. That was the day God made the ground we walk on. He commanded the earth to sprout all kinds of green plants. That was the day all the grass, bushes, and trees were created by God. God looked at the water, the earth, the sky, and all the green plants, and he saw that it was good.

On the fourth day God said, "Let there be stars in the heavens," and the stars appeared. God designed them to sparkle in the night sky and mark the different days and seasons and years. God made the two great lights: the moon to light up the night, and the sun to light up the day. God looked at the water, the earth with its plants, the sky, the planets, the stars, the moon and the sun and saw that it all was good.

On the fifth day God filled the waters and the sky with life. He made all the living creatures of the sea, from the smallest fish to the largest whale. He created all the birds, like sparrows and eagles and ostriches and doves. God made each one special and he saw that all of it was good. God blessed the fish of the sea and the birds of the sky and commanded them to have lots of little babies so that they could fill all the oceans and the whole sky.

On the sixth day God said, "Let the earth bring forth living creatures according to their kinds" (Genesis 1:24). God made the creeping things, like spiders and bugs, and all the animals that walk on the ground, from the smallest mouse to the greatest beast of the earth. And God saw that it was good.

Later in God's gospel story, we learn one special thing from the apostle Paul. Paul wrote that God the Son, who became Jesus, created all that we see. "All things were created through him and for him" (Colossians 1:16). That means that God the Father, God the Holy Spirit, and God the Son were all involved in the creation of the earth—and they made it out of absolutely nothing! The next time you go for a walk on a beach or through a forest, look closely at something God made and you will see just how wonderful it is.

3

God Creates Man & Woman

On the sixth day of creation God said, "Let us make man in our image" (Genesis 1:26). This is special because out of all of God's creation only human beings were made in the image of God. God formed the first human being—a man—out of the dust of the ground. Then God breathed on him and the man came alive! God called the man Adam. He planted a very special garden for Adam to live in, a place called Eden. The garden was beautiful, with rivers and trees. One special tree was called the Tree of Life, and another tree was called the Tree of Knowledge of Good and Evil. God told Adam to take care of the garden, and he spent time with him there. God told Adam he could eat from every tree that grew in the garden but one. If Adam ate from the Tree of Knowledge of Good and Evil, he would die.

But God wasn't finished creating yet. God said, "It is not good that the man should be alone; I will make him a helper fit for him" (Genesis 2:18). Adam needed someone like him to be his best friend, his helper, and his partner. God brought all kinds of animals for Adam to name, but none of them were like Adam to be his helper. So God caused Adam to fall into a deep sleep. While Adam was sleeping, God took out one of his ribs and formed it into a woman. This means that the woman was made from Adam's body. They couldn't be closer, yet they were different from each other too.

When Adam woke up and saw the woman, he was very happy! Now he wasn't alone any longer. Finally he had a helper and a friend! Adam called her Woman because she was made from his own body. Together they became the very first married couple. God blessed them and told them to fill the whole earth with their children and to rule over all the rest of God's creation. God gave them the green plants and the fruits of the trees for food. Then God looked at all that he created and saw that it was very good.

That is how the heavens and the earth, the water and sky, and everything that fills them were created. When God was finished, on the seventh day, he rested from his work.

Did you know that the creation is so amazing that just one look at it, in all its wonder, tells us that God is real and powerful? King David once said, "The heavens declare the glory of God, and the sky above proclaims his handiwork" (Psalm 19:1). The apostle Paul said that God's creation is so amazing that no one can doubt that God is real. Ever since the very beginning of the world, we can see that God is powerful just by looking at the things he made (Romans 1:19–20). The high point—the best part—of God's creation was when he made human beings. All of creation reflects God's glory in its beauty, but human beings are actually created in God's image. This means that people are the only creatures who can live and act like God. We can read God's Word and speak God's Word, and pray to our God. We can write poems, create pictures, and do countless other things that none of the animals can do. But the most important difference between us and the animals is that we can be in a relationship with God as one of his sons or daughters!

Let's Talk About It!

What name did God give to the man?

What animals do you see in the picture?

What makes man and woman different from the animals?

Let's Talk About It!

Why is Eve outside the garden?

Where is Adam?

What is Eve wearing and who gave it to her?

Adam & Eve Disobey God

GENESIS 3:1—24

The wonderful times that the man and the woman enjoyed, living with God in the Garden of Eden, didn't last very long at all. Satan came into the garden in the form of a serpent who wanted to trick them. He went to the woman and tempted her to eat the fruit of the Tree of Knowledge of Good and Evil. That was the only tree God said they should not eat from. If they did, they would die. But the serpent lied to the woman. He said, "You won't really die. What God said isn't true. What will really happen is that you will become like God." The woman believed Satan's lie. She disobeyed God, took some of the fruit, and ate it. She made a terrible decision when she disobeyed God. Then, to make it even worse, she gave some fruit to Adam, who was with her. He ate it and disobeyed God too.

As soon as they realized what they had done, Adam and his wife were ashamed. They took some leaves and tried to make clothes for themselves to cover their nakedness. Later on, when God came walking in the garden, they were afraid and tried to hide from him. But you can't hide from God and you can't hide your sin from God. God went after Adam and asked him why he disobeyed. Adam didn't have a very good answer. He blamed his wife. And when God asked the woman why she disobeyed, she blamed the serpent.

God cursed the serpent for what he had done. Then God told the woman that there would be bad consequences for disobeying him. Now it would be painful when she had babies. And instead of getting along happily with her husband, she would want to rule over him. It would be hard for them to get along. God put a curse on the ground and told Adam that from now on, farming would be hard work. The weeds would fight against him. God also said that one day they would return to the dust of the ground. That meant that Adam and his wife would die. That's what God had said would happen, right from the beginning. God was the one who had told them the truth, not the serpent.

This was a very sad day. God sent the first two people out of the garden he had made for them and placed an angel on guard to keep them out. But in the midst of the sadness, God gave them a great hope. When God was cursing the serpent, he said that someday the woman would have children and one of her children would crush the serpent's head! Satan would be defeated. When Adam heard that promise and understood that they would live to have children, he gave his wife the name Eve. This name meant that she would be the mother of everyone who would ever live.

Did you know that God gave Adam and Eve some clothes made of animal skins to cover their nakedness? There was a secret promise in those first clothes. To make them, God had to sacrifice an animal. That pointed to the day in the future when Jesus, God's only Son, would be born into the world. He would come as a son in the family of Adam—a far, far off great-grandchild of Adam and Eve. Jesus would die on the cross and be punished for the sin of Adam and those who would trust in him, so they could once again be in a relationship with God. And Jesus would be the one to defeat Satan, just as God said.

Cain & Abel

After they were sent out of the Garden of Eden, Adam and Eve discovered how difficult it was to live under the curse that came because they disobeyed. Adam had to work very hard to grow things in the ground. It hadn't been that way before. But then, just like in our gardens today, weeds took over, and insects and animal pests threatened to spoil his crops. Yet even with all the difficulty, Adam and Eve could always remember God's promise that one day, one of their children would crush the head of the serpent. After awhile, Eve did have a baby boy. She named him Cain. Then she had another son and named him Abel. Cain grew up to become a farmer who grew crops for food. Abel raised sheep to give wool for clothes.

One day Cain took some of the things he had grown and gave them to the Lord as an offering. Abel brought an offering to God too—the firstborn and the best animals of his flock. God looked at Abel's offering and accepted it, but he did not accept Cain's offering. This made Cain angry. God tried to help Cain. He said, "Don't be angry, Cain. If you do what is right, you will be accepted. But be careful—sin is close by and you are in danger if you don't say no to it."

But Cain didn't listen. He was still angry that God accepted Abel's offering and not his. Even though God told Cain he would be accepted if he did what was right, Cain didn't care. Instead, he went after his brother Abel and killed him! After that, God found Cain and asked him, "Where is your brother Abel?" Cain lied and said angrily, "I don't know." But God knew what Cain had done. God judged him and disciplined him for his sin. God said that from now on, no crops would grow for Cain. He would wander the land. Cain told God that his punishment was more than he could bear and that he was afraid someone might try to kill him! So God put a mark on Cain to protect him. God said that people would see God's mark and leave Cain alone.

Even though Abel didn't deserve to be killed by his brother, his death couldn't fix the problems that sin brought into the world. But one day, another son of Adam, one of his long far-off grandchildren named Jesus, did fix things. Like Abel, Jesus was killed even though he didn't deserve it. But when he died, Jesus' blood was able to take away the curse of sin for everyone who believes in him. That's why the writer of the book of Hebrews tells us that the blood of Jesus speaks a better word than the blood of Abel (Hebrews 12:24).

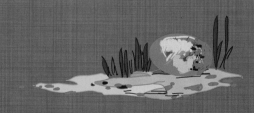

Let's Talk About It!

Who is lying in the bushes, and why is he there?

Why did Cain kill his brother?

How does our anger make us like Cain?

Let's Talk About It!

Name some of the animals that went into the ark.

What else had to go into the ark?

How does the ark remind us of Jesus?

God Chooses Noah

GENESIS 6—7

After Cain killed Abel, Adam and Eve went on to have other sons and daughters. Their children married, had children, and the number of people on the earth began to grow and grow. Some of those people obeyed God, many more did not.

God looked down on the earth and saw that people had become very, very wicked. All the time, their hearts were filled with sinful thoughts. The people were cheaters. They hurt one another and they did not love God. "And the LORD was sorry that he had made man on the earth, and it grieved him to his heart" (Genesis 6:6). That day, God decided to destroy the wicked people, the animals, the insects and the birds, and start again.

But there was one man God was pleased with. His name was Noah. The Bible tells us that Noah walked with God. Noah lived with his wife and three sons, Shem, Ham, and Japheth. He was five hundred years old when he had those sons. God called out to Noah and told him his plan to bring a flood to destroy everything that breathes. He told Noah to make an ark, a great ship that would be large enough to hold all the kinds of animals the Lord had created. God told Noah just how to build the ark and what to bring inside.

It took a long time to finish the ark. Noah was six hundred years old by the time it was done! When it was ready and the time for the flood was near, God commanded Noah to bring the animals and his family into the ark. In seven days the flood would come. Noah obeyed God. Then God brought the animals to Noah, one mommy and one daddy of each kind. When the ark was full, Noah, his wife, and their three sons with their wives entered the ark and the Lord shut the door. Huge amounts of rain poured down from the sky and great underground springs exploded with water. It rained for forty days and forty nights. The whole earth flooded and all the people and animals of the earth died just as God had said. God saved Noah and his family, but they had to stay in the ark for a whole year until the floodwaters went away.

God saved everyone who entered the ark. In Noah's day, the ark was the only way to be saved from God's judgment. Today, Jesus is our ark. The Bible tells us that only those who are safe "in Christ" will be saved from God's judgment. So when you think of Noah's ark that saved him from the flood, remember Jesus, who saves us from our sin.

The Rainbow of God's Promise

As the waters from the flood got lower, the ark came to rest on top of a mountain called Mount Ararat. When the ark had been there for many days, Noah opened a window and sent out a raven. He knew that if the raven found dry land, it would not come back. But for many days it flew back and forth above the ark. Finally, one day it left and didn't return. Then Noah sent out another bird, a dove, but the dove couldn't find a branch to rest on, so it returned to the ark. Noah put out his hand for the tired bird to land on and brought it back inside. After seven days, Noah sent out the dove again. This time the dove returned with a green olive leaf. When Noah saw the fresh green leaf, he knew that the earth was drying out and coming alive again. He waited another seven days and sent out the dove a third time. This time the dove did not return. It had found a dry place to live.

When Noah looked outside the ark, he could see that the water was almost gone. But he stayed in the ark another month, until God said it was time to leave and let the animals go. Noah and his family opened the cages and pens and led out the birds and animals so they could live on the earth and have babies again. When all the animals were gone, Noah, his wife, their three sons and their wives left the ark too. It must have been wonderful to go out into the fresh air. Living in the ark was like living in a giant barn!

To honor God for saving him and his family, Noah built an altar and offered a sacrifice to the Lord. God was pleased with Noah's sacrifice. "God blessed Noah and his sons and said to them, 'Be fruitful and multiply and fill the earth'" (Genesis 9:1). God told Noah that animals could be used for food, but he warned him not to kill other people.

Then God made a special promise to Noah, his sons, and all who would come after them. God called the promise a covenant. God said he would never again send a flood to destroy the earth. God put a rainbow in the sky as a sign of his promise. He told Noah that every time a rainbow appeared in the sky, God would remember the everlasting covenant he made that day. God didn't make that promise because Noah was a good person. Noah was a sinner like all of us. God made that promise because he is a loving God who gives us things we don't deserve. That is called his grace. Today, when we see a rainbow in the sky, it should remind us of God's promise to Noah and the amazing love he showers on sinners, all by his grace.

Did you know that when God saved Noah in the ark, it was a part of his plan to save us? That is true because one day Jesus, our Savior, would be born as a far-off grandchild in Noah's family. There was only one way to be saved from the waters of the flood: you had to go through the door of the ark. And there is only one way to be saved from our sin. Jesus said, "I am the way" (John 14:6). The next time you see a rainbow in the sky, don't just remember the way God saved Noah. Remember Jesus and the way his death brought salvation to us.

Let's Talk About It!

What are Noah and his family looking at?

What happened to all the water?

Why is there a rainbow in the sky?

Let's Talk About It!

How tall is the tower in the picture?

Where are all the workers?

Why did God stop the people from building the tower?

The Tower of Babel

GENESIS 11:1—9

Noah's sons and their wives left the ark and their families grew. Soon the earth began to fill with people again as their children had children of their own and their grandchildren raised families, all in keeping with God's command to fill the earth. All of Noah's children, grandchildren, and great-grandchildren spoke the same language.

There were so many people that they had to spread out. Some moved and discovered a large plain. They called this flat land Shinar. Although God had commanded the sons of Noah to fill the earth, the people didn't want to be scattered. They liked Shinar so they disobeyed God, settled in Shinar, and built a great city there instead. Everyone worked together to make bricks and build the city. They were proud of what they had done—so proud that they decided to build an enormous tower that would reach high into the sky. They didn't build the tower for God and his glory. They built it for their own glory, to make a name for themselves. The people had mostly forgotten about God.

God knew what they were doing, of course. He could see the city and the tower the people had made, and he said, "Behold, they are one people, and they have all one language, and this is only the beginning of what they will do. And nothing that they propose to do will now be impossible for them" (Genesis 11:6). Soon they would forget about God and reject him. So God went down to the city and confused their language. In one moment, everything they were doing suddenly stopped. All at once, the brick makers were speaking a different language from the builders. Or maybe all the bricklayers spoke different languages to each other! Think of how strange and confusing that must have been!

Because they couldn't understand each other anymore, the people stopped their building. They left the city and the great tower and moved away. God scattered them all over the face of the earth, just as he planned. From that day on, people were separated from each other by their different languages. They named the city Babel because that was where all the confusion had started.

Did you know that one day God will gather all the nations back again? People from all tribes, nations, and languages will be gathered together in heaven. On that day, we won't be separated because of our languages anymore. On that day, we will call out together with one voice. Because of what Jesus did on the cross, we will all shout out together, "Hallelujah! Salvation and glory and power belong to our God" (Revelation 19:1).

Abram & God's Promise

GENESIS 12—13

Now that the people of Babel could no longer talk with each other, they spread out over the whole earth. Different nations were formed, each with its own language. Terah, a man whose great-way-back-grandfather was Noah's son Shem, settled with his family in a place called Haran. Terah had a son named Abram. Abram lived in Haran with his wife Sarai and his nephew Lot.

One day the Lord spoke to Abram to take his family and leave. God said, "Go from your country and your kindred and your father's house to the land that I will show you. And I will make of you a great nation, and I will bless you and make your name great, so that you will be a blessing" (Genesis 12:1–2). God told Abram he would use him to bless all the families of the earth. Even though Abram didn't know where God was sending him, he trusted God's words to him. So, when he was seventy-five years old, Abram moved away from Haran with Sarai, Lot, their servants, and everything they owned. Remember, outside his own country, Abram wouldn't have understood the languages of people he would meet, but God gave Abram faith to obey. God was about to start his plan to rescue people from the curse that came when Adam and Eve first sinned. Along the way Abram sinned too, but God didn't leave Abram.

When Abram passed through a land called Canaan, the Lord appeared to him and promised to give the land to Abram and his children. Abram built an altar to the Lord and then continued on his journey. When he arrived safely in Bethel he built another altar to the Lord. After a great famine forced Abram to move to Egypt, he returned to Bethel to live. In all their travels the Lord blessed Abram and Lot. Their flocks of animals grew and grew until they filled the land.

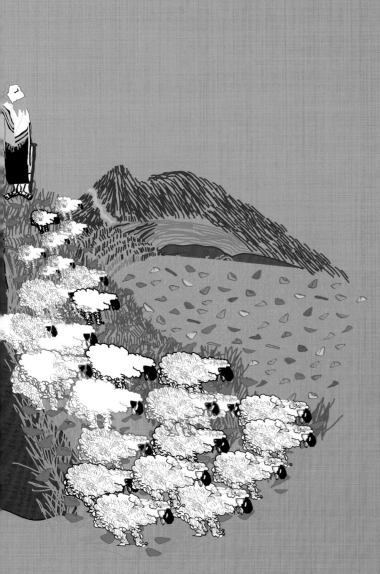

Let's Talk About It!

What is Lot looking at and what is Abram looking at?

Would you rather live in a town or in the country?

What did God give Abram that was better than living in town?

rivers, and streams. With his family and herds, Lot traveled away from Abram. He went to the cities of the valley and pitched his tent near the city called Sodom.

After Lot left, the Lord spoke to Abram and said, "Lift up your eyes and look from the place where you are, northward and southward and eastward and westward, for all the land that you see I will give to you and to your offspring forever" (Genesis 13:14–15). God told Abram he would have so many children and grandchildren that they could not be counted, just like the specks of dust on the earth can't be counted. Lot chose the best piece of land, but Abram received the promise of God. Through Abram we have all been blessed, just as God promised, because it is by the death and resurrection of his great-far-off grandson Jesus that all those who believe inherit the promise of Abram forever!

After awhile, there wasn't enough room for Abram and Lot to stay together. Each of their flocks needed so much land for food and water, even their shepherds began to argue. When Abram saw that they were running out of space, he asked Lot to choose where he wanted to live. If Lot wanted to go to the left, Abram would go to the right. Lot chose to live in a beautiful valley with lots of grass,

17

God Makes a Covenant with Abram

GENESIS 15

Abram, his wife, and all their herds and flocks settled at Hebron. That was the place where God told Abram he would have so many children that they would be like the dust of the earth. But time went by and still Abram did not have a son to fulfill the promise God gave to him. But the Lord did not forget Abram. He spoke to Abram again and said, "Fear not, Abram, I am your shield; your reward shall be very great" (Genesis 15:1). Abram reminded the Lord that he still did not have any children. "Who will carry on for me after I die?" he asked.

The Lord told Abram he would certainly have a son to carry on after he died. He told Abram, "Look up in the sky and count the stars. Can you even do it? That's how many children you will have someday." Abram believed what God told him. The Lord saw Abram's faith and "counted it to him as righteousness" (Genesis 15:6). Abram was a sinner like us, but he put his faith in God's plan.

God told Abram to bring some animals to make a sacrifice. When the sacrifice was all ready, according to the Lord's directions, Abram fell into a deep sleep. Then the Lord told Abram what would happen in the future: Abram's family would end up in another land as slaves and suffer for four hundred years. After that, the Lord would bring them back to Canaan with many possessions. (And that is exactly what God did through Moses hundreds of years later when he delivered God's people from Egypt.)

Later, when the sun was completely down and it was dark, a smoking pot and a flaming torch appeared out of nowhere. They passed down the middle of Abram's offering as it was lying on the ground. The flaming torch was a sign of God's promise to Abram. Again, God promised to give Abram's children all the land around them. God called his promise a covenant, like the promise he made with Noah about the rainbow. And since God always keeps his promises, Abram could be sure he would one day have a son.

Do you know that part of this story is especially for us? The apostle Paul tells us that the words God spoke about Abram's faith—"counted it to him as righteousness"—were written for us (Romans 4:22–24). If we believe that Jesus died for our sins and that God raised Jesus from the dead, our faith will be counted to us as righteousness just like Abram's was. That is God's promise to us. We are not saved by the good things we do. Like Abram, we are saved when we trust in what Jesus did for us. Since God always keeps his promises, we can be sure that if we believe God, we will be saved and spend eternity with God in heaven. Then one day we will even get to talk to Abram!

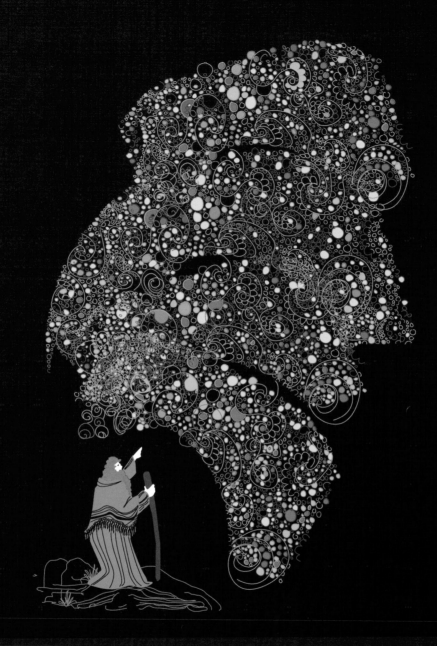

Let's Talk About It!

How many stars can you count?

What did God promise Abram?

How are you and I like the stars in the sky?

God Gives Abram a New Name

GENESIS 17:1—10, 15—21

Almost twenty-five years had passed since God called Abram to go to Canaan. It had been more than ten years since God first promised Abram that he would have a son, but Sarai, Abram's wife, still had no children. Now almost anyone would have said that she was too old to even try. But when Abram was ninety-nine years old, God spoke to him again and reminded him of his promise. He even gave Abram a new name. God said, "Behold, my covenant is with you, and you shall be the father of a multitude of nations. No longer shall your name be called Abram, but your name shall be Abraham, for I have made you the father of a multitude of nations. I will make you exceedingly fruitful, and I will make you into nations, and kings shall come from you" (Genesis 17:4—6).

God told Abraham something very special. He said that his covenant with Abraham would be an everlasting covenant for all generations. That meant it was a promise that would last forever. Again God reminded Abraham of his promise to give him and his children the land of Canaan. Then God commanded Abraham to circumcise all the men

who lived with him as a sign of the covenant. Abraham obeyed God.

God also changed Sarai's name. From now on she would be called Sarah. Not only was Sarah going to have children, but God was going to bless Sarah with a firstborn baby boy! Abraham fell down to the ground and laughed. How could a woman who was ninety years old have a baby? But God assured Abraham that it would all come true. He said that when the son was born, Abraham should name him Isaac. Then God promised to keep the covenant with Isaac and all of Isaac's children after him.

Did you know that God had something very special in mind when he made his covenant with Abraham? When God said he would keep the covenant with Abraham's children, he was thinking all the way to Jesus. That is because Jesus was born as a son in the family line of Abraham! When God told Abraham that kings would come from him (Genesis 17:6), he was looking ahead to the kings that would come, like Saul, David, and Solomon. But most of all he was pointing to the greatest king of all, King Jesus.

Let's Talk About It!

What did God promise Abraham?

Why was God's promise so hard to believe?

Who are some of the people in Abraham's family tree?

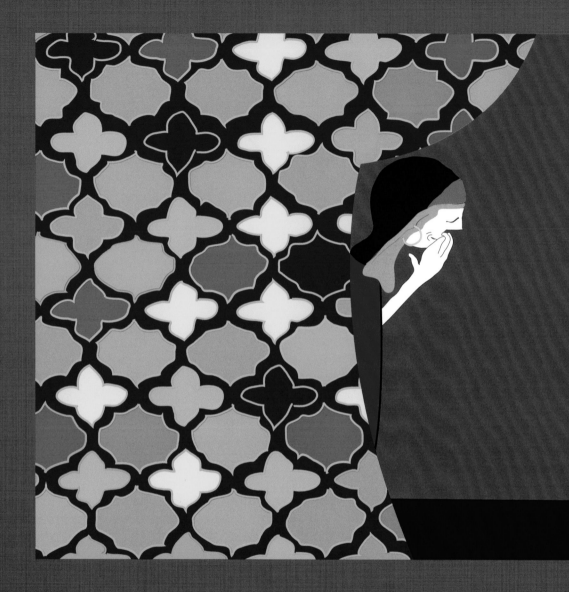

Let's Talk About It!

What did God promise Sarah?

Why did Sarah laugh?

Why did Sarah try to hide her laugh from God?

The Lord Appears to Abraham

After the Lord changed Abram's name to Abraham, he appeared to him again. This time he visited Abraham at his home and brought along two angels. Abraham was resting by his tent during the hottest part of the day when, all of a sudden, he looked up and saw three men standing nearby. As soon as he saw them, Abraham ran to greet them. He bowed down before them and said, "O Lord, if I have found favor in your sight, do not pass by your servant. Let a little water be brought, and wash your feet, and rest yourselves under the tree, while I bring a morsel of bread" (Genesis 18:3–5). The Lord agreed to stay and Abraham ran off to find Sarah.

"Quick," he said to her. "Take some flour and knead it into bread." Then Abraham ran to his herds of cattle, found a calf, and gave it to a young man to prepare for a meal. When the meal was ready, Abraham carried it to the men, who were sitting under the trees that grew near his tents. He set the meal before them and stood by as they ate.

The Lord asked Abraham, "Where is your wife Sarah?" "She is there in the tent," Abraham replied. Then the Lord said, "I will surely return to you about this time next year, and Sarah your wife shall have a son" (Genesis 18:10). Sarah was standing near the tent door, listening to what God was saying. Because she was very old, she laughed at what he said. She thought it was impossible. She told herself, "I am too old to have children." The Lord heard Sarah and asked Abraham, "Why did Sarah laugh? Is anything too hard for the Lord?" Then God repeated his promise that Sarah would have a son next year. Sarah lied and said she didn't laugh because she was afraid. But the Lord corrected Sarah and said, "Yes, you did laugh," yet he did not punish her.

After their meal, the three men stood up to continue their journey. Abraham walked with them to see them on their way. While they were walking, the Lord told Abraham that he planned to make him a great and powerful nation and he chose Abraham that he might obey God and direct his children to follow the way of the Lord.

A year after this meeting, God did give Abraham a son, and through his son Abraham had many children and grandchildren. But God had an even bigger family in mind when he said that Abraham would be the father of a multitude. You see, God calls everyone who follows Jesus a son of Abraham (Galatians 3:7). When the Lord told Abraham his children would be as numerous as the stars of the sky, God had in mind a family of faith even bigger than Abraham's natural family. Everyone who believes in Jesus is a part of God's family of faith and is a child of Abraham.

God Rescues Lot

GENESIS 18:22—33; 19:1—3, 12—29

After the Lord and the two angels finished their visit with Abraham, they headed toward the sinful cities of Sodom and Gomorrah. When Abraham learned that the Lord planned to destroy the cities because they were so wicked, he began to worry for he knew his nephew Lot lived near there. He asked the Lord, "Suppose there are fifty righteous within the city. Will you then sweep away the place and not spare it for the fifty righteous who are in it?" (Genesis 18:24). The Lord replied, "If I find at Sodom fifty righteous in the city, I will spare the whole place for their sake" (Genesis 18:26). Still, Abraham kept questioning the Lord's plan and asked again, "What about forty-five? What about thirty? What if twenty or only ten righteous are found?" Finally, the Lord promised Abraham that if ten righteous people could be found in Sodom, he would spare the whole city.

The two angels went on to Sodom and Gomorrah. Just outside the city, they met Lot and stayed at his house. Even from Lot's home, they could see that the city was a very, very wicked place. There weren't even ten righteous people in the city. The angels warned Lot that the cities would soon be destroyed. They told him to take his family and run away to safety. Lot passed along the angels' warning to the men who were pledged to marry his daughters, but they just laughed. They thought he was joking. When morning came, there was no time left. The angels urged Lot to take his family and run, but even then, Lot was slow to leave.

Finally, the angels grabbed Lot by the hand and pulled his family out of the city. God had mercy on them. The angels urged them to run from the valley and escape to the hills, but because the hills were far away, Lot asked if they could run to the city of Zoar instead. The angels agreed. But they warned Lot and his family not to look back or stop on their journey. When Lot reached Zoar, God rained sulfur and fire down from heaven to destroy Sodom and Gomorrah. When the fiery rains began, Lot's wife disobeyed the angels' warning and turned back to look. Just like that, she turned into a pillar of salt! But Lot and his daughters were rescued because they obeyed the angels.

Did you know that God has a plan to rescue us too? Like Lot, we are all sinners who live in a sinful land. We all need God's merciful rescue. Without it, we will all be punished in the fires of hell that never end. But when Jesus died on the cross, he took the punishment we deserved for our sin. God calls us to believe in what Jesus did, run away from sin, and put our faith in God's plan to save us. But just like Lot, we are stubborn. We want to stay in our world of sin, so God reaches down and gives us the faith we need to believe. Then God draws us away from sin to the safety of his Son Jesus.

Let's Talk About It!

Why are the angels in a hurry?
What will happen if Lot and his family don't leave town?
Where do you think the angels are pointing?

Let's Talk About It!

What do Hagar and Ishmael need to survive?
What is Hagar doing?
What is hidden among the bushes?

Isaac & Ishmael

It was hard for Abraham to keep believing God's promise year after year. While he was waiting for God to give Sarah a son, he took a second wife—Sarah's maid, Hagar—and had a son with her. He named the boy Ishmael. But God had not forgotten his promise to Abraham. Ishmael was not the child God had promised to give Abraham and Sarah. So, one year after God visited Abraham and promised him a son, Sarah had her own baby boy! Abraham and Sarah named him Isaac, just as the Lord had directed them. The name Isaac means laughter. Do you remember when Sarah laughed inside the tent? She couldn't believe it when she heard God promise to give her a son. But now that God's promise had come true, Sarah was filled with joy. She said, "God has made laughter for me" (Genesis 21:6), because she knew that people would laugh with happiness when they heard her story. Imagine a woman older than a grandmother having a baby!

Later, when Abraham had a celebration for his son Isaac, his older son Ishmael laughed in a mocking way. He was jealous of Isaac. When Sarah heard him, she told Abraham to send Ishmael and Hagar away. Abraham didn't like that idea, but God told Abraham he should do what Sarah wanted. God already had a plan to take care of them. God said that Isaac, not Ishmael, would carry on Abraham's name. But God comforted Abraham at the same time. He promised to bless Ishmael and make him into a great nation too. So Abraham sent Hagar and Ishmael away into the wilderness with some bread and a skin of water.

Hagar and Ishmael wandered in the wilderness until they ran out of water. In the hot sun, they would soon die without it. Hagar was afraid for her son and laid him in the shade. She cried out for help and the Lord heard her. Just as he had promised Abraham, God told Hagar, "Don't be afraid. I am going to make your son into a great nation." Then God opened Hagar's eyes to see a nearby well of water. She took the empty water skin, filled it, and gave it to her son to drink. The water saved Ishmael. He grew up in the wilderness and married a woman from Egypt. Soon he began his own family.

Did you know that God waited a long time to give Abraham and Sarah a child on purpose? God always has a reason behind everything he does. God wanted everyone to know that Isaac was born because of God's special promise—not because of Abraham and Sarah's natural strength. God waited until Abraham and Sarah were so old that no one could doubt that Isaac's birth was a miracle of God. Today, everyone who believes in Jesus is adopted into God's family as one of Abraham's children. That is even more of a miracle because, as sinners, all we deserve is punishment. But because of what Jesus did on the cross we can be forgiven of our sin and become a part of the family of God.

Abraham Is Tested

GENESIS 22:1–19

When Isaac was still a boy, God called out to test Abraham. God said, "Take your son, your only son Isaac, whom you love, and go to the land of Moriah, and offer him there as a burnt offering" (Genesis 22:2). Imagine that—God was asking Abraham to kill his only son! Abraham had waited so long for Isaac and now God was asking him to give him up. It didn't seem to make any sense, but Abraham's faith in God's plan was great. So in the morning, Abraham set off to obey God. He took Isaac, cut wood for the offering, saddled up his donkey, and instructed two young servants to travel along with them. Then Abraham and his son began the trip to the place God showed him.

The next day, as they got close to the place, Abraham told his servants to stay behind with the donkey while he and Isaac went on ahead to worship the Lord. We might wonder why Abraham would be willing to kill his only son. That is not something God ever asked anyone else to do! The writer of Hebrews gives us the answer: Abraham believed that God could raise his son from the dead (Hebrews 11:19)! Abraham's faith and love for God were even greater than his love for Isaac. He had no doubt that God would keep his promises, even though he didn't understand God's whole plan. One thing he was sure of: he could trust the Lord.

As they were walking, Isaac could see that they had wood and fire for the sacrifice, but they didn't have a lamb. So he asked his father, "Where is the lamb for a burnt offering?" Abraham replied, "God will provide for himself the lamb for a burnt offering, my son" (Genesis 22:7–8). When they got to the right place, Abraham built an altar and placed the wood on top. Then Abraham tied up Isaac and laid him on the altar. But when Abraham took out a knife to kill Isaac, the Lord called out from heaven, shouting his name. "Abraham! Abraham!" Abraham stopped and said to God, "Here I am." The Lord said to him, "Do not lay your hand on the boy or do anything to him, for now I know that you fear God, seeing you have not withheld your son, your only son, from me" (Genesis 22:12). Abraham looked up, and do you know what he saw? There was a ram whose horns were caught in some bushes. Abraham took the ram and sacrificed it instead of his son. Then God reminded Abraham of his promise to bless him, and Abraham and Isaac traveled home.

Did you know that God gives us a picture of his salvation through this story? Abraham's sacrifice of his only son is a lot like God the Father's sacrifice of his only Son Jesus. There is one big difference. God didn't stop the sacrifice of his Son at the last second like he did with Abraham. Jesus had to die. The ram caught in the bushes is also a picture of our salvation. It was killed instead of Isaac as a substitute. Jesus, the Lamb of God, is our substitute. Jesus died in our place so we could live. Without him, we all deserve death because of our sin against God. The story of Abraham and the sacrifice of Isaac gave Israel a hint of God's saving plan. Now, looking back, it is easy for us to see the connection.

Let's Talk About It!

Where is Isaac in the picture?

Who put the ram in the bushes?

What is Abraham supposed to do to the ram?

God Provides a Wife for Isaac

GENESIS 24

The Lord blessed Abraham, and Isaac grew older. When it was time for Isaac to be married, Abraham sent his most trusted servant to find a wife for him. He told the servant to travel back to the country where his relatives lived. He didn't want him to choose a wife from the local Canaanite people. The servant didn't have as much faith in God as Abraham

did. "What should I do if the woman I choose doesn't want to come back to this land?" Abraham encouraged his servant's faith. He said, "The Lord will send an angel ahead of you to give you success." The servant promised to obey Abraham's directions. He took all kinds of wonderful gifts with him and traveled to the city of Nahor, where Abraham's relatives lived.

When Abraham's servant reached Nahor, he rested his camels near a well outside the city. This was where the women would come in the evening to draw water. The servant prayed, "O Lord, give me success today." He asked God for a sign to guide him to the right wife for Isaac. The servant would ask a woman for a drink. If she offered water to the camels too, the servant would know she was the wife God had chosen for Isaac.

Even before he finished praying, a young woman named Rebekah came to the well to fill her water jar. The servant went to meet her and asked her for a drink. Rebekah quickly poured him a drink and then she said, "I'll draw water for your

camels too." The servant knew she must be the one! When she finished with the camels, he gave her two gold bracelets and a gold ring. He asked her what family she came from. When she told him the name of her grandfather, the servant knew it was Abraham's brother! Rebekah invited him to come to the family home and stay the night. The servant bowed and worshiped God for giving him success.

Rebekah ran all the way home and the servant followed. When he arrived, the servant told Rebekah's family everything that had happened. He told them about his journey, his prayer, and how God answered him. Rebekah's family could see God's blessing in it all. They asked her, "Will you go with this man and marry Isaac?" and Rebekah said yes! So the servant left with Rebekah the very next day. When they got close to home, they met Isaac. The servant told Isaac the whole story. Isaac brought Rebekah home. He loved Rebekah and he married her.

Abraham was right—God provided a wife for his son. You see, by the time Isaac needed a wife, Abraham's faith was strong because it had been tested. He believed God's promise to make his descendants as numerous as the stars and a blessing to all nations. That meant Isaac needed a wife to carry on the promise of many children and grandchildren. One day Jesus would be born into this family, and God's promise to bless all the nations would come through him. Today we are called to believe as well. God promises to give us everlasting life in heaven if we turn from our sin and place our trust in Jesus. Reading the stories of Abraham's life and the ways God kept his promises can help our faith grow because we see that God is a promise-keeping God.

Let's Talk About It!

What did Abraham send his servant to do?

How did the servant know Rebekah was the right woman for Isaac to marry?

What gifts did the servant give Rebekah?

Let's Talk About It!

How are Jacob and Esau different?

What is Jacob cooking?

What did Esau give away to get some food?

Jacob & Esau

GENESIS 25:19—34

Isaac was forty years old when he married Rebekah. The years went by, but Rebekah did not have any babies. She was barren. So Isaac asked God to bless them with children. The Lord heard Isaac's prayer and soon Rebekah became pregnant. She didn't know it at first, but God gave her twin boys. Before they were born, the two babies struggled inside her womb. That made Rebekah a little nervous, so she prayed to the Lord to ask him what was happening. The Lord said to her, "Two nations are in your womb, and two peoples from within you shall be divided; the one shall be stronger than the other, the older shall serve the younger" (Genesis 25:23).

When the two boys were born, they were very different. The firstborn boy had red hair all over his body, so they named him Esau, which means "hairy." Right behind him was his brother, holding onto Esau's heel. They named him Jacob, which means "heel-grabber." It seemed he was trying to keep his brother from being born first! Esau grew up and became a hunter, a man of the outdoors. Jacob was quiet and preferred to stay at home. As they grew older, Isaac loved his son Esau and the meat from the animals he hunted. Rebekah loved her son Jacob, who spent time with her around the tents.

One day Jacob was at home cooking a stew while Esau was out in the field. When Esau came home, he was very tired. He saw the red stew his brother was making and said, "Let me eat some of that red stew, for I am exhausted!" (Genesis 25:30). Jacob made Esau a deal: if Esau agreed to sell Jacob his birthright, he could have some stew. The birthright was a special honor that belonged to the firstborn son. It meant that he would have a greater inheritance when his father died. But Esau didn't care. He told Jacob, "Look, I'm so hungry I'm about to die. What good is the birthright to me?" Jacob challenged him to make an oath to keep his promise. Esau was so hungry that he foolishly agreed, and sold his birthright to Jacob for a piece of bread and a bowl of stew.

Did you know that this story is told again in the New Testament? Paul told the Romans that it was God's plan for Esau to serve his younger brother Jacob (Romans 9:11–12). God wanted everyone to know that he didn't have to follow the traditions of man and choose the oldest son. In fact, even before they were born, God planned to use Jacob to continue the covenant he made with Isaac. That way, everyone would know that God's choice wasn't based on Jacob's good works, but on God's mercy. The same is true for us. When God saves us through Jesus, it's all by his grace. It's not based on who we are or what we have done.

Jacob's Lie

GENESIS 27

When Isaac was old, blind, and close to death, he sent for Esau, his older son. Isaac said, "Take your weapons, your quiver and your bow, and go out to the field and hunt game for me, and prepare for me delicious food, such as I love, and bring it to me so that I may eat, that my soul may bless you before I die" (Genesis 27:3–4).

Isaac's wife, Rebekah, was listening. She wanted her younger son Jacob to receive the blessing. So she came up with a plan to trick her husband. She would prepare the same delicious food that Isaac liked and have Jacob bring it to Isaac. Isaac would think he was Esau and give the blessing to Jacob instead. But when she told Jacob her plan, he was concerned. "My brother Esau is a hairy man and I am a smooth man. If my father touches me, he might think I am mocking him."

So Rebekah planned a disguise for Jacob that would make him smell and feel like his brother. She put goatskins on his arms and neck to make them feel hairy. Jacob put on his brother's clothes so that he would smell like Esau. Then he took the food his mother prepared and went in to his father. He lied and said he was Esau, but Isaac wasn't so sure. "Come closer," he said, "so that I can feel you and be sure that you are really my son Esau." When Isaac touched the hairy goatskins on Jacob's arms and neck and smelled

Esau's clothes, he was fooled. Isaac took the food and gave his blessing to Jacob instead of Esau.

No sooner did Jacob leave when Esau came in. Esau had also prepared a meal, but it was too late. Now the lie was discovered. Isaac realized what Jacob had done, and he told Esau that his blessing had been stolen by his younger brother. Esau cried out and said, "Is he not rightly named Jacob? For he has cheated me these two times. He took away my birthright, and behold, now he has taken away my blessing" (Genesis 27:36). Isaac told Esau that now he, the older brother, would have to serve Jacob because the blessing had gone to him. Esau begged for his own blessing, but there was nothing more to give. Esau became very angry and threatened to kill Jacob. When Rebekah heard this, she made a plan to send Jacob away.

In this story we see that, even in Jacob's sin, God's plan is accomplished. God "works all things according to the counsel of his will" (Ephesians 1:11). God planned for our salvation to come through the line of Jacob, all the way to Jesus. Nothing, not even sin, can mess up God's plan. So even though Isaac ignored God's plan to bless Jacob over Esau, and even though Rebekah deceived Isaac, tricking him into blessing his younger son, God's plan was still accomplished.

Let's Talk About It!

Why is Isaac lying in bed?

Who is kneeling beside the bed?

Why does he have goatskins covering his arms?

Let's Talk About It!

Where does the stairway in Jacob's dream go?

Who is walking up and down the stairs?

Who does the stairway represent?

Jacob's Dream

GENESIS 28:3—22

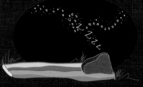

As you can imagine, Esau was pretty angry when he discovered that Jacob had stolen his blessing. When Rebekah heard Esau threaten to kill Jacob because of it, she came up with a plan to protect Jacob. She told Isaac she didn't want Jacob to marry one of the Canaanite women who lived nearby. Isaac listened to Rebekah and called for Jacob. He commanded him not to take a wife from the Canaanites but to return to the land of Paddan-aram, to his uncle Laban's family, and find a wife there. Isaac blessed Jacob again and said, "God Almighty bless you and make you fruitful and multiply you, that you may become a company of peoples" (Genesis 28:3). Isaac asked God to give the blessing of Abraham to his son and then sent him on his way.

So Jacob left his parents and escaped his brother's anger. He traveled toward Paddan-aram, the land where God had called his grandfather, Abraham. When it got dark Jacob set up camp for the night. He used a stone as a pillow for his head and went to sleep. Soon he began to dream. In his dream he saw a kind of ladder or stairway. The steps of the stairway started on the earth and reached up to the heavens. Angels were walking up and down on it and the Lord stood above it all.

The Lord said, "I am the LORD, the God of Abraham your father and the God of Isaac. The land on which you lie

I will give to you and to your offspring. Your offspring shall be like the dust of the earth, and you shall spread abroad to the west and to the east and to the north and to the south, and in you and your offspring shall all the families of the earth be blessed" (Genesis 28:13–14). The Lord told Jacob that he would be with him wherever he traveled. He would never leave him and always protect him.

When Jacob woke up, he felt the Lord's presence. That made him a little afraid because God is so holy and so powerful. He had never experienced anything like that before! When it was time to get up the next morning, Jacob took the stone he had used for a pillow and set it up as a pillar to mark the spot. He named the place "Bethel." He promised God that, if he would protect him on his journey and allow him to return, he would serve the Lord and give back to God a tenth of all God gave him.

Did you know that Jesus connected his life to this story? He told his disciples that he was the stairway that leads to heaven (John 1:51). In fact, Jesus is the only way for us to get to heaven. Jesus said, "I am the way, and the truth, and the life. No one comes to the Father except through me" (John 14:6).

Jacob & Rachel

After his dream, Jacob continued his journey to the land of his relatives, where he would look for a wife. When he was getting close to the land of Laban, his mother's brother, he saw a well where shepherds were gathered. They were waiting until all the flocks arrived. Then together they would roll a large stone from the opening of the well and water their sheep. Jacob walked up to them and asked if they knew a man named Laban. The shepherds answered, "Yes! Here comes his daughter Rachel with his sheep."

When Jacob saw the beautiful Rachel coming to water her father's flock, he went to the large stone and rolled it away all by himself. He gave water to Rachel's sheep, kissed her, and told her who he was. Rachel ran back to her father, who welcomed Jacob as part of the family. Jacob remained with his uncle Laban and worked for him.

Laban had two daughters. Leah was the older and could not see very well. Rachel was the younger daughter and was very beautiful. After a month's work, Laban said he wanted to pay Jacob for his work, but Jacob didn't want money. He wanted Rachel as his wife! "Jacob loved Rachel. And he said, 'I will serve you seven years for your younger daughter Rachel'" (Genesis 29:18). Laban agreed.

Jacob worked for seven years, but the time passed quickly because he loved Rachel so much. When the seven years were over, Laban held a wedding feast. But instead of giving Rachel to Jacob as his wife, Laban deceived him. That evening he gave Jacob his older daughter Leah as his bride instead and Jacob did not notice! The next morning when it was light, Jacob saw he had been tricked. He argued with Laban. "What have you done to me? I wanted to marry Rachel, not Leah!" Laban told Jacob, "In our country, it is tradition for the older daughter to be married first. But you can marry Rachel too—if you work another seven years!"

When Jacob lived at home, he had deceived his father to get his brother's blessing. Now he was the one who had been deceived by his uncle Laban. Jacob married Rachel and worked for Laban another seven years. He loved Rachel but he did not love Leah, which made her very sad. The Lord saw this and blessed Leah with children first, but Rachel remained barren, without children of her own.

Leah named her fourth son "Judah." She would have been very happy if she had known just how special Judah was. You see, Jesus would someday be born from Judah's family line. Jesus is even called the Lion of the tribe of Judah (Revelation 5:5)! This reminds us that God is always at work, even when people like Laban scheme and lie. Laban's tricks did not interrupt God's plan. All along, God planned for his Son Jesus to be born through one of Leah's children.

Let's Talk About It!

How does Jacob feel about Rachel?
What does Leah have that Rachel doesn't?
What is special about Leah's baby?

Let's Talk About It!

Why did Laban chase after Jacob?

If Laban is angry with Jacob, why is he shaking his hand?

What is the pile of rocks for?

Jacob Flees from Laban

GENESIS 31

As Jacob worked during those second seven years, Leah had many children but Rachel had none. Finally, after a long time passed, the Lord blessed Rachel with a son. She named him "Joseph." When Jacob had finished working for Rachel, he asked for Laban's permission to take his wives and children home. Laban didn't want him to go. He encouraged Jacob to stay, offering to pay him. Jacob said he would stay, and in return Laban agreed to give Jacob all the speckled and spotted goats that were born.

God blessed Jacob and he became rich, even though Laban tried to cheat him by changing his wages. If Laban changed the rules and said Jacob could keep only the goats with streaks, God made sure that only goats with streaks were born. If Laban said Jacob could only keep the goats with white streaks, goats with white streaks were born. Because of God's blessing, Jacob's flocks grew so large that Laban's sons were angry. They began to speak against him.

Then God spoke to Jacob in a dream. Jacob told Leah and Rachel what the Lord had said: "I have seen all that Laban is doing to you. I am the God of Bethel, where you anointed a pillar and made a vow to me. Now arise, go out from this land and return to the land of your kindred"

(Genesis 31:12–13). So Jacob drove his flocks away from Laban and headed back to Canaan. He did this secretly, while Laban was away shearing his sheep. Three days later, Laban discovered that Jacob had fled. He went after him and chased Jacob for seven days. But when he got close, the Lord spoke to Laban in a dream, telling him not to harm Jacob.

The next day Laban caught up with Jacob. He questioned Jacob, but there was nothing he could do because the Lord had warned him. So Laban made an agreement with Jacob. He set up a pillar near a heap of stones as a boundary marker. The two men agreed that neither one would cross the marker to harm the other. Then Laban left so Jacob could return to the land of his father.

Laban didn't want Jacob to leave, because he didn't want to give up his daughters or the flocks that had grown so big while Jacob cared for them. But God had a different plan. He planned for Jacob to live in the land God had promised him, his father Isaac, and his grandfather, Abraham. You see, God had special plans for Jacob in the Promised Land. One day, one of his far off grandchildren—Jesus—was to be born there in a town called Bethlehem. There is no way Laban could have stopped that from happening.

Jacob's Wrestling Match

GENESIS 32:1–32

After Jacob and Laban made their agreement, Jacob continued his trip back home. It had been more than fourteen years since he had seen his mother and father. Jacob traveled under the blessing of God, for along the way, the Lord sent angels to meet with him. Jacob knew that the Lord was with him, but he still had his brother Esau to deal with. The last time he had seen Esau, his brother had been furious with him for stealing his blessing. As Jacob drew closer to his homeland, he sent messengers ahead to greet Esau, because he was afraid his brother might still want to kill him. When the messengers returned, they told Jacob that Esau was coming to meet him with four hundred men. Jacob panicked and divided his group in two. That way, if Esau attacked one group, the other would survive.

Jacob asked the Lord to save him as he had promised. Then Jacob thought of a plan. He would send gifts ahead to Esau! Jacob gathered large flocks of goats, rams, camels, and donkeys to present to his brother. The animals were sent ahead, one group at a time, so that Esau would receive present after present after present. Jacob hoped that if Esau was angry, the gifts would calm him down. Then Jacob took his family, moved them across a stream, and spent the night alone.

That night God visited Jacob as a mysterious man who came and wrestled with him. The wrestling match continued for a long time. At dawn, when the man saw he was not winning, he touched Jacob's hip and put it out of joint. He asked Jacob to let him go, but Jacob said, "I will not let you go unless you bless me" (Genesis 32:26). Then the man said, "Your name shall no longer be called Jacob, but Israel, for you have striven with God and with men, and have prevailed" (Genesis 32:28). Then he blessed Jacob. Jacob named that place "Penuel," which means "face of God," because he knew he had seen God face-to-face and survived.

This story tells us how the nation of Israel got its start. The name God gave Jacob would be used for all of Jacob's children and eventually for the whole nation of God's people. Jesus was called the King of Israel as he rode triumphantly into Jerusalem, and he was mocked as the King of Israel when he hung dying on the cross (Mark 15:32). God named Jacob Israel knowing that one day Jesus would die bearing that name—King of Israel.

Let's Talk About It!

Who is Jacob wrestling with?

What happens to Jacob's hip?

Why does the fight go on so long?

Let's Talk About It!

What special gift does Jacob give to Joseph?
Describe Joseph's dreams.
How do Joseph's brothers feel about him?

Joseph's Dreams

GENESIS 37:1—11

Jacob, whom God renamed Israel, returned to Canaan and lived there with his twelve sons: Reuben, Simeon, Levi, Judah, Issachar, Zebulun, Dan, Naphtali, Gad, Asher, Joseph, and Benjamin. One day Joseph, the second youngest son, was tending the flocks with his brothers. He was seventeen years old. When they all returned, Joseph brought his father a bad report about his brothers. I'm sure they didn't like that very much. On top of that, Israel loved Joseph more than his brothers because he was Rachel's son. He gave Joseph a multicolored robe as a gift, but he didn't give any to his other sons. When Joseph's older brothers saw that their father loved him more, they became angry. They hated him and said bad things about him.

One day Joseph had a dream that he told to his brothers. He said that in his dream they were all in a field, tying up bundles of grain called sheaves. Then the bundle that Joseph was tying stood up tall. His brothers' sheaves gathered around and bowed down to Joseph's sheaf. When they heard the dream, Joseph's brothers said, "'Are you indeed to reign over us? Or are you indeed to rule over us?' So they hated him even more for his dreams and for his words" (Genesis 37:8).

Then Joseph had a second dream. This time eleven stars and the sun and the moon were bowing down to Joseph. When Joseph told this dream to his father, he corrected him saying, "What is this dream that you have dreamed? Shall I and your mother and your brothers indeed come to bow ourselves to the ground before you?" (Genesis 37:10). Joseph's brothers were jealous of him, but his father wondered about the dreams.

God gave Joseph his dreams, which seemed wonderful at first. But if Joseph had known all the hard times that lay ahead, he might have talked about the dreams in a more humble way. God was going to take Joseph through slavery and prison before he would finally make him a great ruler in Egypt. There God would use Joseph to save his family from a terrible famine. God would use Joseph to save Israel so that one day Jesus would come from Israel's line and save us all.

Joseph Is Attacked by His Brothers

GENESIS 37:12—36

One day, Joseph's jealous brothers went out to graze the flocks. Israel, their father, sent Joseph to check on his brothers and make sure that they and the flocks were well. Obediently Joseph left for the pastures of Shechem. When he could not find his brothers there, a stranger told Joseph that his brothers and their flocks had moved on to Dothan.

Joseph's brothers saw him coming while he was still a long way off. In their anger, they thought about killing him. "They said to one another, 'Here comes this dreamer. Come now, let us kill him and throw him into one of the pits. Then we will say that a fierce animal has devoured him, and we will see what will become of his dreams'" (Genesis 37:19–20). But Reuben, Joseph's oldest brother, said they should throw Joseph into one of the large empty pits but not kill him. Reuben secretly planned to return to rescue Joseph. The others agreed with what Reuben said. They tore off Joseph's beautiful robe and threw him into the pit, and Reuben left.

While the other brothers were eating, a caravan of Ishmaelites came by with their camels. They were heading to Egypt. Joseph's brothers sold him to the Ishmaelites for twenty shekels of silver and watched as they took him away to Egypt. When Reuben returned, to his surprise, Joseph was gone—sold into slavery! To hide their evil deed, the brothers killed a goat, dipped Joseph's robe in the blood, and showed it to their father. Israel recognized the robe and thought wild animals had killed his son. He was very, very sad. He cried for many days but no one could comfort him. While Israel mourned for Joseph, the caravan of Ishmaelites reached Egypt. Joseph was sold as a slave to Potiphar, the captain of Pharaoh's guard.

Does this story remind you of another person in the Bible who was betrayed? Joseph's life is a lot like Jesus' life. They both were treated badly by people who should have known better. Joseph's brothers were jealous of him. They didn't stop to think that maybe Joseph's dream came from God and was a part of God's plan. Many Jews didn't believe Jesus' teaching either. In the end, one of his closest friends betrayed him. He sold Jesus to his enemies, like Joseph's brothers did, for a few silver coins.

Let's Talk About It!

Point to Joseph in the picture.
What did his brothers do to him?
How do you think Joseph felt?

Let's Talk About It!

What is Joseph riding in?

Describe what Joseph is wearing.

Who has been helping Joseph all along?

Joseph Interprets the Dreams

GENESIS 40—41

Joseph's troubles didn't end when he was sold to Potiphar, the captain of the guard. Working for one of Pharaoh's officers was a wonderful job for a slave and God blessed Joseph as he worked there. But Potiphar's wife fell in love with Joseph and wanted him to love her back. Of course, that was wrong. When Joseph refused, Potiphar's wife became angry at Joseph. She lied and said he had done something wrong, and he was sent to prison. Even so, the Lord was with Joseph in prison and blessed all that he did. Some time later, Pharaoh became angry with his chief cupbearer and baker and threw them into the same prison. Joseph was asked to take care of their needs while they were there.

One night the cupbearer and the baker both had strange dreams. When Joseph heard about the upsetting dreams, he asked the two officials to tell him about them. Joseph knew that the Lord could show him what the dreams meant, and he trusted God to help him. Joseph told the cupbearer his dream meant that the king would forgive him and bring him back to the palace. Joseph asked the cupbearer to remember him when he returned to the king. But the baker's dream was not so nice. Joseph told him that he would be killed by the king. Everything happened just as Joseph said, but the cupbearer forgot about Joseph when he went back to the palace.

Two years later, Pharaoh, king of Egypt had his own strange dreams. When the cupbearer overheard the king speak of them to his wise men, he remembered Joseph and told the king about him. The king sent for Joseph and told him two very strange dreams. In the first he saw seven skinny cows rise up out of the Nile River to eat seven fat cows. In the second dream seven plump ears of corn were swallowed up by seven withered ears. Joseph warned Pharaoh that the dreams meant there would be seven years with plenty of food followed by seven years of terrible famine, when no food would grow. Joseph told Pharaoh to tell his leaders to store away food during the good years so that in the years of famine, Egypt would have food to eat.

Pharaoh was pleased with the way Joseph explained the dreams. He knew God had helped him. He said, "Since God has shown you all this, there is none so discerning and wise as you are." Pharaoh continued, "You shall be over my house and all my people shall order themselves as you command" (Genesis 41:39–40). The king gave Joseph his ring and royal robes to wear. He had Joseph ride in a chariot behind him for all of Egypt to see.

Who do you think protected Joseph and helped him while he was in prison? That's right, God helped Joseph! You see, God wanted to use Joseph as a special part of his plan. God often turns bad things around for good. One far-off day from Joseph, God would use the death of his Son Jesus, which seemed very bad, to do something very good—save us from our sins. Nothing can stop God's plan to save his people—not prison, or even death!

God Provides for the Israelites in Famine

GENESIS 42

God gave Egypt seven years with plenty of food, just as Pharaoh's dream foretold. Joseph collected the grain and stored it in the cities of Egypt. He gathered food in each city from all the surrounding fields. There was so much stored away that no one could count it. When the seven years of famine hit the land, Egypt had plenty to eat. The Egyptians came to Joseph and he sold them grain from the storehouses. Word spread and soon people from the surrounding countries were traveling to Egypt to buy food too.

When Joseph's father heard that people could buy food in Egypt, he sent his ten older sons to buy grain. When they arrived, the brothers bowed down to Joseph. They did not know he was the brother they had sold as a slave years before. But Joseph recognized them! He remembered his dreams and what his brothers had done. Joseph accused them of spying on Egypt. He questioned them harshly and put them in prison for three days. Are you surprised he did that? Do you think it was because he was angry? That wasn't the reason. God was using Joseph to show his brothers their sin against their younger brother. And Joseph was testing them to see how much their hearts had changed since then. Were they any different now?

On the third day Joseph told his brothers to prove their innocence by bringing back their youngest brother, whom Jacob had kept at home. The brothers told each other that God was punishing them for what they had done to Joseph. They did not realize that Joseph could understand what they were saying. They thought he didn't speak their language. Then Joseph had Simeon tied up in front of them and hauled away to prison until they returned. Joseph told his servants to give the brothers their grain and secretly return their money, hiding it in their sacks, and send them on their way. Joseph knew that when his brothers found their silver in their sacks, they would be afraid of God because of what they had done to Joseph. Once again God would use this to help them be sorry for what they had done against their brother.

On their journey, one of the brothers opened a sack to get some grain for his donkey and found the money in the sack! All the brothers were afraid. When they returned to their father, they discovered the money in each of their sacks, and they were even more afraid. They asked to bring Benjamin with them when they returned to Egypt so Simeon could be freed, but their father refused. He was afraid he would lose Benjamin just like he had lost Joseph.

Even though Joseph's brothers sinned against their younger brother, Joseph was kind and showed mercy to them when he gave them grain to keep them alive during the famine. Joseph's life is a reflection of the way God deals with us. Like Joseph's brothers, we all deserve to be punished for our sins, but God doesn't treat us as our sins deserve. Instead, God gave up his only Son Jesus for our salvation. Just as Joseph's brothers needed grain for food, we need Jesus—who said he was the bread of life (John 6:35)—to save us from our sins.

Let's Talk About It!

What is stacked up in the picture?

Who is the man dressed like a king?

How is this picture like the dream Joseph had before his brothers sold him into slavery?

Joseph Reveals Himself to His Brothers

GENESIS 43–46

When his family ran out of food again, Israel had no choice but to send his sons back to Egypt to buy more grain. This time he had to send Benjamin with them. As soon as they arrived, the brothers returned the money that had been placed in their sacks after their first journey. Joseph released Simeon from prison when he saw that his brothers brought along Benjamin as he had commanded.

Joseph treated his brothers to a special meal and then sent them on their way with more grain. Secretly, he again commanded his servants to put their money back in their sacks. He also ordered them to hide a silver cup in Benjamin's sack. When his brothers found it, they would fear God even more for what they had done against Joseph.

Not long after his brothers left to travel home, Joseph ordered his men to catch them, find the cup and bring them back. Soon the brothers were standing before Joseph again. How frightened they must have been! Joseph accused them of stealing the cup and ordered Benjamin to become his servant, since the cup was in his sack. Judah offered to take Benjamin's place for he had promised his father he would take care of his younger brother. He explained that his

father loved Benjamin so much that losing him would surely kill their father.

At that point, Joseph began to cry. Now he could see that his brothers were sorry for what they had done all those years before. He sent the Egyptians out of the room to speak to his brothers alone. He said, "I am your brother, Joseph, whom you sold into Egypt. And now do not be distressed or angry with yourselves because you sold me here, for God sent me before you to preserve

life" (Genesis 45:4–5). Joseph kissed and forgave his brothers and they talked together for some time. After so many years, the brothers were friends. Joseph told his brothers that the famine would last for five more years. With Pharaoh's blessing, he sent them home with food and gifts, and an invitation to bring back their father.

When the brothers told Israel that Joseph was alive, he did not believe them until he saw the gifts from Pharaoh. Israel offered a sacrifice to the Lord, and that night God spoke to him in a vision. He said, "Do not be afraid to go down to Egypt, for there I will make you into a great nation. I myself will go down with you to Egypt, and I will also bring you up again" (Genesis 46:3–4). So Israel and his family traveled to Egypt and were saved from the famine. Later, Joseph explained to his brothers that even though they meant him harm when they sold him into slavery, God meant it all for good, to save many peoples' lives.

Did you notice that it was Judah who offered his life in Benjamin's place (Genesis 44:33)? Does that remind you of the way Jesus offered to die in our place? Some might say it was a coincidence that Judah—Jesus' far-off great grandfather—was the one who offered his life in exchange for his brother's. But in God's amazing plan, nothing happens by accident!

Let's Talk About It!

What was hidden in the sacks?

How do Joseph's brothers feel about seeing him?

How does Joseph help his brothers?

Let's Talk About It!

What is baby Moses floating in?

Can you point to the cross in the picture?

What special job does God have planned for Moses?

STORY 27

God Protects Baby Moses

EXODUS 1:1—2:10

Because of the famine Israel and his family settled down to live in Egypt. Over time they had more and more children and grew to be a great people. Joseph died and after awhile, a new pharaoh came into power who did not remember Joseph or what he had done to save Egypt. This new king thought there were too many Israelites. He thought they would rise up and attack Egypt. So Pharaoh turned the Israelites into slaves. He put slave drivers over them who made them carry heavy loads, work in the fields, make bricks, and build cities. But God blessed his people in the midst of all this trouble, and their families continued to grow.

When Pharaoh saw this, he was unhappy. He told the midwives who helped mothers when they were having their babies to kill all the baby boys. But the midwives feared God more than Pharaoh and they did not obey. God blessed the midwives and the Israelites had even more children! Not long after that, Pharaoh commanded that every Israelite baby boy should be thrown into the Nile River. Only daughters were spared.

There was one Hebrew woman who had a fine baby boy. She was afraid he would be killed, so she hid him for three months. When she couldn't hide him any longer, she made a basket out of reeds and coated it with black tar to keep out the water and help it to float. She put her baby son in the basket and hid it among the reeds of the riverbank. She assigned her daughter to watch him. That morning Pharaoh's daughter came to the river and found the baby in the basket. The baby's sister came out from where she was hiding and offered to find a woman to nurse the infant. Pharaoh's daughter agreed and sent the baby back to his mother to care for him until he was older. Later, when the boy came to live with her, she named him Moses and raised him in Pharaoh's courts. God saved Moses because he was a part of God's plan to help his suffering people.

Did you know that the word God used for Moses' basket is the same word that is used for Noah's great boat, the ark? Just like God used the ark to save Noah, God used the little basket to save Moses. God protected baby Moses from Pharaoh's order because God planned to use him to rescue his people from their slavery in Egypt. Many years later, God protected baby Jesus from another evil king. King Herod tried to kill him, but God warned Joseph in a dream to go to a place of safety. Jesus, like Moses, grew up to rescue God's people from slavery. But it was a different kind of slavery—a slavery to sin.

55

God Calls Moses

EXODUS 2:11 – 4:31

As Moses grew up to be a man, the slavery of God's people in Egypt continued. Their lives were very hard, and Moses could see how much they suffered. One day Moses even killed a cruel Egyptian who was beating one of the Hebrew men. The Hebrews were his people, and he wanted to help them. But when Pharaoh found out what Moses had done, he planned to kill Moses. So Moses ran away from Egypt into the wilderness, to the land of Midian. There he met a family with seven daughters. They welcomed Moses. In fact, Moses married the oldest daughter! Moses and his wife lived with her father, Jethro, and Moses helped tend Jethro's flocks of sheep.

One day, Moses was with the sheep on the side of a mountain called Horeb. He noticed a bush full of flames, but the fire was not burning up the branches! That was strange, so he decided to take a closer look. As he walked nearer, God called to him from inside the bush. "Moses, Moses," the Lord called out.

"Here I am," Moses answered.

"Do not come near. Take the sandals off your feet for the place on which you are standing is holy ground. I am the God of your Father, the God of Abraham, the God of Isaac, and the God of Jacob."

When he heard God speak, Moses just hid his face. He was afraid to look at God.

"I have seen the suffering of my people and I have heard their cries for help. I am going to deliver them," God told him. Then God said something to Moses that really surprised him. "I will send you to Pharaoh to bring my people out of Egypt."

"Who am I that I would be able to lead the people out of Egypt?" Moses asked. He didn't think he could rescue the people by himself! God assured Moses, "I will be with you."

Moses knew the people back in Egypt would not so easily believe he was God's deliverer, and they would have a ton of questions. So he asked God, "When people ask me who sent me, what should I say? What is your name?" "I AM WHO I AM," the Lord told him (Exodus 3:14). God was too big to use an earthly name like Bob or Henry to describe himself. But the name "I AM" was a wonderful way for God to describe himself, for he has always been around and will always be.

Even though God said he would be with Moses, Moses still did not believe. He said, "What if they don't believe me or listen to my voice?"

God told Moses to throw his staff to the ground. When he did, it turned into a snake. "Catch it by the tail," God said, and as Moses obeyed, the snake became a staff again. "That will help them believe that the God of their fathers has appeared to you." But Moses was still afraid to go. He didn't think he was very good at speaking and said, "Oh, my Lord, please send someone else."

God was angry with Moses for not trusting him but he sent his brother Aaron to help him speak to Pharaoh.

So, Moses and Aaron made their way back to Egypt. They gathered the elders or rulers of Israel together and told them what God was about to do. The elders believed Moses and Aaron and thanked God for hearing their cries for help.

The book of Hebrews tells us that when Moses first

left Egypt, he had an idea that God had a plan to save his people. Instead of enjoying the pleasures of Egypt as Pharaoh's son, Moses chose to live as one of God's people and to trust the Lord (Hebrews 11:24–26). By saving Israel, God's promise to Abraham was preserved so that one day Jesus would be born to save us too.

Let's Talk About It!

What is unusual about the bush in the picture?

Why has Moses taken his sandals off?

What does God say to Moses from out of the bush?

Moses Confronts Pharaoh

EXODUS 5:1—7:13

When it was time to deliver God's message to Pharaoh, Moses and Aaron went to Pharaoh and boldly said, "Thus says the LORD, the God of Israel, 'Let my people go so that they may worship me.'" But Pharaoh answered proudly, "I do not know the Lord and I will not let Israel go."

Then Pharaoh told his taskmasters not to give the Hebrew slaves any straw to make their bricks. Pharaoh's order forced the Israelites to gather their own straw, but still Pharaoh forced them to make the same number of bricks. If they made fewer bricks, they would be beaten!

The Israelites complained to Moses saying, "You haven't helped us at all! Things are even worse now because of you." Moses was sad. He cried out to the Lord and asked him why this terrible thing had happened. The Lord comforted Moses and told him to tell the people, "I am the LORD, and I will bring you out from under the burdens of the Egyptians, and I will deliver you from slavery to them, and I will redeem you with an outstretched arm and with great acts of judgment. I will take you to be my people, and I will be your God, and you shall know that I am the LORD your God" (Exodus 6:6–7).

The Lord sent Moses back to Pharaoh to tell him again to let the Israelites go. God warned Moses that Pharaoh would not listen, but God would then show his power and rescue Israel. To prove to Pharaoh that God's power was with Moses, the Lord told Moses to have Aaron throw his staff down on the ground in front of Pharaoh. Then it would become a serpent. Moses and Aaron did just what the Lord told them, and when Aaron threw down his staff, it turned into a snake! Pharaoh quickly called his magicians to see if they could do what Aaron had done. When they threw down their staffs, they turned into serpents too, but Aaron's serpent swallowed up and ate the other snakes! Even though God revealed his power, Pharaoh did not want to obey him. He hardened his heart, which means he decided not to believe God and would not let God's people go.

It may seem like things were not going well for Moses, but we can't forget that God's plan can never be stopped. Even when things don't seem to go right, God is in control behind the scenes, working out his purpose. Think about Jesus. When he was arrested, the disciples didn't think things were working out either. But God knew exactly what he was doing. Even when the bad guys seemed to be winning, God's plan to save us was working perfectly.

Let's Talk About It!

What message did Moses and Aaron bring to Pharaoh?

Who are the men wearing the green hats?

What are the snakes doing?

Let's Talk About It!

Point to the picture of the first plague, where God turns water into blood.

How many plagues can you identify?

What do you think is the most terrible plague God sent against Egypt?

God Sends Plagues Against Egypt

EXODUS 7:14—11:1

God hardened Pharaoh's heart and he refused to let the Israelites go. Because of this, God told Moses to strike the water of the Nile River and turn it into blood. Moses obeyed the Lord and the Nile—and all the water in Egypt—turned to blood. Now there was no water to drink! But when Pharaoh saw that his magicians could do the same thing, he refused to let God's people go.

Seven days later, God sent Moses back to Pharaoh. Moses said, "Thus says the LORD, let my people go. If you refuse I will fill your country with frogs."

Again Pharaoh refused, so Moses turned to Aaron and said, "Stretch out your staff over the rivers, canals, and pools and make frogs come up out of the land." When Aaron did, suddenly frogs were everywhere! Pharaoh pleaded with Moses to take the frogs away and he promised to let the people go. But once the frogs were gone, he changed his mind again. Next, God sent a plague of gnats to Egypt. The gnats attacked the Egyptians but left God's people alone. Pharaoh tried to bargain with Moses. He said the Israelites could offer their sacrifices to God in Egypt. But Moses said that the Lord's command was to let the people go. Finally Pharaoh agreed, but when the gnats were gone, he changed his mind again!

The Lord brought plague after plague to Egypt. Every time he did, they never bothered the Israelites, just the Egyptians! God sent flies, caused the Egyptians' animals to die, made the people sick with boils, sent hailstorms, then swarms of locusts that ate everything in sight, and even darkness that covered the land. As he sent plague after plague, God was creating a story for the Israelites to tell their children and grandchildren. By the time God was finished with Pharaoh, everyone would know God's mighty power and share the story of God's victory.

But in spite of the plagues, Pharaoh would not listen. Again and again, he hardened his heart. He kept trying to bargain with Moses, but when Moses refused, Pharaoh told him to leave and never return. Otherwise, he would die. There was only one plague left. After that, God said Pharaoh would obey.

Did you know that the plagues were especially designed by God to show that he was the true God over Egypt? The Egyptians worshiped all kinds of gods. They had a god of the Nile, a god of the sun, and even a goddess named Heqt who was called the frog goddess! When God showed that he was in control of the Nile River, the sun, and the frogs, he was telling the people of Egypt that their gods were false. Today, thousands of years later, when we read this story we see how powerfully God saved his people to open a way for Jesus to come.

The Last Plague & the First Passover

EXODUS 11–13

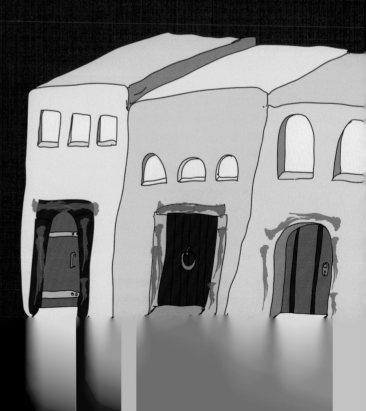

The last and worst plague was still to come. Moses warned Pharaoh one final time that he had to let Israel go. He told Pharaoh that around midnight that very night, the Lord would travel through the land of Egypt. Every firstborn son would be struck down and killed, from the firstborn son of Pharaoh to the firstborn son of the slave girl. If Pharaoh didn't obey God, all of Egypt would suffer, but God would protect his people. Moses told Pharaoh that once this happened, Pharaoh's officials would bow to Moses and Israel would be free to go. Moses left Pharaoh very angry, because Pharaoh would not listen even though the next plague was going to be very bad.

The Lord said to Moses and Aaron, "Each man is to take a perfect male lamb for his family and kill it on the fourteenth day of the month. Then he should take the blood from the lamb and put it on the sides and tops of the doorframes of your houses. On that day I will pass through Egypt and strike down every firstborn—both men and animals. But the blood will be a sign for you. For when I see the blood on the doorframes, I will pass

Moses listened carefully to the instructions the Lord gave him and shared them with God's people. Moses told them to eat quickly, to put sandals on their feet and a staff in their hand. The Lord called the meal the Lord's Passover, because even though all the firstborn of Egypt would be killed, God would pass over the firstborn of Israel. God told Moses to celebrate the Passover every year so that all generations would remember what the Lord had done.

Moses told all these things to the Israelites and they obeyed the Lord's command. They prepared the meal and dabbed the blood on their doorframes. At midnight, God brought the last plague to Egypt and struck down all the firstborn sons, including Pharaoh's son. Then Pharaoh sent for Moses and said to him, "Up, go out from among my people, both you and the people of Israel; and go, serve the LORD, as you have said" (Exodus 12:31).

Because the people of Egypt were so afraid, they urged the Israelites to leave right away.

Did you know that the lambs slain during the Passover are a picture of Jesus? In the New Testament, Jesus is called the Lamb of God who takes away the sin of the world (John 1:29) and the Lamb who was slain (Revelation 5:6, 12). Just as the blood on the doorposts protected Israel from God's judgment then, the blood of Jesus takes away God's judgment now. The apostle Paul even calls Jesus our Passover lamb (1 Corinthians 5:7).

Let's Talk About It!

What is painted on the doorframes?

What happened in the homes that didn't have the blood on the doorframes?

How is the blood on the doorframes like Jesus' blood shed on the cross?

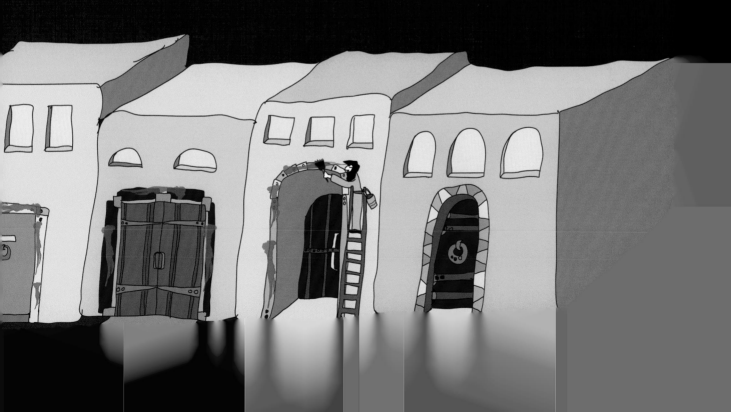

God Parts the Red Sea

All over the land the people of God hurried out of their homes as God led them out of Egypt. They headed into the wilderness toward the Red Sea. As the people gathered, a large pillar of cloud formed. The Lord was in the cloud and moved ahead of the people to show them where to go. At night, the Lord led them with a pillar of fire that burned brightly, giving light for them to see. That way God's people could travel by day or by night. Over one million Israelites left Egypt, along with their sheep and cattle. It was a very big group!

When they reached the Red Sea, God told them to set up camp there. He spoke to Moses and said, "I will harden Pharaoh's heart and he will pursue you, thinking you are trapped by the sea. But I will get glory over Pharaoh, and all of Egypt will know that I am the LORD."

It happened just the way God said it would. When Pharaoh was told that the Israelites had gone, he changed his mind again. He called his army together and took six hundred chariots to chase after the Israelites. When the Israelites saw the Egyptians coming, they were afraid. But Moses told them, "Fear not, stand firm, and see the salvation of the LORD, which he will work for you today" (Exodus 14:13). Then God moved the pillar of cloud from the front of the crowd to the back. Now it stood between Israel and the Egyptians. Moses stretched his hand out over the sea. A great east wind blew all night, blowing the water out of its normal place. The floor of the sea became dry land. The people walked through the sea on dry ground, with a wall of water on the left and another on the right.

When the Egyptian army saw what was happening, they tried to chase after the Israelites. But the Lord clogged up the wheels of their chariots and they could not move quickly through the pathway in the sea. The Egyptians became frightened, because they knew God was fighting against them. When God's people were safely on the other side, the Lord told Moses to stretch his hand over the sea again. When he did, the sea rushed back into its place and all the Egyptians were drowned. So the Lord saved Israel that day, just as he had promised. When God's people saw his great power at work and the dead Egyptians on the shore, they were filled with awe for the Lord. They celebrated in worship and song, safe on the other side.

Before God parted the Red Sea, the Israelites were trapped. They could not save themselves from the Egyptians. But God opened a way through the sea and the Israelites walked through by faith. We are trapped too. We are dead in our sin with no way to save ourselves. God opened a way of escape for us through Jesus. The Bible tells us that if we trust in him and his sacrifice on the cross for our sin, we will be saved—forever!

Let's Talk About It!

Why does God divide the Red Sea?

What holds the Egyptians back until the Israelites complete the crossing?

How would you feel walking through a sea between two high walls of water?

Let's Talk About It!

What is Moses doing in the picture?

Where has the water come from?

Why does God give water to the people instead of punishing them for their complaining?

God Provides Food & Water for Israel

EXODUS 16:1–17:7

Even though God performed many wonders to rescue his people from Egypt, they were quick to forget all he had done—and even quicker to complain when there was a problem. When they were thirsty, they complained instead of asking the Lord for water. When they were hungry, they said terrible things to Moses like, "You have brought us out into this wilderness to kill this whole assembly with hunger" (Exodus 16:3). In spite of their grumbling, the Lord was kind to them and provided water for them to drink. He even gave them special bread from heaven, called manna, to eat each day. Every morning they gathered enough manna for one day. (Any leftover bread would rot and get worms in it.) But on the sixth day, God told them to gather a two-day supply so they could rest on the Sabbath day. God prevented the manna for the Sabbath from rotting and growing worms.

Moses warned the people that when they grumbled, they were really grumbling against the Lord. But the people didn't listen. They forgot Moses' warning. After they moved from the place where God first brought the manna, they became thirsty again. Right away, they started quarreling and complaining. They started saying bad things about Moses again and asked him, "Why did you bring us up out of Egypt, to kill us and our children?" (Exodus 17:3). Moses cried out to the Lord for help. He told the Lord, "The people are almost ready to stone me!"

The Lord told Moses to take some of the elders of Israel to the rock at Horeb. You might remember that this was where God first spoke to Moses in the burning bush. This time God said, "I will stand before you there on the rock at Horeb, and you shall strike the rock, and water shall come out of it, and the people will drink" (Exodus 17:6). Moses did just as the Lord commanded and, sure enough, water flowed from the rock, plenty for all of God's people and their animals.

God could have punished the people for their grumbling, because it was wrong. Instead, he told Moses to strike the rock right where the Lord himself stood. Instead of judgment, the people received the blessing of water. In the New Testament, the apostle Paul tells us that the rock Moses struck is meant to remind us of Jesus (1 Corinthians 10:4). Instead of striking Israel for their sin, God struck the rock, which represented Jesus Christ. Even way back in the day of Moses, God knew that his salvation would come through the sacrifice of his Son Jesus. Through this story God gave Israel a hint of how he was going to save his people. Instead of punishing us for our sin, God brought the rod of his judgment on Jesus at the cross. When God saved Israel and gave them water, he was looking ahead to the sacrifice of his Son. When God saves us, he looks back to Jesus on the cross.

God Gives Moses the Ten Commandments

EXODUS 20:1—24

After three months of walking through the desert, the people of Israel came to Mount Sinai. They camped at the foot of the mountain while Moses went up to meet with God. God told Moses to set up a boundary at the base of the mountain and to warn the people not to cross it. In three days, God said he would come down where the people could see him. If the people even touched the edge of that boundary, they would die because his presence was holy and the people were sinful.

On the third day, the mountain shook with thunder and lightning filled the sky. Suddenly, the people heard a loud trumpet blast, and the mountain was covered with smoke. No one had ever seen anything like that before! Courageously, Moses went up to meet with God. God spoke to him in the thunder. He gave Moses the Ten Commandments and Moses brought them back to the people. Here is what they said:

I am the LORD your God. You shall have no other gods before me.

You shall not make an idol for yourself in the shape of anything at all.

You shall not take the LORD's name in vain.

Remember the Sabbath and keep it holy.

Honor your father and mother that you may live long in the land.

You shall not murder.

You shall not take your neighbor's wife for yourself.

You shall not steal.

You shall not lie and bear false witness against your neighbor.

You shall not covet your neighbor's house or anything he owns.

When the people heard the thunder, the lightning, and the loud trumpet, they trembled! They said they were afraid to talk with God. Moses said to the people, "Don't be afraid. God has come to test you. He wants you to respect and honor him so that you won't sin." Then Moses walked closer to God, and God gave him these words to tell Israel: "You have seen for yourselves that I have talked with you from heaven. Do not make gods of silver or gold to worship along with me." After Moses gave Israel God's message, the people agreed to obey all that God said and Moses wrote down the words the Lord gave him.

Do you know why God gave Israel (and us) the commandments? The apostle Paul said that God's commandments, which we call the law, taught him what sin was. He said that if God had not given us the law, we would not know what sin is (Romans 7:7). Paul also said that the law was our schoolmaster to teach us about Christ (Galatians 3:24). You see, once we know God's law and we see how many times we break it, we realize that we are sinners who need a Savior. That is where Jesus comes in. How about you? Have you broken God's law? None of us can obey God perfectly. None of us except for Jesus! When we put our faith in him, Jesus takes away our sin and gives us his perfect record of obedience. That is how we can be saved from God's judgment for breaking his law.

Let's Talk About It!

What is Moses holding?

Where did he get them?

What is happening to the mountain?

Let's Talk About It!

What does the ark represent?

What room in the tabernacle is made especially for the ark?

What does God say to put inside the ark?

The Tabernacle

EXODUS 25–26

After God gave Moses the Ten Commandments, he told Moses to build a tent. This was no ordinary tent, because God was going to live in it! He was going to have a place to stay right in the middle of the Israelites' camp, and he was going to travel with them as they entered their new home in Canaan. God said this tent would be called a tabernacle. Inside, there would be special pieces of furniture, and God told Moses exactly how they should be made. Since this was God's house, everything had to be just right. God said to Moses, "Go and ask the people for the things we need to make the tabernacle and everything in it. I want each of them to give what their hearts want to give. I want everyone to have a part in making this place where I will live. We will need gold, silver, bronze, jewels, fine cloth, animal skins, and many other things." Do you know how the Israelites had gotten such valuable things? They were some of the gifts the Egyptians had given them when they left Egypt.

Certain people were chosen to build the tabernacle and everything in it. The tent was one large room divided into two by a special curtain called a veil. The larger section was called the Holy Place and the smaller, square room was called the Most Holy Place, because that was where God's presence stayed. The veil or curtain that separated the Most Holy Place from the rest of the tabernacle helped the Israelites understand that God was holy—he could not live among sinful people. The outside walls of the tabernacle were not like the walls of our houses, because it was a tent. Instead, the walls were heavy curtains that hung on wooden poles. Layers of cloth and animal skins formed the roof of the tent to keep out the rain. Whenever God told the people to move their camp, the tabernacle could be taken apart to travel with them. Men from the tribe of Levi would pack up the main tent, the courtyard fence, and everything inside, and set it up again wherever God commanded.

Inside the Most Holy Place, where God's presence lived, was a special piece of furniture called the ark. The ark was a reminder of God's presence. It was a chest made of acacia wood, covered with a thin layer of pure gold. On each side were two gold rings and two wooden poles covered with gold to slide through the rings. These poles were used to carry the ark so that no one would need to touch it, since this was where God's presence rested. The cover to the ark was called the mercy seat. It was made of solid gold! It had statues of two cherubim or angels, one on each side. They faced each other with their wings spread out over the mercy seat. God said to Moses, "Put the mercy seat on the top of the ark, and inside the ark, put in the things I will give you. That is where I will meet with you and give you the commands I have for the people of Israel."

Did you know that in John's Gospel, God uses the word "tabernacle" to describe how Jesus came to earth? He tells us that Jesus came down from heaven to live or "tabernacle" among us (John 1:14). When God told Moses to make the tabernacle as a place for him to live, it pointed ahead to the day when Jesus would come to live with us. One of his names is Emmanuel, which means "God with us."

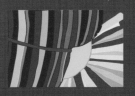

The Golden Calf

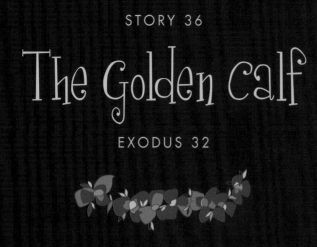

God spent a lot of time telling Moses about the tabernacle and the objects that would go inside it. The tabernacle would help the people understand more about him and teach them how to worship and serve him. So God gave Moses a detailed design for a golden lampstand, an altar, the priests' clothing, and many other items. God even told Moses the names of the people who should make them. Then God wrote the laws he gave to Moses on stone tablets.

But while all this was happening, the people in the camp grew tired of waiting for Moses to come down from the mountain. They went to Aaron and said, "We don't know what has happened to Moses! He brought us out of Egypt, but he has been gone a long time. We need some new gods to take us where we need to go. We want you to make them for us." Think about that! God was busy planning to live with the Israelites, and they were already forgetting about him.

Aaron did what the people asked. He collected gold from the people, melted it, and formed it into an idol in the shape of a calf. Then Aaron said to the people, "Here you are! This is the god who led you out of Egypt! Tomorrow we will have a special feast to worship him." Did you think that Aaron would forget the Lord so quickly after all he had done for them? Imagine how God felt! He knew what was happening even while he was talking with Moses.

The Lord told Moses that the people had made a golden calf and they were worshiping and offering sacrifices to it. This made the Lord very angry. He said he would destroy the people who had turned their backs on him and make a great nation out of Moses' family instead. But Moses remembered that God gave him the job to take care of the people and speak up for them when they were in trouble, just like they were now. So Moses reminded God of his promise to Abraham, Isaac, and Jacob. He asked God not to destroy them, because they were the people God had promised would become as many as the stars in the sky. The Lord listened as Moses pleaded for the people, and he decided not to destroy them. Then Moses left the mountain to go down to the people. He carried with him the tablets of stone that had God's Word written on them.

When Moses saw the golden calf, he threw down the stone tablets and broke them into pieces. He burned the golden calf with fire, ground the gold into powder, and scattered it on the water. Then Moses made the people drink it as a punishment.

God used Moses as a mediator for Israel. That means he was a man in the middle, with Israel on one side and God on the other. God would speak to Moses, and Moses would tell the people what God had said. Moses also stood in the middle in times of trouble. When Israel sinned, Moses asked God to forgive them. Moses was a sinner too, but God listened to him as a mediator. In

the future, Jesus became the perfect and sinless mediator between sinful people and a holy God. Though Moses stood in the middle for the people, he could not take Israel's sins away. He could not take the punishment they deserved. Only Jesus could do that, and he did that for anyone who trusts him. Even today, Jesus remains our mediator, praying for us before the Father in heaven.

Let's Talk About It!

While Moses meets with God on the mountain, what trouble do the people get into?

Why was making the golden calf such a bad thing?

What did Moses do to the golden idol when he returned from meeting with God?

God Has Mercy on Israel

EXODUS 33—34

After Moses destroyed the golden calf, he said to the people, "You have sinned a great sin. I am going up to the Lord to see if I can make up for your sin." So Moses climbed back up the mountain and stood in God's presence. He asked God to forgive the people for making the golden idol. He even said to God, "If you can't forgive them, Lord, please punish me instead. Please take my name out of your book." The Lord heard Moses and did not destroy the people, even though Moses could not take the punishment for the people's sin.

But the trouble was not over yet. The Lord told Moses he didn't want to lead Israel anymore! God said, "The people are so stubborn and rebellious, I might destroy them while we travel together." When Moses told the people the terrible news, they were very sad. To show God they were sorry, they took off all the fancy clothing they had worn for the celebration with the golden calf.

Moses went back to the Lord and reminded him that the Israelites were his special people, the ones God had promised to bless. Moses said, "We don't want to go anywhere if you do not go with us. We want everyone to know we are your chosen people." Moses said that God's presence was what made the people of Israel special and different from all other nations. Moses was being a mediator again, just as God wanted.

The Lord heard what Moses said and he agreed to go with the people and give them another chance. Then Moses asked for a very surprising thing. He asked if he could look at God. But God would not allow that because Moses was sinful and God was holy. A sinful man could not see God's face and live. Instead, God told Moses to bring two new stone tablets to the top of the mountain. Then he placed Moses in the rocks with a crack to look through. As the Lord passed by, he covered the crack with his hand. After he had passed, he took away his hand so that Moses could see the last part of his glory.

Moses stayed with God on the mountain for forty days and nights. God wrote the Ten Commandments on new stone tablets and gave them back to Moses. When Moses returned to the people, his face shone with the glory of God because of the time he had spent with him.

Do you know what the greatest display of God's glory is? It is when Jesus died on the cross for our sin and rose from the dead! By dying on the cross, Jesus displayed God's mercy and grace for all to see. That gave God great glory! Moses tried to take the punishment Israel deserved, but he couldn't because he was a sinner. But Jesus did what Moses could never do. He lived a sinless life and then gave it up for us. Now that is glorious!

Let's Talk About It!

Why is Moses' face lit up?

How do you think Moses felt after seeing the last part of God's glory?

What has been the greatest display of God's glory in history?

Let's Talk About It!

What kind of bird did God give Israel to eat in the desert?

What else did the people eat in the desert?

What are the people thinking about?

The People of Israel Complain

When the tabernacle was completed, the pillar of cloud that led Israel by day moved above it. At night it glowed with fire. The pillar of cloud stayed above the tabernacle until God said it was time to move on. Then the pillar of cloud would leave the tent and start moving in the direction God wanted his people to go. The Levites would pack up the tabernacle and all Israel followed the cloud until it stopped. Wherever it stopped, the Levites would put the tabernacle back together again so that God would always be living among his people.

Still, it wasn't always easy to travel through the desert. Some people began to complain and the Lord heard them. God was providing for all their needs, so it wasn't right to complain. God sent fire down from heaven and some of the outer parts of the camp were burned. When the people saw the fire, they called out to Moses for help. Moses prayed to God and the fire died down, but the people didn't learn from their mistakes.

You might remember that every day, as the dew settled on the ground, the Lord sent manna down from heaven for the people to eat. The people gathered the manna, ground it into flour, boiled it in pots, and made cakes out of it for their food. But some of the people really wanted meat to eat, and they started complaining about it—even though the Lord had just punished complaining by sending fire to the camp! They said, "Oh, we wish we had meat to eat! We remember the fish we ate in Egypt—it didn't cost us anything! And we had cucumbers and melons and leeks and onions and garlic too. But now there is nothing but this manna. We are tired of looking at it!"

When Moses heard the people complaining again, he said to the Lord, "Leading these people is too much for me. I can't do it anymore!" The Lord told Moses to choose seventy godly men—elders—to help him. God gave his Holy Spirit to those men, and they began to prophesy. When Joshua heard two of the men prophesying, he didn't know what to think. He was concerned that people might not respect Moses as their leader anymore. But Moses corrected Joshua. He said he wished God would pour out his Spirit on everyone! Now Moses had help to lead the people.

What do you think happened to the people who complained about wanting meat? The Lord heard and gave them quail to eat. Not just a few birds, but tens of thousands of quail. And not just for one or two days, but every day for a month! There were so many quail that those who gathered up the birds filled six sacks each. But the grumblers who caused the trouble were struck down by the Lord before they even finished eating.

Many years later the prophet Joel said that a day would come when God would give his Holy Spirit to all people, just as Moses had hoped would happen (Joel 2:28). That day came after Jesus went back to heaven on the day of Pentecost. The hope of Moses and the prophecy of Joel came true. Now, when God forgives people for their sins, he puts his Spirit to live in them. Instead of God's Spirit just being on a few men, God's Spirit lives inside all believers.

Miriam

Aaron and Miriam, Moses' brother and sister, fell into the same sin of complaining as the rest of the people. They became jealous of Moses and complained about him. They said, "It's not as if the Lord has only spoken through Moses, is it? Hasn't he spoken through us too?" There was no reason for Miriam and Aaron to complain against Moses. Even though he was the leader, Moses did not brag about it. In fact, the Bible says Moses was the most humble man on the face of the earth.

Still, they did complain and, just as before, the Lord heard what they were saying. Suddenly, the Lord spoke. He called Aaron, Miriam, and Moses to the Tent of Meeting. The Lord came down to the entrance of the tent in the pillar of cloud and stood there. He called Aaron and Miriam forward and corrected them. He told them that Moses was no ordinary prophet. God spoke to other prophets through dreams and visions, but with Moses, God said, he spoke face-to-face. The Lord rebuked them for speaking against Moses as they had, because it showed that they did not honor God's choice. When the cloud lifted from that place, Miriam's face turned white as snow from a very dangerous disease called leprosy.

Aaron turned to Moses and repented for what he had said and done. He appealed to Moses to keep his sister from suffering such a cruel disease. Moses cried out to the Lord to heal his sister. Normally, a person with leprosy would not be allowed to live with other people. But the Lord said that Miriam should only be shut out of the camp for seven days. Then she would be healed and she could return again. So Moses and the people waited the seven days. Once Miriam returned to the camp, they set out again.

God spoke to his people in the Old Testament in many ways. He used the pillar of cloud to tell them when to move and when to stay still. He spoke to them through the prophets and through Moses. But the writer of Hebrews tells us that today God speaks to us through his Son Jesus (Hebrews 1:1–3). Jesus is the Word of God who came down to live among us. His words are preserved for us to read again and again in the New Testament. Jesus' words are "living"—that means they still affect people who read them today. Unlike other books of history, the Bible's words can actually change our lives because they have the power of God. The gospel, the Bible tells us, is the "power of God for salvation to everyone who believes" (Romans 1:16).

Let's Talk About It!

Why is Miriam sitting alone far outside the camp?

Why is she so sad?

Who prays to God for Miriam?

Let's Talk About It!

What report did the fearful spies bring back to the people?

What are the names of the two spies who told the people they could trust God?

Who do you think Joshua and Caleb are pointing to?

Israel Spies Out the Land

NUMBERS 13 – 14

Eventually, the people reached the land of Canaan. God said to Moses, "Send some men to explore the land I am giving you. Choose one man from each tribe to go." So Moses picked twelve men, one from each tribe, to spy out the land. He told them, "See what the land is like, and whether the people who live there are strong or weak, few or many. What kind of land do they live in? Is it good or bad? What kind of towns do they live in—do they have walls around them? Is the soil good for farming? Are there trees? Do your best to bring back some of the fruit of the land too." So the spies left the camp and explored the land of Canaan for forty days.

When they came back, they brought a bunch of grapes big enough that two men had to carry it! Then they gave their report to Moses, Aaron, and all the people, but it was not what Moses was expecting. Ten of the spies said, "The land is rich and beautiful, but the people who live there are powerful. The cities are big with high walls around them. We are not strong enough to fight them!" They were afraid and did not believe that God would give them what he had promised. But two of the spies, Joshua and Caleb, trusted the Lord. Caleb said, "Don't listen to these men! We should go up and capture the land, just as God wants us to. We can certainly do it!" But the fearful spies argued with Caleb and Joshua. "We can't attack those people! They are stronger than we are! They are so big that we look like tiny grasshoppers compared to them. It will never work!"

Who do you think the people believed? They believed the ten fearful spies. They even said, "If this is what is ahead, it would be better to return to Egypt. We should choose a leader to take us back!" Joshua and Caleb said, "The Lord has a wonderful land he is ready to give us. If he is pleased with us, he will give it to us, a land that flows with milk and honey. Don't rebel against the Lord! Don't be afraid of the people living there. We will swallow them up because God has removed their protection and he is with us!" But the people refused to listen. In fact, they said that Joshua and Caleb should be stoned to death! Then, suddenly, everything stopped. The glory of the Lord appeared at the Tent of Meeting. God had something to say too!

The Lord said, "How long will this people despise me? And how long will they not believe in me, in spite of all the signs I have done among them?" (Numbers 14:11). God knew that the people were afraid because they did not trust or believe him. Again, God threatened to destroy all of Israel and start over with Moses alone. But again Moses was the mediator between God and the people, and he reminded God of his forgiveness.

Ten of the spies gave a bad report because they forgot about God. But Joshua and Caleb didn't forget that God was with them. They had faith in God's power to save. Did you know that putting faith in God is the way we please God too? Just as Joshua and Caleb put their faith in God's power to deliver them from their enemies and give them the Promised Land, we are called to put our faith in Jesus, who saves us from our greatest enemies: sin and death.

Moses Disobeys God

NUMBERS 20:2–13

The people of Israel did not believe God would help them conquer the land he had promised to give them. What happened next was very, very different from what might have been. Now God said that the people of Israel were not allowed to enter the Promised Land. Instead, they were sent back into the wilderness, where they would wander for forty years until a new generation, their children, would have the blessing of living in the land God had promised them. So because of their lack of faith, they lived in a dry wasteland instead of enjoying the milk and honey of the Promised Land.

Life in the wilderness was tough. After a month of travel, Moses' sister Miriam died and was buried. And once again, instead of trusting the Lord and accepting the consequences of their sin, the people quarreled against Moses and Aaron. They said, "Why did you ever make us leave Egypt to bring us to this evil place? Nothing grows here—no grain, no figs, no vines, no pomegranates—and there's no water to drink."

When Moses and Aaron heard this, they went before the Lord at the Tent of Meeting and fell facedown in prayer. The glory of the Lord appeared to them and the Lord told Moses, "Take your staff and gather the people. Then speak to a rock and tell it to give up its water for the people to drink." Moses didn't say a word. He just took his staff and assembled the people. But there was a problem: Moses was angry! And because he was, he didn't obey the Lord and simply speak to the rock. Instead, he hit the rock twice with his staff. And instead of telling the people that the water came from the Lord, Moses and Aaron complained and said that they were the ones who had to give them water! Despite their disobedience, God was merciful. Water came out of the rock for all the people and their animals to drink.

Because they disobeyed, the Lord had something to say to Moses and Aaron, and it must have been very hard to hear. "Because you did not believe in me or honor me as holy before the people of Israel, you will not bring them into the Promised Land when the time comes. You will never enter it."

Moses was a wonderful mediator for Israel, but even he was a sinner, just like you and me. Because of that he was not allowed to lead God's people into the Promised Land. One day, long after Moses died, another mediator came. This one never sinned—not once! He obeyed God's Word perfectly. His name is Jesus. The apostle John tells us that Jesus only did what he saw the Father do. That is what allowed him to take the punishment for our sins. Since Jesus never did anything wrong, he could take our place and receive God's wrath for our sins—so that we never would have to!

Let's Talk About It!

Why did God send the people to the wilderness instead of the lush green Promised Land?

What do you think it was like to live in the wilderness?

Why was Moses angry?

Let's Talk About It!

When the people complained, what did God send to punish them?

What do the people have to do to be saved?

How is Jesus like the bronze snake on the pole?

God Heals Israel with a Bronze Snake

NUMBERS 21:4–9

As the people of God continued wandering in the desert, God led them to Mount Hor. There God said that Aaron would soon die. He would not be allowed to enter the Promised Land because he and Moses had rebelled against the Lord. They did not follow his command when Moses struck the rock instead of speaking to it. God directed Aaron and his son Eleazar to climb up the mountain with Moses. Once they were on top, God told Moses to take away Aaron's garments and give them to his son Eleazar. Then Aaron died on top the mountain and all of Israel was very sad for a whole month.

When Israel moved on from that place, they were attacked by Arad, a Canaanite king. This time, instead of complaining, they cried out to the Lord and promised to destroy Arad and his cities if God would give them victory. The Lord heard their prayer. He gave them victory over the king and the people destroyed his cities. From Mount Hor they traveled back toward the Red Sea to go around the land of Edom. This was because the people of Edom were strong and did not allow Israel to walk across their land.

Once again the people grumbled against the Lord and against Moses. This time they said, "Why have you brought us up out of Egypt to die in the wilderness? For there is no food and no water, and we loathe this worthless food" (Numbers 21:5). Because of their complaining, the Lord sent fiery serpents among the people. The snakes bit them and many people died. When the people realized that they had sinned against the Lord in their complaining, they went to Moses as their mediator and asked him to ask the Lord to take away the snakes. Moses prayed for the people, and God answered him in his mercy.

But instead of taking the serpents away, God said to Moses, "Make a fiery serpent and set it on a pole. Everyone who is bitten should look up at it. When he sees it, he shall live." Moses did as the Lord commanded. He made a snake out of bronze metal, set it on top of a pole, and lifted it up so the people could see it. Whenever a snake bit someone, he or she could look up at the serpent on the pole and be healed.

Jesus once compared himself to that snake lifted up on the pole. When he spoke to Nicodemus he said, "As Moses lifted up the serpent in the wilderness, so must the Son of Man be lifted up, that whoever believes in him may have eternal life" (John 3:14–15). Just like the people in the desert, we have been wounded by our sin. The sting and bite of our sin is eternal death and we can't save ourselves from it. We can only be forgiven if we look up to Jesus on the cross and believe that God will save us through his death. Just as the people looked to the serpent on the pole for their forgiveness, we look to Jesus on the cross for ours.

Rahab's Help

JOSHUA 1–2

Moses was a very special servant of the Lord. The Bible says there was no one else like him. He even spoke to God face-to-face, yet he was not allowed to take the people into the Promised Land because of his sin. When he was 120 years old, God led him to the top of Mount Nebo so he could see the Promised Land from a distance. Though he could not enter the land, God allowed him to see that the promise was about to come true. There Moses died, and God buried him. Soon after, God chose Joshua to take Moses' place. He was one of the spies who had believed God's promise forty years before. After the people mourned Moses' death, the Lord told Joshua to cross the Jordan River and conquer the land. "Everywhere you put your foot, I will give you that land just as I promised," God said. "I will be with you just like I was with Moses. I will never leave you or forsake you."

Like Moses, Joshua sent spies into the land. But this time only two spies were sent. Joshua told them to spy on the city of Jericho. The men entered the city and spent the night at the house of a woman named Rahab. But the king of Jericho had his own spies, who discovered that Joshua's men were at her house. When Rahab heard that the men from Israel were in danger, she took them up to the roof and covered them with stalks of flax to hide them. When the king's men came, she told them, "The men have already left. I don't know where they went, but if you hurry, you might still catch them." So the king's men hurried away, searching for the spies all the way to the Jordan River. But they closed the gate of the city behind them, shutting the men of Israel in.

Rahab went back up to the roof and told the men what had happened. She told them that everyone in her city had heard about the powerful God of the Israelites, who had dried up the Red Sea and conquered the Egyptians. The people of Jericho were so afraid that their hearts were melting with fear. But Rahab felt differently. She said, "I know the Lord has given this land to you. Your God is the true God of heaven and earth. Please be kind to me and my family as I have been kind to you. Please spare our lives when your people come to Jericho." The spies promised that Rahab and her family would be safe if she helped them get away, and here is what they did. Rahab's home was on the wall of the city, so her window opened outside the city wall. It was the perfect way to escape. Rahab lowered a rope out her window and the two spies climbed down, landing safely outside the city. They told Rahab to hang a scarlet cord outside her house. When Israel came back to conquer Jericho, she and her family should stay inside her home and they would be safe. After hiding in the hills for three days, the spies returned to Joshua. They told him, "The Lord has surely given the land into our hands, because the people are filled with fear because of us!" Back in Jericho, Rahab tied the scarlet cord to her window.

Did you know that God had special plans for Rahab? She became King David's far-off grandmother. That means she also became the great, far-off grandmother of Jesus! Just as the blood on the doorposts kept the Israelites safe during Passover, the scarlet cord in Rahab's window protected her and her family from the judgment God brought to Jericho. One day her far-off grandson Jesus would die on the cross. His scarlet blood covers our sins so that we too can be saved from the judgment of God.

Let's Talk About It!

How does Rahab help the spies from Israel?
What does she hang from the window?
Why did she put it there?

Jericho Falls

JOSHUA 3—6

The day after the spies returned, Joshua set out for Jericho with the people of Israel. When they reached the Jordan River, they camped there for three days because the river was very high and they could not cross it. The Lord told Joshua to send the ark of the covenant into the waters first. The priests who carried the ark were to stand with it. As soon as their feet touched the water, God caused the floodwaters far upriver to stop. Soon the mighty river dried up and Israel walked across it on dry ground. When the kings of the Amorites and Canaanites heard that the Lord had dried up the floodwaters so that Israel crossed over on dry ground, their hearts melted with fear.

For the first time, Israel was in the land God had promised to give Abraham's descendants hundreds of years ago. It was a very special day, so the people celebrated by marking the place where they crossed with a pile of stones. They also circumcised the new generation and celebrated the Passover, because these both marked them as God's chosen covenant people. Then it was time to move against Jericho. As Joshua drew near the city, the Lord appeared. He stood before him as a man with a sword and said, "I am the commander of the army of the LORD." When Joshua heard that, he fell down and worshiped. The commander of the Lord's army said to Joshua, "Take off your sandals from your feet, for the place where you are standing is holy."

(Joshua 5:14–15). Joshua obeyed right away. The Lord told Joshua, "I have given the city into your hands." He told Joshua to have the people march around the city for six days. Then, on the seventh day, they should march around it seven times, have the priests blow their trumpets and shout, and the walls of Jericho would fall.

Joshua obeyed the Lord. For six days, the people marched around the city once. The ark of the covenant with its armed guards led the way. Seven priests blew their trumpets, but the people were completely silent. Then everyone returned to camp. On the seventh day, they marched around the city seven times. Then, at Joshua's command, everyone in Israel gave a great shout. At once, the walls of Jericho broke apart and fell flat to the ground! Joshua told the people to invade the city and destroy everything in it, except the silver, gold, bronze, and iron. Joshua said that these were holy and must be saved for the Lord. What happened to Rahab and her family? Joshua sent the two spies to rescue them, just as they had promised. So the men of Israel destroyed the whole city and set it on fire, but Rahab and her family were saved. They became part of the people of Israel.

God's plan of attack—marching around the city and shouting—showed everyone that it was God's strength and power that brought down Jericho's mighty walls. God wanted Israel to know that their victory did not come from themselves. All the glory went to God. The Lord's plan of attack against the curse of sin and death is the same. None of us can save ourselves from sin and death. Only by the sacrifice of Jesus on the cross can we find victory over those enemies. Just as it was for Israel, our salvation does not come by our own works. We don't deserve it. We can't earn it. Our good works cannot demand it. Salvation for Israel and for us is completely undeserved. It comes to us by the grace of God alone, by the power of God alone, for the glory of God alone.

Let's Talk About It!

In the picture, what is happening to the walls of Jericho?

Are the trumpet blasts and shouting of Israel making the walls collapse?

Who will be praised for this great victory?

Let's Talk About It!

Where did Achan hide the stolen treasure?

Who did Achan steal from?

Why can't we hide our sins from God?

Israel & Ai

When the walls of Jericho fell, the men of Israel were to give all the silver, gold, bronze, and iron to the Lord and destroy everything else. And everyone obeyed...except for one man named Achan. When he saw two hundred shekels of silver, a large gold bar, and a beautiful cloak, he disobeyed the Lord and took them for himself. Achan dug a hole inside his tent and hid the things he stole, thinking that no one would ever know.

But the Lord knew what Achan had done. His holy anger burned against all Israel, not just Achan. When Israel went to attack the next city, Ai, they lost! Although Ai was much weaker than Jericho, Israel was defeated because the Lord did not help them win. When Israel heard they had lost the battle and thirty-six men had been killed, the people were filled with fear. What had gone wrong? Why hadn't the Lord blessed them? Joshua fell down before the Lord and asked why Israel had lost the battle. The Lord answered, "Israel has sinned. They have taken some of the things that were supposed to be devoted to me and hidden them with their own belongings. This must be made right." The Lord told Joshua to assemble the people the next day. Step by step, the Lord would show who had stolen the devoted things. Everyone would pick a lot, with something like a straw. The one who picked the shorter straw would be the chosen one, the guilty one.

The next morning Joshua brought Israel together. Each tribe stood together, and when they cast the first lot, the tribe of Judah was taken. Then, of all the clans of Judah, the Zerahites were chosen. Then, from among the Zerahites, the household of Zabdi was chosen. Finally, Achan was chosen from all the men of that household. Joshua ordered Achan to confess what he had done. Achan said, "I have sinned against the Lord. When I saw the beautiful robe, the gold, and the silver shekels, I wanted them for myself, so I took them. They are hidden inside my tent." Messengers went to Achan's tent and brought back the devoted things. Then all of Israel stoned Achan and his family to death. They burned everything they owned and put a great pile of stones over that place.

After Achan was killed, the Lord commanded Israel to attack Ai again. This time Israel defeated Ai because the Lord helped them win the battle. Afterwards, Joshua built an altar and sacrificed peace offerings to the Lord. Then he read the Law of Moses to the people to remind them of God's law.

Did you know that God sees everything we do, good and bad? Like Achan, we all deserve to be punished for our sins—and the punishment we deserve is death. But instead of punishment, God made a way for us to be forgiven by sending his Son Jesus to die on the cross in our place. There is a wonderful mercy hidden in this story about Achan. God could have destroyed all of Israel or at least all of Achan's tribe, but he didn't. That is because God had a special plan for Achan's tribe. God planned that one day, out of Achan's tribe, the tribe of Judah, God would bring his salvation. Jesus would be born into that same tribe! Achan's punishment helped preserve the holiness of God's people so that one day, Jesus, the Lion of the tribe of Judah, would be born.

God Calls Gideon

JUDGES 6:1—35

After their victory over Ai, Joshua led the people to many victories against their enemies. But after Joshua died, the people of Israel disobeyed the Lord. Instead of driving the Canaanites out of the land, they lived alongside these idol worshipers. God said to Israel, "What is this you have done? So now I say, I will not drive them out before you, but they shall become thorns in your sides, and their gods shall be a snare to you" (Judges 2:2–3).

Since Israel had not driven out their enemies, God allowed those enemies to conquer them. But when Israel cried for help, God delivered them. Sadly, they did not learn their lesson. Again and again Israel turned away from the Lord to serve false gods. There came a time when the Lord allowed the Midianites to overpower Israel because of their sin. The Midianites ruled them for seven years and the people were so afraid of them that they made caves in

attacked, stole their crops, and raided their land, leaving little food for the people of Israel to eat. So the people cried out to the Lord for help again.

Once again God heard their cry for help and appeared to a man named Gideon who was hiding from the Midianites because he was afraid. The Lord called out to Gideon and said he would be the one to save Israel from their enemies. Gideon thought the Lord should find someone else. "How can I save Israel?" he asked. "My clan is the weakest clan and I am the weakest in my family." But the Lord said to Gideon, "I will be with you and you will strike down the Midianites." This was hard for Gideon to imagine. He asked the Lord to show him a sign to help him believe that what God said was true. The Lord agreed and Gideon went to prepare a meal for him. When he returned, the Lord told him to set the food on a rock and pour some broth over it. Fire sprang up out of the rock and consumed the food, and the Lord disappeared. Then Gideon knew he had seen the Lord face-to-face!

The Lord told Gideon to destroy the idols his father had in their home. Gideon broke down his father's altar to Baal and cut down his wooden Asherah pole. But because Gideon was afraid, he waited until night to do it. Then he built an altar to the Lord on top of the broken idols. He sacrificed a bull to the Lord and burned it up with the wood from the Asherah pole. When everyone woke up and saw what Gideon had done, they wanted to kill him. But Gideon's father stopped them. "If Baal is a real god," he said, "let Baal punish Gideon!" But of course Baal was a false god, so nothing happened to Gideon.

In spite of Israel's sinful ways, God gave them Gideon to save them from their enemies. Israel did not deserve to be rescued. God did it because he loved them. And that is the same reason God sent Jesus to save us, even though we are sinners who disobey God like Israel did.

Let's Talk About It!

What did God tell Gideon to do with his father's idol, an Asherah pole?

Why did Gideon do this at night?

What happened in the morning when the people saw what he had done?

Let's Talk About It!

What are the enemy soldiers doing to one another?

What did Gideon and his men have to fight with?

Who really won the battle for Gideon that day?

Gideon's Victory

JUDGES 6:36—7:25

After Gideon tore down his father's idols, the Midianites crossed the Jordan River to attack Israel. The Spirit of the Lord came upon Gideon. He blew the trumpet and called for God's people to gather. But Gideon was still not sure God would help him defeat the Midianites. So Gideon laid out a fleece of sheep's wool on the threshing floor and said to God, "If it's really true that you will use me to save Israel, please show me with this fleece. If you allow dew to fall on the fleece but it is dry on the ground, then I will know you will use me to save Israel, as you have said." In the morning the fleece was wet and the ground was dry, just as Gideon had asked. But Gideon still did not believe, so this time he reversed his request. The next morning, the ground was wet but the fleece was dry. Then Gideon knew God was with him. He gathered thirty-two thousand men of Israel to fight the Midianites.

But God didn't need or want that many men to fight with Gideon. He wanted Israel to see it was his power alone that would rescue them. So the Lord said that anyone who was afraid should go home. After that, only ten thousand men were left! But that was still too many men. So when the men went to the river to drink, the Lord told Gideon to keep only those men who lapped water up from the river with their tongues like a dog. That left only three hundred men! Now, when God defeated the whole Midian army with just three hundred men, God alone would get the glory. Gideon and all Israel would know it was only by God's strength that they were saved from their enemies.

With only three hundred men to fight with him, the Lord knew Gideon was afraid. So he sent him to the Midianite camp to listen to what they were saying. Gideon heard two soldiers talking. One soldier shared a dream and another soldier told him what it meant. The one interpreting said that the God of Israel was going to give a man named Gideon victory over them! When Gideon heard this, his confidence and faith in God's plan grew. He went back to his camp and prepared his three hundred men to attack.

Gideon divided the men into three groups. He gave each man a trumpet and a clay jar with a burning torch inside. Then Gideon's men surrounded the Midianites. At Gideon's signal, everyone blew their trumpets and smashed their jars. They held up their torches and shouted, "A sword for the LORD and for Gideon!" (Judges 7:20). The Lord confused the enemy so much that they began killing each other. Then the Midianites ran away. Gideon sent messengers to the rest of Israel who chased the Midianites down and defeated the enemy as they ran.

Did you know we are saved by God's grace today just like Israel was in Gideon's day? God saved Israel with only three hundred men so they could see that it was by God's grace, not their own work. They could not boast in their own efforts. Our salvation comes when we, like Gideon, believe in God's plan to save us. We can't do it by our own work either. None of us can boast and say, "I saved myself!" The apostle Paul wrote, "For by grace you have been saved through faith. And this is not your own doing; it is the gift of God, not a result of works, so that no one may boast" (Ephesians 2:8–9). Even with us, God gets all the credit.

God Gives Samson Strength

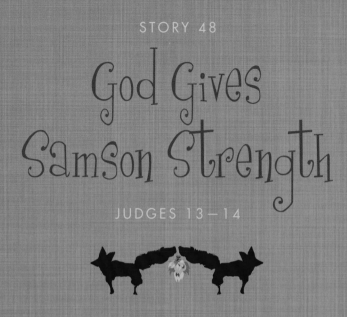

After Gideon died, the people fell back into their sinful ways. God chose others like Gideon to rescue Israel and lead them, but again and again the people fell into wickedness. So the Lord allowed the Philistines to conquer Israel and rule over them for forty years.

Then one day the Lord appeared as an angel to an Israelite woman who was married to a man named Manoah. He said to her, "You have been waiting for a child for a long time, but now the time has come for you to have a son. He will be special from the moment of his birth. I am going to use him to rescue Israel from the Philistines." God told Manoah's wife never to cut the boy's hair. This was to show that he was set apart for service to God. In time, Manoah's wife had a son. She named him Samson and left his hair to grow long. When Samson became a young man, the Spirit of the Lord began to stir in him. One day while he was walking, a roaring lion jumped out at him. But the Spirit of the Lord rushed upon Samson, who killed the lion with his bare hands.

But instead of living for God's glory, Samson became proud. He was disrespectful to his parents, demanding they get him a wife from among the Philistines instead of God's people. When they tried to correct their son, Samson did not listen to them. But even though Samson was sinful, God used him to judge the Philistines who were ruling over God's people.

Once Samson caught three hundred foxes and tied their tails together. He put torches between each pair and lit them. Then he sent pairs of foxes running off to burn down the crops of the Philistines. When the Philistines found out what had happened, they came to fight the people of Judah. They demanded that Samson be tied up and given over to them. Samson agreed to be tied up with strong, new ropes. After his hands were bound, the Israelites took Samson to the Philistines. The Spirit of the Lord fell upon him again, and he easily broke the ropes.

Then he saw a jawbone of a donkey lying on the ground. Samson picked it up and used it as a weapon to strike down a thousand men!

Long after the days of Samson, another angel appeared to another couple. He announced that their son would rule over God's people and deliver them from another enemy. The couple was Mary and Joseph, their Son was Jesus, and he delivered them—and us—from sin. Just as it happened with Samson, the Spirit of the Lord came upon Jesus. But instead of fighting an earthly battle, Jesus fought a spiritual one. And unlike Samson who was proud and often did what he wanted, Jesus obeyed God perfectly, even when it meant dying on the cross for our sins. By his death, Jesus defeated death for everyone who believes.

Let's Talk About It!

What is Samson holding?

What does he do with it?

How can one man defeat so many without getting hurt himself?

Samson Loses His Strength

JUDGES 16

Samson made many enemies as a judge over Israel, especially among the Philistines. But he was too strong for them to fight, so they set traps for him instead. Even then, Samson escaped. Finally the Philistines came up with a plan. Samson loved a Philistine woman named Delilah. The Philistines promised her a treasure of silver coins if she could find out the secret of his great strength. Delilah agreed and the new trap was set.

The next time Samson came to visit Delilah, she asked, "Tell me the secret of your great strength. Is there any way you can be tied up so that you can't escape?" Samson lied. He said, "If anyone ties me up with seven fresh bowstrings, I will lose my power." So, while Samson slept, Delilah tied him up just as Samson had said. Then she shouted, "Samson, the Philistines are here to capture you!" Samson woke up and snapped the bowstrings as if they were nothing. Delilah complained, "You lied to me! Now tell me the truth. What is the secret of your strength?" Samson lied again. This time he said, "If anyone ties me with new ropes that have never been used, I will become as weak as any other man." But when she tied him up with new ropes and called in the Philistines, Samson broke the new ropes easily.

A third time Delilah asked Samson the secret of his strength. A third time Samson lied and, when the Philistines came, Samson escaped. Day after day Delilah pestered him to tell him the truth: "How can you say you love me if you won't tell me your secret?" Finally, Samson was so tired of arguing that he told her about his vow to God to never shave his head. Samson should not have done this, but in his pride, he thought he would not lose his strength. This time, while he slept, Delilah had a man shave his head. When the Philistines came in, Samson was easily captured, because God left Samson to fight in his own strength. The Philistines gouged out Samson's eyes and put him in prison.

After Samson had been in prison for awhile, the Philistines brought Samson to the temple of their god to mock him and to praise their god for his defeat. The Philistines were sure this would be a great day, but they forgot something. While Samson had been in prison, his hair had grown long again, as God had wanted it to be. When Samson entered the temple, he asked the attendant to put his hands on the pillars that held up the building, so they could help him stand. Then he prayed, "O God, please strengthen me just once more." God heard his prayer, and when Samson pushed against the pillars, his great strength returned. The whole roof of the building tumbled down on Samson, the Philistine rulers, and all the people who gathered there. They all died.

Although God used Samson to save Israel from their enemies, Samson fell into the sin of pride. He thought he could be strong all by himself, without God's help. He became distracted with the pleasures of the world. This story teaches us that no ordinary man could ever bring lasting salvation to God's people, for we are all sinners. One day, though, God sent a deliverer named Jesus who was very different. Unlike Samson, God's Son Jesus did not fall into sin. Though he was God, he humbled himself and came as a man to live a perfect life and die on the cross in our place, to provide a salvation that lasts forever!

Let's Talk About It!

What has God forbidden Samson to do?

What happens to Samson when he wakes up and finds his hair cut off?

Can you remember a time when you disobeyed?

Let's Talk About It!

Who are the three people in the picture?

What does Boaz do to help Ruth and Naomi?

Who is Ruth and Boaz's special great-grandson?

Ruth

RUTH 1—4

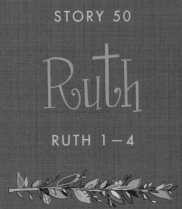

In the days when judges like Samson and Gideon ruled the land of Israel there was a famine. Because there was no food, Elimelech, a man from God's people in Judah, moved to the pagan land of Moab. He took his wife Naomi and their two sons. In time, Elimelech died and his sons married women from Moab. But it wasn't long before the sons died too. This left Naomi all alone with her sons' widows, Ruth and Orpah. There was no man to care for them.

After awhile, Naomi received word that the famine in Israel was over. There was food again in Judah. So Naomi decided to travel back home. She urged Ruth and Orpah to return to their families and gods. Orpah left, but Ruth refused. She said, "Where you go I will go, and where you live I will live. Your people will be my people and your God my God." So Naomi and Ruth returned to Bethlehem together. Since they had no food or money, Ruth went to the fields to gather the leftovers the harvesters missed. God led her to the field of Boaz, a relative of Naomi, just as he came to visit his men. When Boaz saw Ruth, he welcomed her and kindly invited her to eat with him. He told the men to leave plenty of grain behind for her to gather.

When Ruth told Naomi about Boaz and his kindness, Naomi explained that Boaz was a close relative. This meant he was one of their "redeemers," who could marry Ruth and care for her since her husband had died. In those days, there were special rules about those things. Naomi was happy that Boaz had showed Ruth such favor. She sent Ruth back to him, hoping he would marry her. And that is just what Boaz did! He went to the elders of the city and promised to "redeem" and take care of the two widows, by marrying Ruth and buying back Naomi's land to give her a place to live and grow food. Later, when Ruth and Boaz had a son, the women said to Naomi, "Blessed be the LORD, who has not left you this day without a redeemer!" (Ruth 4:14). They named the boy Obed. When he grew up, Obed became the father of Jesse, who became the father of David, who became king of Israel!

Did you know we have a Redeemer too? A redeemer in Naomi's day would buy back the land a widow had lost when her husband died. He would pledge to care for her. Jesus is our Redeemer in an even greater way. By dying on the cross for our sins, Jesus paid the price to redeem us from the curse of our sin. Now all those who trust in the Lord are redeemed. They will live with God in heaven and he will take care of them. In Galatians, Paul tells us that God sent his Son "to redeem those who were under the law, so that we might receive adoption as sons" (Galatians 4:5).

God Hears Hannah's Prayers

1 SAMUEL 1:1 — 2:11

When Ruth's grandson Jesse grew older, he married and had his own children. During that same time, the Lord allowed a prophet to be born named Samuel. It happened this way: Every year a man named Elkanah traveled to Shiloh to worship the Lord and offer sacrifices with his wives, Hannah and Peninnah. Peninnah had sons and daughters, but Hannah had no children. This made Hannah sad because she wanted children very much, and Peninnah made fun of Hannah about it. When they all traveled to Shiloh, Peninnah would irritate Hannah, year after year.

Finally, Hannah was so sad that on one of their trips she went to the temple to pray. She pleaded with the Lord in silent prayer and made a vow. "O Lord, if you will give me a son, I will dedicate him to serve you all the days of his life." When Eli, the priest, saw Hannah's lips moving but heard no sound, he thought she was drunk. He scolded her, but Hannah explained that she was very sad and she was pouring out her soul to the Lord in prayer. When Eli heard this, he replied, "Go in peace. God give you what you have asked of him." When Hannah heard Eli's encouragement, she was no longer sad. She went home with Elkanah. And the Lord remembered Hannah and gave her a son. Hannah named the baby boy Samuel.

When Samuel was old enough, Hannah returned to Eli with her little boy. She presented Samuel to the priest and said, "I am the woman who stood here beside you praying to the Lord. I prayed for this child and the Lord has given me what I asked of him. Now I give him to the Lord. For his whole life, I want Samuel to serve God." Then she prayed a beautiful prayer that started out with the words, "My heart rejoices in the Lord; my strength is lifted up in him. I can boast over my enemies because I rejoice in your salvation." Then Hannah left Samuel to be cared for by Eli at the temple. Every year she would visit Samuel at the time of their yearly sacrifice and take him clothes she had made for him. She kept her promise to God, but even she could not have predicted all that God would do through her firstborn son. God planned to call Samuel as a prophet to speak for God to his people.

One day, much later, God blessed another woman with a very special son who spoke the words of God. Her name was Mary, the mother of Jesus. Did you know that Mary prayed a prayer of joy very similar to Hannah's? While she was pregnant with Jesus, her cousin Elizabeth confirmed what God's angel had told Mary about her baby. Mary replied with a prayer that began, "My soul magnifies the Lord, and my spirit rejoices in God my Savior" (Luke 1:46–47). Perhaps Mary remembered Hannah's prayer, recorded in God's Word. Both Hannah and Mary's sons, Samuel and Jesus, grew up as prophets who served the Lord. In this way Samuel's life points forward to Jesus.

Let's Talk About It!

How does God answer Hannah's prayers?

What is Hannah doing in the picture?

What is the name of her son?

Let's Talk About It!

Who is calling to Samuel?

Who does Samuel think is calling his name?

What did God tell Samuel about Eli?

God calls Little Samuel

1 SAMUEL 2:12–3:21

I wish I could tell you that little Samuel was surrounded by people who loved the Lord when he went to live with Eli. But, sadly, that was not true. Although Eli served God, he had two wicked sons, Hophni and Phinehas, who did not. They were worthless men who did not obey their father or the Lord. But Samuel was different. He "continued to grow both in stature and in favor with the LORD and also with man" (1 Samuel 2:26). This means he was growing up to be a person who loved and pleased God, and people could see it.

One day the Lord sent a prophet to warn Eli about his wicked sons. He told Eli that both sons would die on the same day and that Eli's family would not be blessed. Through the prophet, the Lord said, "I will raise up for myself a faithful priest, who will be obedient to the things that are in my heart and in my mind. His house and family will serve me forever." But even then Eli did nothing about his sons.

One night in the temple, just before Samuel fell asleep, the Lord called out to him. Samuel answered "Here I am!" and hurried to Eli. But Eli said, "I didn't call you. Go back and lie down." The Lord called out a second time, "Samuel!" Again Samuel woke Eli, thinking he had called. Then the Lord called out a third time, "Samuel!" When Samuel went to Eli again, Eli knew it must be the Lord calling

Samuel's name. So Eli told Samuel to lie down again. This time he said, "If he calls you, say, 'Speak, Lord, for your servant is listening.'" Samuel lay down again and, when the Lord called him a fourth time, Samuel answered, "Speak, for your servant is listening."

The Lord told Samuel he was going to punish Eli and his household. This would fulfill the word the prophet brought, because Hophni and Phinehas had sinned against the Lord and Eli had not stopped them. The next morning Eli insisted that Samuel tell him everything the Lord had said. Though Eli knew it was the Lord who had spoken, he did nothing to turn away from his sins or correct his sons. So in a short time God's judgment came to Israel. The ark of the Lord was captured, and Eli and his two sons died. But the Lord was with Samuel. All Israel knew that Samuel was the Lord's prophet.

Did you know we can see a glimpse of Jesus in the story of Samuel? The prophet who spoke to Eli said that God would raise up a faithful priest to serve him forever. No ordinary man can serve as a faithful priest forever, because they all die! But Jesus is the faithful high priest who lives forever (Hebrews 7:24). There is another interesting connection to the life of Jesus in this story. When Jesus was growing up, Luke says that "Jesus increased in wisdom and in stature and in favor with God and man" (Luke 2:52). Those are almost the exact words used to describe young Samuel as he grew. In the midst of Eli's sinful household, God raised up Samuel to be a faithful priest. His life points us to Jesus, who is our faithful priest forever.

The God of Israel Cannot Be Captured

1 SAMUEL 4—7

Some time after Samuel told Eli that God would judge him and his sons, Israel went to war against the Philistines. Instead of asking the Lord for help, they went into battle in their own strength. Israel lost the battle and four thousand men died. The elders could not understand why they lost! To make sure they won the next battle, they took the ark of God with them, and Hophni and Phinehas were glad to follow along. The problem was that everyone treated the ark as though it had a secret power of its own, like a good luck charm. Again they went into battle without asking the Lord for help—and lost. This time even more people died. Hophni and Phinehas were killed, and the ark of God was captured. When Eli heard this terrible news, he fell over, broke his neck, and died.

The Philistines treated the captured ark like one of their gods and put it in their temple with their god Dagon. The next morning they found the statue of Dagon knocked to the ground, facedown in front of the ark of God. The Philistines stood Dagon back up, but the next morning Dagon was on the ground again! This time his head and arms were broken off too. After that, the people of the city became very sick. So they sent the ark away from that place, but no matter where they sent it, the people became very sick.

In desperation, the Philistines asked their priests for help. Their priests told them to return the ark to Israel. So they put the ark on a cart pulled by two cows and sent the cart away. Even without a driver, the cows carried the ark straight back to Israel. When the people of Israel saw the ark returning, they rejoiced. The Levites unloaded the ark, broke apart the cart, and sacrificed the cows as a burnt offering to the Lord. But some men who looked upon the ark were struck down and killed because the ark of God was holy. The others said, "Who is able to stand before the LORD, this holy God?" (1 Samuel 6:20). Then even the Israelites sent the ark away to another town.

When Samuel learned about the ark, he commanded the people to put away their false gods and turn their hearts to the Lord. Samuel sacrificed a lamb for the people's sins and called out to the Lord for Israel. While Israel was gathered for the offering, the Philistines came in a surprise attack, but the Lord heard Samuel's prayers and defeated the Philistines with a mighty, thunderous sound that sent them into confusion. From that day on, during Samuel's rule, Israel had peace with the Philistines.

Do you know why God knocked over the statue of Dagon? The ark represented God's presence, and the idol to Dagon represented the false worship of the Philistines. No false god would be allowed to stand above the Lord God! So God himself tore down the Philistine idol. Sin cannot stand in God's presence. That is why the cross is so important for us. As sinners, we cannot live in the presence of a holy God. We need our sin taken away. That is what Jesus did for us on the cross. He took the punishment for our sin so we could be forgiven. Once we are forgiven, we can enter God's presence without fear.

Let's Talk About It!

Where is Dagon's head?

Why is it broken off his body?

What does God want to teach the Philistines by knocking down their idol?

Let's Talk About It!

What is Samuel doing in the picture?

Why do the people want a man to be king instead of God?

How does God plan to use the new king to help his people?

Israel Demands a King

1 SAMUEL 8—10

When Samuel grew to be an old man, he appointed his sons to be judges over Israel. But Samuel's sons were not faithful to God. Instead of ruling honestly as their father had done, they took bribes of money from people and ruled unfairly to please them. Because of this, the elders of Israel gathered together and demanded that Samuel appoint a king to rule over them, so they could be like the other nations. Samuel knew that the Lord was the King over Israel, and he prayed to God and told him what the people said. The Lord said to Samuel, "Listen to what the people are saying to you. They have not rejected you; they have rejected me as their King." The Lord told Samuel to warn Israel that a king would demand their work and their time, their money, their servants, and the best of their land. They would be like slaves. But the people didn't believe these warnings. They insisted on a king so they could be like the nations around them. They wanted an earthly king who could judge them and fight their battles for them. They were rejecting God, who wanted to do both of those things for Israel himself.

God gave them what they wanted. The Lord chose Saul, a tall, handsome man from the tribe of Benjamin, to be king. God sent Saul to Samuel and instructed Samuel to anoint him king over Israel. In spite of Israel's sin, the Lord told Samuel he would use Saul to deliver Israel from the Philistines. So Samuel anointed Saul king and presented him to the people. "All the people shouted 'Long live the king!'" (1 Samuel 10:24). He looked like just the kind of king they had in mind, and they were even more excited when Saul helped them defeat their enemies, the Ammonites.

Samuel rebuked the people. He told them that when they chose a king, they had rejected God. Then he called upon the Lord to bring thunder and rain. When the people heard the storm, they were afraid. They repented for demanding a king. Samuel comforted them. In spite of their sin, God would not reject them, he said, because he had chosen them as his own special people. Samuel warned Israel, "If you and your king obey the Lord, it will go well with you. But if you disobey the Lord, you will be swept away, along with your king."

Did you know God planned for a king to reign over Israel long before Israel demanded one? He even gave Moses instructions on how to choose a king (Deuteronomy 17:14–20). The problem with Israel's desire for a king was that they had rejected God, their true Sovereign King. If they had followed the Lord, they would have discovered that one day the Sovereign God would send his Prince to rule over Israel. He would be called the Prince of Peace because he would bring an everlasting peace to God's people. There would be no end to his rule and reign. That Prince is Jesus, whom God sent to redeem Israel's sin. King Jesus led God's people to the ultimate victory—a victory over Satan, sin, and the curse of death.

Saul Disobeys the Lord

1 SAMUEL 13:1—14; 15:1—26

One day Samuel told Saul to go to the town of Gilgal and wait seven days. Samuel would meet him there and offer a sacrifice. Then, Samuel explained, he would tell Saul what to do. While Saul waited for Samuel, he gathered the people to get ready for a Philistine attack. The Philistines came with thirty thousand chariots and six thousand horsemen with swords. With all those warriors on the way, the army of Israel grew afraid and started to scatter. By the seventh day, Saul was impatient. He was afraid he was going to lose all his soldiers. So instead of waiting for Samuel, Saul offered the sacrifice himself, something a king was not allowed to do. Samuel arrived just as Saul finished. When he saw what Saul had done, he rebuked him. He told Saul that because he did not keep the Lord's commandment, Saul would not be king for long. God would choose another man to be king, a man after God's own heart.

Saul went on to win many battles over Israel's enemies, but he didn't always follow the Lord. Once, God sent Samuel to Saul with a message to attack the Amalekites and completely destroy them, including all their oxen, sheep, cattle, and donkeys. Saul gathered a great army and defeated the Amalekites, but then he disobeyed the Lord again. Saul and the army destroyed everything that was worthless, but they kept for themselves the oxen, the best of the sheep, the fattened calves, the lambs, and all that was good, and they spared the life of Agag, the wicked Amalekite king.

Then the Lord said to Samuel, "I am sorry that I made Saul king, because he has not followed me or carried out my commands." The next day Samuel went to Saul to ask him why he disobeyed the Lord. Saul tried to hide what he had done and said, "I have carried out the Lord's instructions!" But Samuel could hear the bleating of the sheep Israel had spared. He confronted Saul, but instead of admitting his sin, Saul blamed the people for taking the animals. Samuel said to Saul, "Because you have rejected the word of the LORD, he has also rejected you from being king" (1 Samuel 15:23). Finally Saul became sad at this news and confessed his sin. He asked Samuel to return home with him to worship the Lord. But Samuel refused because God had rejected Saul. When Samuel turned to leave, Saul grabbed his robe and tore it. Samuel looked at Saul and told him that, just as the robe was torn, "The Lord has torn the kingdom of Israel from you this day and has given it to a neighbor of yours, who is better than you."

Even though God warned Saul and promised him that all would go well if he obeyed his commands, Saul failed as king. In fact, all of Israel's kings sinned against the Lord. But one day another king would come to Israel who would obey God's commandments perfectly. The apostle Paul tells us that our great King Jesus obeyed the commandments of the Lord, even though it meant he would die a terrible death on the cross (Philippians 2:8). Jesus was tempted like every other man, but he obeyed God perfectly. Now he offers to trade his perfect life for our sinful lives if we will place our trust in him.

Let's Talk About It!

How does Saul disobey God?

What does he do to Samuel's robe?

What does Samuel say to Saul?

Let's Talk About It!

Which one of Jesse's sons does God choose?

Why doesn't Jesse think David can be a king?

Why does God choose David?

God Chooses a New King

1 SAMUEL 16:1–13

After Samuel rebuked Saul and told him God would find a new king, Samuel finished the task Saul failed to carry out. He killed King Agag of the Amalekites. Then Samuel left that place very sad. He would not see Saul again until the day of Saul's death.

Then God said to Samuel, "How long will you grieve over Saul, since I have rejected him from being king over Israel? Fill your horn with oil, and go. I will send you to Jesse the Bethlehemite, for I have provided for myself a king among his sons" (1 Samuel 16:1). But Samuel was afraid. "How can I go?" he asked the Lord. "If Saul hears, he will kill me." The Lord told Samuel to plan a sacrifice and invite Jesse and his sons to come. That way, no one would know he was traveling to anoint a new king. God promised to show Samuel which son was the one.

Samuel did as the Lord instructed and traveled to Bethlehem. When he arrived, he announced a sacrifice and invited Jesse and his sons. When it was time for the sacrifice, Samuel looked at Jesse's sons to see which one he thought would be anointed king. When Samuel saw Jesse's oldest son Eliab, he was impressed with how tall and strong he was. Samuel thought for sure Eliab was the one! But the Lord told Samuel that Eliab was not the one. He told Samuel not to be fooled by outward appearances. He explained that the Lord sees things differently than people do. He said, "Man looks on the outward appearance, but the LORD looks on the heart" (1 Samuel 16:7).

One by one, Jesse brought his sons to Samuel. Each time Samuel said, "The Lord has not chosen this one." From the oldest to the youngest, the sons stood before Samuel, but none of them were chosen by the Lord. Finally, Samuel asked Jesse if all his sons had come. Jesse replied, "There is only one left. He is the youngest, and he stayed home to care for the sheep." Samuel said, "Send and get him. We won't sit down until he comes." When David, the youngest son, arrived, God told Samuel to anoint him. God chose David that day as the next king of Israel! As soon as Samuel poured the horn of oil on David, the Spirit of the Lord rushed upon him and remained with him for the rest of his life.

Do you know how this story points forward to Jesus? David was the youngest son and probably the smallest, but the Lord chose him because he was a man after God's own heart (1 Samuel 13:14). Like David, Jesus was a man after God his Father's own heart. Jesus obeyed his Father perfectly, and by his death he delivered God's people from their greatest enemies. Jesus came as a baby, born in a humble stable in the same town of Bethlehem that David came from. Jesus was born in the family line of David. That means Jesus was the great, far-off grandson of David.

David & Goliath

1 SAMUEL 17

Not long after David was anointed king, the Philistines gathered their armies to attack God's people again. Saul was still king, but the Spirit of the Lord had left him. The Philistines were on one mountain and King Saul's army was on another, with a valley in between. The Philistines had a great warrior named Goliath on their side. He was nine feet tall and wore heavy armor. Each morning for forty days Goliath came out to the soldiers of Israel and made fun of them and their God. He dared them to fight and said, "Choose a man for yourselves, and let him come down to me. If he is able to fight with me and kill me, then we will be your servants. But if I prevail against him and kill him, then you shall be our servants and serve us" (1 Samuel 17:8–9). The men of Israel were terrified and no one volunteered to fight Goliath.

From time to time, David traveled to the battlefield to bring food for his brothers in the king's army. One day, David was there to hear Goliath mocking Israel and daring the soldiers to fight him. David asked the soldiers, "Who is this uncircumcised Philistine, that he should defy the armies of the living God?" (1 Samuel 17:26). David's oldest brother scolded David. "Who do you think you are to be talking to us like this? You don't have the right to say anything."

But when Saul heard about David he called for him. David told Saul, "I will go and fight this Philistine," but Saul saw that David was just a boy. Still David did not give up. He told Saul how the Lord had helped him kill lions and bears all by himself. He said, "The Lord who delivered me from the lion and the bear will deliver me from this Philistine." So Saul at last agreed. He offered David his own armor to wear, but it was too heavy for David. Instead he took only his staff, five smooth stones, and a sling as he went out to meet Goliath.

When Goliath saw David coming toward him, he mocked him and said, "Am I a dog, that you come to me with sticks?" (1 Samuel 17:43). David replied, "You come to me with a sword and a spear and a javelin, but I come to you in the name of the Lord of hosts. He will deliver you into my hand and I will strike you down. Everyone on earth will know it is the Lord who saves." As Goliath moved toward David, David put a stone in his sling and hurled it at Goliath. The rock hit him on the forehead and the mighty Goliath fell to the ground. Then David ran to Goliath, took out his sword, and cut off his head, killing the great giant. When the Philistines saw that Goliath was dead, they ran in fear. The men of Israel chased them until they won a great victory.

When we read this story, we like to compare ourselves with David. But really, we are more like the men of Israel, afraid to fight and in desperate need of a champion to save them. David was God's man for the job. He did what the Israelites could not do. The salvation David brought Israel should remind us of Jesus. Like David, Jesus was a king who went to battle on our behalf. His victory was over sin and death. Before David delivered the men of Israel from Goliath, they stood helpless against him just as we are helpless to save ourselves and need Jesus to deliver us from our sin. David's life points to Jesus, and this story helps us see that we are not saved by our own strength, but by God's power.

Let's Talk About It!

What does Goliath say against God?
Why doesn't anyone want to fight Goliath?
How is David different from all the other soldiers?

Let's Talk About It!

Why does the ark start to fall?

What mistake does Uzzah make?

Why couldn't anyone touch the ark?

The Ark of God

2 SAMUEL 6—7;
1 CHRONICLES 13

After King Saul died David took the throne as king of Israel. One of David's first desires was to bring the ark of God back to Jerusalem. Saul had forgotten about the ark while he was king, so for twenty years it remained in the house of a man named Abinadab, cared for by Eleazar, Abinadab's son, until David came with his men to bring it home.

In those twenty years, the instructions God gave Moses about the ark were forgotten too. Instead of using the Levites to carry the ark with its poles, David and his men placed the ark on a cart pulled by a team of oxen, led by Uzzah and Ahio, Abinadab's sons. David and the people with him did not realize anything was wrong. They rejoiced with all their might as they traveled with the ark, singing to the music of trumpets, tambourines, lyres, harps, and cymbals. When they came to a certain spot in the road, the oxen stumbled. To keep the ark from falling, Uzzah put out his hand and took hold of it to keep it steady. But Uzzah was a sinful man and the ark of God was holy. So immediately God struck Uzzah down dead. Not even the priests were supposed to touch the ark! David was angry that God killed Uzzah and he questioned how he would ever get the ark back home to Jerusalem. Until David knew the answer, he left the ark in the home of a man named Obed-edom. The Lord blessed Obed-edom and his household while the ark was there.

After returning to Jerusalem, King David prepared a place for the ark and set up a tent for it. David discovered he had not followed the Lord's instructions on how to carry the ark, which Moses had written out. So David gathered the Levites and his commanders and went back for the ark. This time they did as God had commanded. The Levites carried the ark with the poles on their shoulders and did not touch it with their hands. After six steps, David stopped to offer a sacrifice to the Lord, and then led the ark back to Jerusalem. There was singing and rejoicing as David returned with the ark, and he danced with all his might. The Levites brought the ark inside the tent and offered burnt offerings and peace offerings to the Lord. David blessed the people in the Lord's name and gave every man and woman bread, meat, and a cake of raisins to celebrate the ark's return.

After the ark was brought into Jerusalem, God established his covenant with David through the prophet Nathan. God said, "Your family line and your throne will last forever." When David heard this, he was humbled and prayed to the Lord.

The story of Uzzah and the ark teaches us something very important about God. We learn about God's holiness and we get a hint of God's plan to set up an eternal kingdom. It might seem harsh that God took Uzzah's life, but it was important for the people to understand that God is holy and he must punish sin. Yet, though the people were sinful, God promised to establish David's throne forever. With that we get a glimpse of God's plan of salvation through Jesus. For Jesus is the King in David's family line that lives forever! Unless we trust in Jesus to take our sins away, like Uzzah we will die. But once God saves us, we become a part of his eternal family and can even touch the Lord in heaven without fear.

David the Psalmist

1 CHRONICLES 16:1–36;
1 SAMUEL 16:14–23; PSALM 23

After the ark of God was brought into the tent David made for it, King David chose men from the priestly tribe of Levi to lead a worship celebration. David wrote a song and asked Asaph, the chief musician, to sing it. The words of the song told the story of all God had done for Israel. The song ended with the prayer: "Save us, O God of our salvation, and gather and deliver us from among the nations, that we may give thanks to your holy name, and glory in your praise. Blessed be the LORD, the God of Israel, from everlasting to everlasting!" (1 Chronicles 16:35–36).

From the time David was a boy, God had blessed him with musical talents. When Saul was still king and was tormented by an evil spirit, young David was called to play music for him. When David played his harp, the king felt better because the evil spirit would leave. Today, the words for many of David's songs are preserved in the book of Psalms. *Psalm* is just another word for "song," and many of David's psalms or songs spoke about his life, the nation of Israel, and their relationship with God. Psalm 23 is like that. Here are the words:

"The LORD is my shepherd; I shall not want. He makes me lie down in green pastures. He leads me beside still waters. He restores my soul. He leads me in paths of righteousness for his name's sake. Even though I walk through the valley of the shadow of death, I will fear no evil, for you are with me; your rod and your staff, they comfort me. You prepare a table before me in the presence of my enemies; you anoint my head with oil; my cup overflows. Surely goodness and mercy shall follow me all the days of my life, and I shall dwell in the house of the LORD forever" (Psalm 23).

It is fun to compare the words of David's psalms to the Bible's stories about his life and wonder which of the events each psalm is describing. For instance, in Psalm 23 David is talking about walking through a valley in the presence of his enemies. Could this be about the time David walked into the valley to fight Goliath? We don't have the musical notes that go with the different psalms, but the words to David's songs can still help us grow in our faith and walk through the hard times we face in life.

Did you notice that the last line of Psalm 23 tells us that David will live in the house of the Lord forever? There is only one way we can live in heaven with God forever, and that is by trusting in Jesus and what he has done on the cross. Often David's psalms give us a hint of the Lord's coming salvation through Jesus. And some of his psalms, like Psalm 22, are wonderful prophecies foretelling God's plan to save us through Jesus.

Let's Talk About It!

What did David write songs about?

What incident is David possibly recalling?

How can we tell that David loved the Lord?

Let's Talk About It!

What fills the completed temple?
What does God use for a temple today?
How can we be filled with God's Spirit?

Solomon & the Temple of God

1 CHRONICLES 28—29;
2 CHRONICLES 1:1—7:10

Even King David sinned against the Lord, yet unlike so many of the kings who came after him, he did not turn away from the Lord to worship false gods. David served the Lord and God gave him victory over his enemies. After they were defeated, David wanted to build a temple for the Lord. But God did not allow it because David was a man of war. Instead, the Lord told David that Solomon his son would succeed him as king, and he would be the one to build the Lord a temple.

When David heard this, he gathered all his officials and told them that the Lord had chosen Solomon to be king after him. He said that if Solomon obeyed the Lord, God would establish his kingdom forever. Then, in front of his commanders and officers, David said to Solomon, "My son, it is important that you serve God with your whole heart and mind, because the Lord searches our hearts and he knows every plan and thought. Seek the Lord and do not walk away from him, because if you do he will cast you off forever. Be careful, for the Lord has chosen you to build him a house. So be strong, my son, and do it."

Then God gave King David detailed plans for the temple, which he passed along to his son. David took up a great offering and collected gold, silver, bronze, iron, and precious stones for the building of the temple. After Solomon became king, the temple construction began. Over 150,000 men were assigned just to cut and move the stone! Still, it took seven years to build the temple. The rooms inside were designed by God to be like the tabernacle, with a special room called the Most Holy Place for the ark of God.

When the temple was finally completed and the ark of God was moved into the Most Holy Place, King Solomon prayed and fire came down from heaven to burn up the offering the priests had prepared. The glory of the Lord filled the temple, and all the people worshiped and praised the Lord. King Solomon and the people celebrated for seven days and sacrificed 142,000 animals to God.

Everyone who saw the temple Solomon built could hardly believe how wonderful it was. But did you know that this temple of stones was nothing compared to the spiritual temple God would build out of people? In the New Testament, the apostle Paul tells us that everyone who trusts in Jesus becomes a part of God's temple and God's Spirit lives inside them (1 Corinthians 3:16). But because we are sinful, something had to happen first to allow our holy God to live with us. God sent his only Son Jesus to take the punishment we deserved for our sins. Those who trust in what Jesus did for their salvation have their sins forgiven and are filled with the Holy Spirit. Together, all believers form a spiritual house where God lives. The Bible calls them a temple built with living stones (1 Peter 2:5).

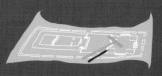

The Kingdom Is Divided

1 KINGS 11—12

Although Solomon built the Lord a beautiful temple and was wiser than any other man, he disobeyed the Lord and married hundreds of foreign wives. These women pulled him away from the Lord and persuaded him to worship foreign gods, just as God had warned. As Solomon grew older he did evil things like building altars to these false gods on the high places around Jerusalem. He did not follow the Lord as his father David had done.

Therefore God said to Solomon, "Since this has been your practice and you have not kept my covenant and my statutes that I have commanded you, I will surely tear the kingdom from you and will give it to your servant. Yet for the sake of David your father I will not do it in your days, but I will tear it out of the hand of your son" (1 Kings 11:11–12). Because of David, who did not serve idols, God planned to allow Solomon's son to rule over one tribe yet tear the others away. Meanwhile, the Lord sent the prophet Ahijah to Solomon's servant Jeroboam. Ahijah told Jeroboam that God was about to take ten tribes away from Solomon's son. He said Jeroboam was the man God had chosen to rule over these tribes. When Solomon found out about this he tried to kill Jeroboam, but Jeroboam escaped and lived in Egypt until Solomon's death.

When Solomon died his son Rehoboam became

king over all God's people. They asked him to be kind to them and reduce the hard labor his father had forced on them. The older men advised Rehoboam to do as the people asked, but the young men told Rehoboam to be even tougher! They said he should treat the people harshly and demand even more from them. Rehoboam took the advice of the younger men and made harsh threats when his people came to talk with him. Because of this the people turned away from Rehoboam and did not follow him. Ten tribes of Israel rejected Rehoboam and left to form their own kingdom. When they heard that Jeroboam had returned from Egypt, they made Jeroboam their king. Only the people of Judah stayed loyal to Rehoboam, just as the prophet had foretold.

After Jeroboam was made king over the ten northern tribes, he worried that his people might return to Solomon's son when they traveled back to Jerusalem to worship at the temple there. Instead of trusting the Lord about this, Jeroboam made golden calves for the people to worship in the cities of Bethel and Dan. He told his people, "Now you don't need to go to Jerusalem to worship. You can worship these gods right here!" Jeroboam told the people that these were the gods that led them out of Egypt. So the tribes that broke away from Rehoboam worshiped the false gods Jeroboam created. They did not worship the Lord in Jerusalem.

Do you remember why God spared the tribe of Judah and kept it loyal to the king in Jerusalem? Ever since God had spared Judah and his brothers from the famine in Egypt, God protected Judah's family. God promised Judah that there would always be a king from his tribe on the throne. And God also promised David, who was from the tribe of Judah, that his throne would last forever. One day another king from the tribe of Judah, named Jesus, would sit on the throne of David. Jesus is the crucified King of the Jews, who rose again on the third day to rule as king over God's people for ever and ever!

Let's Talk About It!

Point to Jeroboam in the picture.

What is he telling the people he leads away from Jerusalem?

Can you remember another time God's people worshiped a golden calf?

God Provides for Elijah in Miraculous Ways

1 KINGS 16:29—17:24

The kingdom of Israel remained divided after God took the ten tribes away from Solomon's son. These northern tribes kept the name *Israel* that God had given Jacob, but they did not follow the Lord. The tribe of Judah lived in Jerusalem along with the priests of Levi, who cared for the temple. They were called the people of Judah. After awhile, a sinful man named Ahab became Israel's king. He married a sinful woman named Jezebel. They served the false god Baal and even built a house for Baal.

Because Ahab was so wicked, the Lord sent a prophet named Elijah to deliver this message from the Lord: From now on, there would be no more rain or dew in Israel unless the Lord spoke through Elijah. Without rain, there would be no water to help fill the streams, and no water for crops to grow or for animals and people to drink. Then the Lord sent Elijah away. He said, "Depart from here and…hide yourself by the brook Cherith….You shall drink from the brook, and I have commanded the ravens to feed you there" (1 Kings 17:3–4). With Elijah gone, Ahab could not call on the Lord for help when the rain stopped. All he had were his false idols. He would discover Baal could not help him. When

the drought began, God kept his promise to Elijah. Elijah drank from the waters of the brook and was fed bread and meat carried by ravens each day.

But then one day, the brook dried up for lack of rain. God sent Elijah to Zarephath, where God said a widow would feed him. Sure enough, when Elijah arrived, he saw a widow gathering sticks. He called out to her, "Would you bring me a little water in a jar so I may have a drink? And please bring me a piece of bread." The woman replied, "I don't have any bread, just a handful of flour in a jar and a little oil in a jug. When I gather these sticks, I am going home to make a meal for me and my son, and after that we will die." Elijah said, "Do not fear; go and do as you have said. But first make me a little cake of it and bring it to me, and afterward make something for yourself and your son. For thus says the LORD, the God of Israel, 'The jar of flour shall not be spent, and the jug of oil shall not be empty, until the day that the LORD sends rain upon the earth'" (1 Kings 17:13–14). The widow obeyed Elijah and the Lord provided food for her, her son, and Elijah for many days. The jar of flour did not empty and the jug of oil did not run dry.

Then one sad day the widow's son got sick and died. Elijah asked the Lord to raise her son. The Lord heard Elijah's prayers and brought him back to life! This had never happened before. When the widow saw her son alive she told Elijah, "Now I know that you are a man of God, and that the word of the LORD in your mouth is truth" (1 Kings 17:24).

Do you know what was special about the widow who helped Elijah? She was not an Israelite, but God still cared for her. Jesus said, "There were many widows in Israel in the days of Elijah, when…a great famine came over all the land, and Elijah was sent to none of them but only to Zarephath, in the land of Sidon, to a woman who was a widow" (Luke 4:25–26). Elijah didn't realize it, but God's choice of this widow reflected his wonderful plan to save people from every tribe and nation through Jesus.

Let's Talk About It!

What are the ravens bringing to Elijah?
How do they know he's hungry?
Who is really providing food for Elijah?

STORY 63

Elijah & the Prophets of Baal

1 KINGS 18

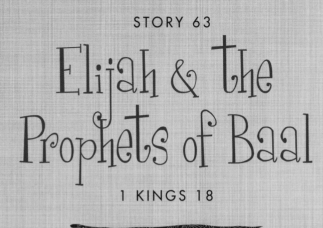

The long drought caused a terrible famine in Israel in the days of King Ahab. But the prophet Elijah, the one man who could ask the Lord to bring rain, was nowhere to be found. God had hidden him. Jezebel, Ahab's wicked wife, had captured all the prophets of the Lord she could find and killed them. But she didn't find them all because a servant of the king named Obadiah saved one hundred of them by hiding them in a cave.

After Elijah spent many days at the widow's home, God told him to return to Ahab and say that the Lord was about to send rain. So Elijah left the widow and started back to Israel. Along the way, he met Obadiah and told him to go and tell the king he was returning. When Ahab heard

the news, he came out to meet Elijah and said, "Is it you, you troubler of Israel?" Elijah answered, "I have not troubled Israel but you have, because you have abandoned the Lord and followed Baal." Elijah told Ahab to summon the people of Israel and gather the 850 prophets of Baal and Asherah to meet him at Mount Carmel.

The king gathered the prophets at Mount Carmel. Elijah challenged them to a contest. "Bring two bulls for sacrifices, one for me and one for you. Gather two piles of wood and lay one bull on each pile. Then you prophets of Baal can call out to your god to send down fire to burn up the sacrifice. I will call on the name of the Lord. Whichever god answers by sending fire is surely the true God." The prophets and the people agreed. When the bulls arrived, Elijah told the prophets of Baal to go first. They prepared their sacrifice and their altar and called on Baal all day long, but Baal didn't answer. Elijah made fun of them. "Maybe your god is sleeping! Maybe he is on vacation!" The prophets yelled louder and even cut themselves with knives, but still Baal did not answer.

Then it was Elijah's turn. He repaired an old altar of the Lord that had twelve stones representing the twelve tribes of Israel. He dug a trench around it and placed the wood and the bull on top. Then Elijah had four jars filled with water and poured on top of the altar. Three times Elijah had water poured over the offering, so that it even filled the trench. The wood and the sacrifice were dripping wet, making them difficult to set on fire. Then Elijah prayed, "O LORD, God of Abraham, Isaac, and Israel, let it be known this day that you are God in Israel….Answer me, O LORD, answer me, that this people may know that you, O LORD, are God, and that you have turned their hearts back" (1 Kings 18:36–37).

While Elijah was praying, the Lord sent fire from heaven upon the offering. It burned up the wood, the bull, and even the water in the trench. When the people saw it, they cried out, "The Lord, he is God! The Lord, he is God!" Elijah told the people to capture the false prophets and kill them. Only then did the Lord give Israel rain.

God rescued the people of Israel from their idolatry by showing them that he alone was the one true and powerful God. The prophets of Baal were destroyed, but God showed mercy to his people despite their sin. Each time we see God rescue sinful Israel in the Old Testament, it points to the way God rescues sinners through the death and resurrection of Christ. Jesus' crucifixion and resurrection are the greatest demonstration of God's power and mercy. And through them, God draws us away from the idols in our lives as well.

Let's Talk About It!

Point to the prophets of Baal.

Why didn't their sacrifice get burned up?

What did Elijah do to his offering to make sure everyone would know his God was all-powerful?

Let's Talk About It!

Who are the two men in the picture?

What is happening?

How do you know that Elisha gets the double portion he wants?

Elijah Is Taken Up to Heaven

2 KINGS 2

King Ahab died, and some time later it was time for Elijah to leave this earth too. But God had a special plan for him. The Lord planned to take Elijah up to heaven in a whirlwind! On the day this was going to happen, Elijah and his assistant Elisha set out on a journey from Gilgal. Elijah said to Elisha, "Please stay here, because the Lord has sent me all the way to Bethel." But Elisha answered, "As the LORD lives, and as you yourself live, I will not leave you" (2 Kings 2:2). Elisha knew the Lord was going to take Elijah away and he wanted to be with him. So they traveled on to Bethel together.

When they arrived, the local prophets went up to Elisha. "Do you know that today the Lord will take away your master?" "Yes, I know it. Keep quiet," Elisha said, for he did not want to be distracted from following his master. Then Elijah asked Elisha to stay in Bethel while he went to Jericho. Once again Elisha refused. "As the LORD lives, and as you yourself live, I will not leave you" (2 Kings 2:4). So they traveled to Jericho together. When they arrived in Jericho, the prophets there asked Elisha if he knew God was going to take Elijah away. Elisha told them to be quiet too. As he did earlier, Elijah told Elisha to stay behind in Jericho while he went to the Jordan. Again Elisha refused. So they traveled

When Elijah came to the Jordan River, he took off his cloak, rolled it up, and struck the water. Instantly the river parted and he and Elisha walked across on dry ground. When they reached the other side, Elijah asked Elisha, "What shall I do for you before I am taken from you?" Elisha replied, "Please let there be a double portion of your spirit on me," for he wanted God to use him like God had used Elijah. "You have asked a hard thing," Elijah said, "But if you see me as I am being taken from you, you will receive it. If not, you will not receive it." Suddenly, chariots of fire with horses of fire raced down from heaven and separated the two men. In a moment Elijah was taken up into heaven by a whirlwind, so fast that he dropped his cloak. Elisha saw it all and cried out, "My father, my father! The chariots of Israel and its horsemen!" Then Elijah disappeared from sight.

Elisha picked up Elijah's cloak and walked back to the Jordan River. Just as Elijah had done, he struck the water. Miraculously it parted, just as it had done for Elijah. God had passed Elijah's ministry to Elisha. When the fifty prophets who were watching saw Elisha cross, they said, "The spirit of Elijah now rests upon Elisha." They bowed down to him and then left to search for Elijah, but of course they never found him.

Did you know that the prophet Malachi said Elijah would return one day (Malachi 4:5)? Malachi's prophecy kept the Jews in Jesus' day looking for Elijah's return. Some even thought Jesus was Elijah. Malachi's prophecy was fulfilled in Jesus' day when the angel who appeared to Zechariah told him that his son would come in the spirit and power of Elijah. Zechariah's son, John the Baptist, became a great prophet used by God to bring the most important message of all: that Jesus was the promised Messiah. What's more, a few years later during Jesus' ministry, Elijah did reappear. It happened during Jesus' transfiguration on a mountain when Elijah appeared with Moses to talk with Jesus.

Elisha's Ministry

2 KINGS 4:1—37

After Elijah was taken up into heaven, God's favor rested upon Elisha. Elisha received his request, a double portion of Elijah's spirit, and he became the Lord's prophet. Like Elijah, he performed many signs and wonders in the name of the Lord.

One day a widow came to Elisha asking for his help. Her husband had died and now she was in debt to some men. They were threatening to sell her two children into slavery as payment for the money she owed. Elisha listened carefully and then asked the woman, "What do you have in your house?" "All I have is one jar of oil," the widow replied.

Elisha told her, "Go and borrow as many empty jars as you can from your neighbors. Don't ask for just a few! Bring them back to your house and shut the door behind you. Then pour oil into all the empty jars, one by one." The widow obeyed Elisha and gathered the empty jars. She and her sons went inside her home, shut the door behind them, and began pouring oil from their one jar to fill all the empty containers. The oil kept flowing and flowing so that all the empty jars were filled! When the last one was full, the oil ran out. Elisha told her, "Go, sell the oil, pay your debts, and use the leftover money to live on." Her sons were saved from the bill collectors.

As Elisha traveled around, a man and his wife invited him to stay at their house. The wife prepared him meals to eat and, in time, they even built an addition to their home for Elisha to use when he was in town. This couple had one problem. They didn't have a son and the husband was very old. When he died, there would be no one to care for the wife. Elisha wanted to bless the woman for her kindness to him. He told her that in one year she would give birth to a son. And then it happened, just as Elisha had said.

Several years later, the boy was helping his father in the field when he cried out in pain, "My head! My head!" So the boy was taken home, where his mother cared for him. But by noon her son had died. Without telling anyone the reason, the woman said she must go to the prophet of God. When she finally reached Elisha, he could see she was terribly upset. She told him what had happened and refused to leave until he came back with her. When he arrived, Elisha found her son lying dead on his bed. Elisha prayed to the Lord and then lay down on the child with his face on the little boy's face. Soon the boy's body got warmer, but still he did not wake up. Elisha walked around the house and then lay on the child a second time. When he did this, the child sneezed seven times and opened his eyes. He was alive again!

Elisha's life, like all the prophets of old, points forward to Jesus. Jesus was called a "great prophet" by those who saw him raise a widow's son from the dead (Luke 7:16). But while the Old Testament prophets spoke God's words, Jesus was the Word of God (John 1:1). Prophets like Elisha did miracles by God's power, but Jesus did miracles by his own power, for Jesus is God.

Let's Talk About It!

How many jars does the woman collect?

How is she going to fill all those jars with just one little jar of oil?

What do we learn about God from this story?

Let's Talk About It!

Why is Naaman standing in the river?

What is going to happen to him when he begins to wash?

What do we need to do to have all our sins washed away?

Naaman Is Cured

2 KINGS 5

During the time Elisha was a prophet, a man named Naaman commanded the army of the king of Syria. He was a brave and courageous soldier, but he had a terrible problem that courage could not solve. Naaman suffered from the skin disease of leprosy. Naaman's wife had a servant girl who had been captured in a raid into Israel. One day she told Naaman's wife that the prophet Elisha could heal Naaman of his disease. When Naaman's wife told him about the prophet, he told the king. The king urged Naaman to go to Israel and find Elisha. He even gave Naaman a letter to the king of Israel, asking for help. Right away Naaman left for Israel with the letter and silver, gold, and clothing as payment for his healing.

When the king of Israel read the letter, he was afraid and tore his clothes. "I am not God!" he said. "I have no power to heal this man!" He forgot about the Lord's prophet. Instead he thought the letter was a trick by the king of Syria, designed to start a fight. When word about the request reached Elisha and he heard that the king had torn his clothes, Elisha sent for Naaman. So Naaman traveled to Elisha's house with his chariots behind him, carrying the silver and the gold. He rode right up to Elisha's door, but Elisha did not come out. Instead Elisha sent a messenger to tell Naaman to wash in the Jordan River seven times. Then he would be healed.

At first Naaman was angry and refused. He was an important man and he had traveled a long way. "I thought he would come out to me and call upon the name of the Lord his God and wave his hand and cure me. Our rivers at home are much better than Israel's rivers. Why can't I wash in one of them and be healed?" But his servants urged him to obey Elisha's command. Naaman listened and obeyed the instructions. He washed in the Jordan seven times and suddenly, the leprosy disappeared! Naaman returned to Elisha and said, "I know that there is no God in all the earth but in Israel" (2 Kings 5:15). He offered Elisha a gift, but Elisha refused. Naaman promised to worship the Lord and left for home.

When Elisha's servant Gehazi saw his master refuse the gifts, he followed Naaman to get something for himself. He lied to Naaman, saying that Elisha needed gifts for two visitors. He asked for some silver and special robes. Naaman was happy to help. But even before Gehazi returned, the Lord showed Elisha what Gehazi had done. When Gehazi came back, he lied about his meeting with Naaman. Elisha told Gehazi that Naaman's leprosy would now come upon him. Gehazi left Elisha, white as snow with leprosy.

Jesus told the story of Naaman to show that God's plan of salvation was for all people. Jesus said, "There were many lepers in Israel in the time of the prophet Elisha, and none of them was cleansed, but only Naaman the Syrian" (Luke 4:27). Jesus wanted the Jews, who refused to believe in him, to know that God planned to save people from every nation, not just the people of Israel. It is by believing in Jesus' death and resurrection that people from every nation can have their sins washed away.

The Fall of Israel

This story is not a happy one. From the time Jeroboam began his reign as king over Israel, he and the kings who followed him sinned against the Lord. Instead of worshiping the true God, they followed false gods and secretly did things that should not be done. They built high places to worship the Canaanite gods all through their towns and cities. They set up pillars and Asherim as idols on every high hill and under every green tree. They made offerings to false gods at these places and served their idols, the very things God told them not to do. Yet the Lord kept warning Israel and Judah through every prophet he sent, saying, "Turn from your evil ways and keep my commandments and my statutes, in accordance with all the Law that I commanded your fathers, and that I sent you by…the prophets" (2 Kings 17:13).

In spite of these warnings, Israel did not listen. They followed the gods of the nations around them and wor-shiped their golden calf idols. They did evil things and even burned their children as offerings to the false gods. Because of this, God's righteous anger rose up against Israel and he used the nations around them to punish them.

Here's what finally happened: When Hoshea was king over Israel and doing evil in God's sight, God brought Shalmaneser, the king of Assyria, to defeat him. At first, Hoshea held off an attack by paying Shalmaneser lots of money. But later, Hoshea stopped the payments and tried to get the king of Egypt to help him fight Assyria. When Shalmaneser found out, he attacked Israel, arrested Hoshea, and sent him to prison. He surrounded Israel's capital city of Samaria with soldiers so that no one could get out. Finally the Israelites gave up and they were carried away as prisoners to Assyria. This disaster came because Jeroboam set up idols in the land and all the kings after him followed his wicked ways. The people of Israel did not turn away from this sin, so the Lord sent them to Assyria as captives. After that, the people of Judah in Jerusalem were all that was left of God's people in the Promised Land.

The people of Judah resented their brothers in Israel because they worshiped idols instead of worshiping God in Jerusalem. The two countries hated each other for a long time. But one day, many years later, a man from the tribe of Judah reached out to the Samaritans (another name for the people of the northern kingdom of Israel) with a special message called the gospel. That man, of course, was Jesus the Son of God who died on the cross for our sins, even the sins of Samaritan people. Do you remember the story of the woman at the well? She was a Samaritan whose ancestors had worshiped idols in Samaria, refusing to worship the Lord in Jerusalem. Instead of rejecting her, Jesus asked her for a drink and touched her life with his words. She believed and told all her friends about Jesus. As a result, many Samaritans from her town trusted in the Lord (John 4:39).

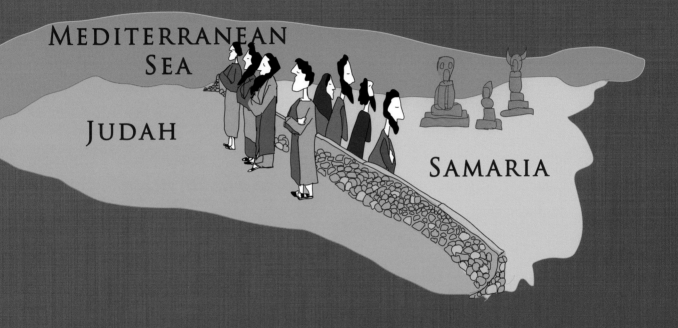

Let's Talk About It!

Why are God's people standing with their backs against one another in the picture?

Who does God send to warn them to turn away from their sin?

Who does God send to take away sin and bring his people back together again?

Good King, Bad King

2 CHRONICLES 28–29; 33

While the kings of Israel in the north did what was evil in God's sight and were finally captured by the Assyrians, another group of kings ruled over Jerusalem in the south. The first southern king, Rehoboam, allowed high places for idol worship to be set up on the hills. His son Abijah did the same wicked things his father did. At first, it seemed like the kings of Judah would be just as wicked as the ones in Israel. But in spite of the bad start, God raised up some good kings over Judah too. Kings like Asa, Jehoshaphat, and Uzziah followed the Lord. One of the best kings was Hezekiah, but his father Ahaz and his son Manassah were two of the worst.

Ahaz set up idols in Jerusalem to the false god Baal. He messed up God's temple and shut its doors. While he was king, God allowed the king of Syria to conquer Judah and many people were captured. When Ahaz died, his son Hezekiah took the throne. Hezekiah did what was right in the eyes of the Lord. He commanded the Levites to clean out the temple and open its doors. When the temple was ready, Hezekiah and his officials took seven bulls, seven lambs, and seven male goats for a sin offering.

Then Hezekiah invited all the people to offer their own sacrifices. There were so many animals sacrificed that there were not enough priests to handle them all. Afterwards, Hezekiah called the people to celebrate the Passover. Because Hezekiah followed the Lord, God blessed Hezekiah and gave him victory over his enemies.

When Hezekiah died, his twelve-year-old son Manasseh became king. At first, Manasseh did not serve the Lord. He did what was evil and rebuilt the high places his father Hezekiah tore down. Manasseh also rebuilt altars to the false god Baal. Because of this the Lord sent the king of Assyria to fight against Judah. Manasseh was captured and taken to

Babylon as a prisoner. But then something unexpected happened. Manasseh turned away from his sin, humbled himself before the Lord and prayed to God for help. The Lord heard Manasseh's prayer and put him back on the throne in Judah. He took down all the foreign gods he had erected, but his son Amon put them right back up after Manasseh died. After that, even the book of God's law was lost!

While Ahaz, Hezekiah, and Manasseh were ruling as kings, Isaiah served as God's prophet. Many bad things were happening, but Isaiah brought a word of hope. He said that one day God would bring a king who would reign in righteousness (Isaiah 32:1). You probably know who that was. Unlike the kings of Judah, Jesus never sinned. Even the best of the kings were sinners, but Jesus never was. He is the righteous king Isaiah said would come. The sacrifices Hezekiah offered in the temple held back God's judgment for awhile, but only the blood of King Jesus shed as a sacrifice for our sins can save his people forever.

Let's Talk About It!

What are the kings in the picture doing?

Which king is worshiping idols?

How can you tell if you love something more than God?

Jonah & Nineveh

JONAH 1—4

While Elisha the prophet was serving God in Israel, God raised up another prophet named Jonah. One day God called Jonah and said, "Get up and go to Nineveh, that great city, and warn them that judgment is coming because of their evil ways." Nineveh was an Assyrian city and its people were Israel's enemies. So Jonah was not happy. He didn't want to warn them! He wanted God to punish them instead. Jonah knew that if Nineveh turned away from their sin, the Lord would forgive them because he is kind, merciful, slow to get angry, and full of love. He didn't want Nineveh to experience that. So instead of obeying the Lord, Jonah ran away. He got on a ship sailing in the opposite direction, to Tarshish. He even told the crew he was running away from the Lord.

But God sent a storm so fierce that it threatened to destroy the ship. After praying to their gods with no success, the sailors woke Jonah. They cast lots to see who was responsible for the danger they were in. This is like drawing straws: whoever got the shortest one was the one who was to blame. When the lot fell to Jonah, the sailors remembered he was running away from God. Jonah admitted that the storm was his fault. He said the sailors could save their ship by throwing him into the sea. Although they tried to row to shore, the storm was too powerful, so at last they picked up Jonah and threw him overboard. Right away, the sea calmed.

What happened to Jonah? The Lord sent a great fish to swallow him, and Jonah was in its belly for three days and three nights. Jonah knew it was the Lord who had saved him and he prayed to God for help. The Lord commanded the fish to spit Jonah out onto dry land. Afterward the Lord again told Jonah to go and warn Nineveh.

This time Jonah obeyed. He traveled to Nineveh and gave them the Lord's warning.

What do you think happened next? When they heard Jonah's words, the whole city of Nineveh turned away from their sin and asked God for mercy. And just as Jonah predicted, God accepted their repentance and saved them from the disaster he had threatened. The only problem was that Jonah still didn't like it! He left the city angry and stopped to rest on a nearby hill. God allowed a plant to grow and shade Jonah from the hot sun. This made Jonah happy. But to teach Jonah a lesson, God sent a worm to eat the plant and a hot wind and sun to destroy it. When Jonah got angry that the plant was destroyed, the Lord said to him, "If you can have pity for a plant, why shouldn't I care about the thousands of people in Nineveh?"

Did you know that Jesus compared himself to Jonah? He said, "Just as Jonah was three days and three nights in the belly of the great fish, so will the Son of Man be three days and three nights in the heart of the earth" (Matthew 12:40). Just as the Lord sent a fish to swallow Jonah, so the Lord sent Jesus to die for our sin. Just as the Lord ordered the fish to release Jonah, so the grave had to release Jesus—it could not hold him. The gospel story was hidden in the story of Jonah until Jesus opened it up for us to see. Also, God's mercy to Nineveh gave a hint that God planned to save people from every nation, not just Israel.

Let's Talk About It!

How does Jonah disobey God?

How do you think Jonah feels to be back on land again?

How does God show forgiveness to Jonah?

Let's Talk About It!

If you were king, what commands would you give your people?

What does Josiah do to honor and obey God with his life?

What can you do to honor and obey God?

Josiah, the Eight-Year-Old King

2 CHRONICLES 34—35

In the kingdom of Judah we saw that King Hezekiah followed the Lord and tore down the idols in his country. Then his son Manasseh and grandson Amon put them up again. By the end of Amon's reign as king, the celebration of the Passover and even the book of God's law were lost and forgotten. When King Amon died, his eight-year-old son Josiah became king in Jerusalem. Little Josiah followed the Lord and walked in the righteous ways of King David before him.

When he was sixteen years old, Josiah tore down the false gods in the city of Jerusalem and the surrounding countryside. He ordered the altars to Baal chopped down. His men toppled the Asherim and the other idols, broke them up, and ground them into pieces while he watched. Then Josiah scattered the little pieces on the graves of the idol worshipers who had sacrificed to the false gods. That way the idols would never be used again. When Josiah had cleansed the land of idols, he returned to Jerusalem.

When Josiah was eighteen, he ordered Shaphan, the governor's son, to repair God's temple, which the kings before him had allowed to fall apart. While they were working, Hilkiah the priest found the book of the law that God had given Moses. He took it to Shaphan, who took it to the king and read it out loud to him. When Josiah heard the words of the law, he was so upset that he tore his clothes. He called for the priests and said to them, "Go seek the Lord for all of us who are left in Israel and in Judah. God's anger must be great because our fathers disobeyed the words written in this book." So Hilkiah went to the prophetess Huldah to see what the Lord would say.

Huldah told Hilkiah that the Lord was angry with the people of Judah because of their sin. But because Josiah had repented, the Lord would delay the disaster he planned for Judah. During Josiah's lifetime there would be peace. Hilkiah shared these words with the king. In response, Josiah gathered the people and read the book of the law to them. He made a covenant to follow the Lord and commanded the people to obey the Lord as well. Josiah brought back the Passover celebration and gave thirty thousand of his own lambs and young goats to be sacrificed. "No Passover like it had been kept in Israel since the days of Samuel the prophet" (2 Chronicles 35:18). Because of his example, people followed the Lord while Josiah was king, and they did not turn away.

Although King Amon lost the book of the law, God preserved it through Josiah. Why? Because God's plan to save his people wasn't finished yet! The law and the Passover would not be forgotten because they point us to Jesus. One day Jesus would come as the last lamb to be sacrificed when he died on the cross for our sins. Jesus talked about God's desire to preserve the law when he said, "For truly, I say to you, until heaven and earth pass away, not an iota, not a dot, will pass from the Law until all is accomplished" (Matthew 5:18).

The Fall of Jerusalem

2 KINGS 23:31 – 25:30;
2 CHRONICLES 36

After King Josiah died the Lord brought his judgment against Judah. Josiah's son Jehoahaz became king, but he did not follow his father's good example. He was an evil king, so the Lord sent the pharaoh of Egypt to war against him. He captured Jehoahaz and took him to Egypt. His brother Jehoiakim took his place as king, but Jehoiakim did not follow the Lord either. He too did what was evil in God's sight. This time the Lord sent Nebuchadnezzar, king of Babylon, to fight against him. Nebuchadnezzar made Jehoiakim his servant and took away vessels from God's temple to use in his palace.

Jehoiakim was king, but he was like a puppet—he had to do whatever Nebuchadnezzar said. During this time the Lord sent bands of raiders to attack Jerusalem. The Chaldeans and Syrians, the Moabites and Ammonites all fought with Judah, and the warnings many prophets had given came true. The Lord had sent prophets like Jeremiah to warn Judah of the coming dangers. Jeremiah told them that if Israel turned from their sins God would let them remain in their land (Jeremiah 7:3). But the people did not listen. Instead they made fun of God's messengers and ignored God's warnings. Finally, things had gone too far and God expressed his anger against them. Jeremiah told the people that God would bring a disaster on them that they could not escape. And even if they cried out to God he would not listen. Israel would cry to their false gods and then see that they couldn't save them from their trouble (Jeremiah 11:11–12).

When Jehoiakim died, his son Jehoiachin took his place. He was wicked just like his father. Not long after he became king, Nebuchadnezzar returned and surrounded Jerusalem. He took the new king prisoner and carried off the rest of the treasures in the temple and the king's palace. Nebuchadnezzar arrested the mighty men, the officials, and the craftsmen of Jerusalem and took ten thousand of them as captives into Babylon. A young man named Daniel was captured at that time. Zedekiah was made king, but even after all that, he did not listen to Jeremiah. Zedekiah did what was evil in God's sight and even rebelled against Nebuchadnezzar. Because of this, Nebuchadnezzar killed many in Jerusalem, burned the temple, set the city on fire, and broke down Jerusalem's walls. Those who survived were carried into exile to Babylon. Only a few of the poorest people were left behind to farm and tend the vines.

Those were terrible times. God brought such destruction to Jerusalem because his people had ignored his warnings through the prophets for hundreds of years. But even then, God gave some hope. Although his people were taken captive to Babylon for seventy years, he did not abandon them. Jeremiah brought a promise from the Lord, telling Israel that a day would come when he would raise up a new

king who would bring justice and righteousness to their land. God said he would do it to keep his word to David. This righteous branch would save Judah, and Israel would live securely. He would be called "The LORD is our righteousness" (Jeremiah 23:5–6). Can you guess who this wonderful king would be? That's right! Jesus is the king God promised. Jesus is the righteous Branch God would one day bring from the family line of King David.

Let's Talk About It!

What is happening to Jerusalem and the people of God in the picture?

Why does God allow bad things to happen to his people?

What about our sin? Does it bring good or bad consequences for us?

Nebuchadnezzar's Dream

DANIEL 1 – 2

When King Nebuchadnezzar conquered Jerusalem, he captured the most talented young men and sent them off to Babylon to be educated and then put into service for the king. Daniel, Shadrach, Meshach, and Abednego were four of the men sent off to Babylon. When their training was complete, the king found that these four men were ten times wiser than his enchanters and magicians. This was because the Lord blessed them with wisdom and knowledge. Daniel could even understand and interpret dreams.

One night, King Nebuchadnezzar had a dream that troubled him. He called his magicians, enchanters, and sorcerers to see if they could tell him the dream and its meaning. They answered, "O king, tell us the dream and we will tell you what it means." But the king said, "No! I want you to tell me both the dream and its meaning! If you don't, I will have you torn apart and your houses destroyed!" The magicians were afraid. They said, "There is not a man on earth who can meet the king's demand" (Daniel 2:10). But that answer made the king so angry he ordered that all the wise men of Babylon should be killed.

Now Daniel was also one of the king's wise men. When he heard this bad news, he asked for a little more time to interpret the dream for the king. Then he and his three friends prayed and asked the Lord to reveal the mystery to Daniel. And God answered their prayers. Daniel went to see the king and said, "No wise man can know this dream by himself, but there is a God in heaven who can make it known." Then Daniel told the king his dream. There was a mighty statue with a head of gold, a chest of silver, a thigh of bronze, legs of iron, and feet of iron and clay. There was also a stone not cut by human hands that came and struck the statue. It broke it into such tiny pieces that the wind blew them away. Then the stone became a great mountain that filled the whole earth.

Then Daniel told the king the dream's meaning. Each part of the statue was a different kingdom that would rule over the one that came before it. It started with the golden head and ended with the stone that represented the kingdom of God. God's kingdom would break all the others into pieces and God's kingdom would last forever.

When the king heard this, he dropped to the floor and fell on his face. He said to Daniel, "Truly, your God is God of gods and Lord of kings, and a revealer of mysteries, for you have been able to reveal this mystery" (Daniel 2:47). The king was so grateful that he appointed Daniel ruler over Babylon and chief over all the other wise men. Shadrach, Meshach, and Abednego were put in charge of Babylon under Daniel.

Did you know that Jesus is the rock in Nebuchadnezzar's dream? Daniel said this rock would destroy earthly kingdoms and bring in an everlasting kingdom. Paul said that Jesus was the one Isaiah meant when he talked about "a stone of stumbling, and a rock of offense; and whoever believes in him will not be put to shame" (Romans 9:33). Jesus is the King of kings and Lord of lords. His everlasting kingdom crushes the sinful kingdoms of the world, but reaches out with salvation to all who put their trust in him.

Let's Talk About It!

Describe Nebuchadnezzar's dream.

Why is it so hard for the wise men to tell the king the meaning of his dream?

What is the rock doing to the statue, and what does the rock represent?

Let's Talk About It!

Who are the three men that King Nebuchadnezzar has thrown into the fiery furnace?

Who is the fourth man?

How does God save Shadrach, Meshach, and Abednego?

Four Men in the Furnace

DANIEL 3

At first, King Nebuchadnezzar was so amazed by Daniel's interpretation of his dream that he fell down and worshiped the Lord. But he soon forgot about Daniel's God. Instead, he built a huge golden statue of himself that was ninety feet tall and nine feet wide. When it was ready, the king sent for all his officials. His messenger proclaimed, "At the sound of the music of the horn, pipe, lyre, and all other instruments, the king commands everyone to bow down and worship his golden image. Anyone who refuses will be thrown into a fiery furnace." When they heard that warning, all the officials and people in Babylon fell down and worshiped the golden image.

Well, not everybody. Some Chaldeans hurried to bring a bad report about some of the Jews. "O king," they said, "some of the Jews you have appointed to rule in Babylon have refused to obey your order to bow down! Shadrach, Meshach, and Abednego have said they will not serve your gods or worship your image."

The king was furious. "Bring them to me!" he said. When Shadrach, Meshach, and Abednego arrived, the king gave them a choice: "Either bow down to the golden image or be thrown into the fiery furnace." Even then, the three men refused to bow down. They said, "Our God whom we serve is able to deliver us from the burning fiery furnace, and he will deliver us out of your hand, O king. But if not, be it known to you, O king, that we will not serve your gods or worship the golden image that you have set up" (Daniel 3:17–18).

When he heard those words, Nebuchadnezzar became even angrier! He ordered the furnace to be heated seven times hotter than before, and he sent some of his strongest men to throw Shadrach, Meshach, and Abednego into the flames. The furnace was so hot that the fire killed the men who threw Shadrach and his friends into the fire. Then King Nebuchadnezzar looked into the fire to see what was happening to the three men. What he saw amazed him. He said, "I don't see three men tied up in the fire. I see four men, untied and walking around in the flames! The fourth one looks like a son of the gods."

At this, the king commanded the men to come out of the furnace. Everyone saw that not even a hair on their heads was singed. Their clothes didn't even smell like smoke! The king said, "Blessed be the God of Shadrach, Meshach, and Abednego" (Daniel 3:28). Then Nebuchadnezzar made a decree saying, "Any people, nation, or language that speaks anything against the God of Shadrach, Meshach, and Abednego shall be torn limb from limb, and their houses laid in ruins, for there is no other god who is able to rescue in this way" (Daniel 3:29). Then he gave promotions to the three men.

Did you wonder who the fourth man in the fire was? God's presence was in the fire with the men. God didn't just save the men from the fire, he went into the fire with them to save them. One day the Son of God would leave heaven and come into this sinful world to save us too. The fourth man in the fire gives us a hint of how God planned to save us. Jesus would come to earth and experience temptation and suffering just like we do. When we think of the fourth man in the fire, we should think about Jesus. Jesus came to earth to rescue us from everlasting punishment in the fires of hell.

The Glory Belongs to God Alone

DANIEL 4

Although King Nebuchadnezzar was amazed by the escape of Shadrach, Meshach, Abednego, and the fourth man he saw in the furnace, he still did not follow the Lord. So the Lord gave Nebuchadnezzar a dream to warn him. The dream frightened the king and he called on his wise men to interpret it, but no one could tell him what it meant. Finally, with the help of the Lord, Daniel came to interpret the king's dream.

In his dream, the king saw a large tree that reached to the heavens. The tree provided fruit for everyone to eat, shade for the animals, and a place for birds to build their nests. But God ordered the tree to be cut down and destroyed so that only the stump of the tree was left. Then God said the stump was a man who should be bound with iron and sent to live with the cattle in the field. He should eat grass with them and his mind would be like the mind of a beast in the field. In this way he would learn that God rules over men.

When Daniel heard the dream, he was frightened by what it meant. But the king wanted to hear the interpreta-tion, no matter how bad it was. So Daniel explained, "O king, the tree stands for you and your power. God is going to cut you down and send you away from men, so that you will live out in the field to eat grass like an ox. But," Daniel explained, "after you repent of your sins, God will restore you. Then you will know God rules over the kingdoms of men." Daniel urged the king to turn from his sins to avoid this disaster, but the king did not repent.

One year later, as the king walked along his roof, admiring all his work, he proudly said, "Is not this great Babylon, which I have built by my mighty power…for the glory of my majesty?" (Daniel 4:30). Before the king even finished speaking, God spoke from heaven: "The kingdom has been taken from you. You will be sent away to live with the animals until you know that God is the one who rules the kingdoms of men." And that is exactly what happened. Nebuchadnezzar's human reason left him and he was driven out of his palace to live among the animals. His hair grew long like an eagle's feathers. His nails grew long like a bird's claws, and he ate grass like an ox. He stayed that way until he repented of his pride.

Only then did his reason return. After that, instead of praising himself, he praised God and said, "Now I, Nebuchadnezzar, praise and extol and honor the King of heaven, for all his works are right and his ways are just; and those who walk in pride he is able to humble" (Daniel 4:37).

When we read about Israel's captivity in Babylon, it can seem as though God's plan for his people failed. But God used the kings who defeated Israel to discipline his people and rescue them from the destruction their sin would bring. So you see, Israel's capture was part of God's plan. God kept his people safe in Babylon until the promised day of their return. Though many in Israel were destroyed, God preserved those who were taken to Babylon, and one day he would use them to carry out his plan of salvation.

Let's Talk About It!

According to Daniel, whom does the tree represent?

What does God warn Nebuchadnezzar is going to happen to him?

Why doesn't Nebuchadnezzar listen to God's warning?

Daniel in the Lions' Den

DANIEL 6

King Nebuchadnezzar and his son King Belshazzar died, and Babylon was taken over by a new group of people, the Medes and the Persians. Darius the Mede became the new king. Darius chose 120 leaders to rule over the kingdom, and he picked Daniel and two other men to be presidents over them. Daniel served the king so well that the king planned to put Daniel in charge of the whole kingdom. But when the other leaders discovered the king's plan, they were jealous. They looked for a way to make Daniel look bad, but they couldn't find anything. So they came up with an evil plan to trap him.

They came to the king and suggested he make a new law. "O king, you should make a law that anyone who prays to any god or man but you should be thrown into a den of lions." They lied to Darius and said that all the presidents of the kingdom had agreed—but no one had asked Daniel. The other leaders knew Daniel prayed to the Lord every day. Once the king signed the law it could not be changed, so the trap was set for Daniel. What do you think Daniel did when he heard about the new law? He didn't stop praying! Daniel opened his window and knelt down in front of it so he could look toward Jerusalem as he prayed. And just like always, Daniel gave thanks to God, no matter who was watching.

Soon the evil men came to spy on Daniel. They caught him praying just as they had hoped, and they hurried to tell the king. Since Daniel had broken the law, he had to be thrown into the den of lions! The king was very troubled by this news. He looked for a way to save Daniel, but the law could not be changed. Sadly, the king ordered Daniel thrown into the lions' den, but he said to Daniel, "May your God, whom you serve continually, deliver you!" (Daniel 6:16). After Daniel was thrown to the lions, a stone was laid across the opening and the king sealed it with his ring so that no one could open it.

All that night, the king did not eat or sleep. As soon as morning came he rushed to the den and called out, "O Daniel, servant of the living God, has your God, whom you serve continually, been able to deliver you from the lions?" (Daniel 6:20). Soon a voice came up from the lions' den. It was Daniel! "My God sent his angel and shut the lions' mouths, and they have not harmed me," he said (6:21). Daniel came out of the lions' den without a scratch! The king commanded the wicked leaders to be thrown into the lions' den themselves. Before they reached the bottom, the lions attacked and tore them to pieces.

Did you know we can trust the Lord to save us just as Daniel did? God saved Daniel from certain death by closing the lions' mouths. God saves us from our sin and death through the cross. Daniel's salvation points to the greater salvation Jesus would one day bring. The apostle Paul wrote to Timothy, "Christ Jesus came into the world to save sinners" (1 Timothy 1:15). The book of Hebrews tells us that Jesus is able to save completely those who come to God through him (Hebrews 7:25). We all need to be saved—not from lions, but from our sin.

Let's Talk About It!

What is the angel in the picture doing to the lions?

What can we learn from this story about God?

What can we learn from Daniel's example?

Let's Talk About It!

What part of the temple did God's people rebuild first?

Why are the older men in the front so sad?

Who does the temple point us to?

The Exiles Return

EZRA 1; 3:1–13

When Cyrus, king of Persia, ruled over Babylon, in the very first year of his reign, God worked in Cyrus's heart to make this proclamation: "The LORD, the God of heaven, has given me all the kingdoms on earth, and he has commanded me to build him a house at Jerusalem, in Judah. If you are one of his people, may God be with you! You may go back to Jerusalem and rebuild the house of the LORD." God did this to fulfill the promise he had made through the prophet Jeremiah years before. God had said he would bring the exiles back to Jerusalem after seventy years of captivity (Jeremiah 29:10). Now it was happening.

As the people prepared to go, Cyrus gave them back the things Nebuchadnezzar had stolen from God's temple. He commanded the people of Babylon to give the Jews who were returning to Jerusalem silver and gold and other things they would need. God touched the hearts of many priests, Levites, and other Jews living in Babylon so they wanted to return home. When they reached Jerusalem, they took up an offering to rebuild the temple.

The very first thing they did was to repair the altar of the Lord and make burnt offerings to God. They were afraid of the nations surrounding them and they knew they needed God's help. In the second year they were back in Jerusalem, the people came together to start building the temple again. Zerubbabel and Jeshua were in charge of the work.

The first job was to lay a new foundation for the temple. When it was finished, they planned a celebration. The priests, Levites, and the sons of Asaph (the great psalm writer) came together to praise the Lord. They followed the instructions King David had given many years before. All the younger people shouted and praised the Lord to celebrate the new temple. But the older men, who remembered how wonderful Solomon's temple had been, were sad. They wept out loud when they saw how much smaller this new temple would be. The sounds of the shouting and praising and the weeping and crying all blended together, and people could hear it from far away.

God sent the prophet Haggai to encourage the people and tell them that God would fill this new temple with his glory. Then Haggai shared another wonderful promise about the future. He said that a day was coming when the glory of the temple would be even greater than it was in Solomon's day. In that day, God would bring peace to his people (Haggai 2:9). Many years later, Jesus brought the peace God promised through Haggai. By dying for our sins on the cross, Jesus satisfied God's wrath, making peace with God for sinners who trust in him. Jesus also introduced a greater temple—a living temple, not one made out of stone. This temple is made of God's people, with Jesus as the head. Today, instead of God's presence resting in a stone building, God lives in the hearts of his people. Now, that is a greater glory!

The Temple Is Completed

EZRA 4–6

After the temple's foundation was finished, it wasn't long before trouble began for God's people. Enemies from the nearby countries did not want the temple to be rebuilt. There was a new king now, and the enemies of Israel wrote him a letter to complain about what the Jews were doing. When the king ordered the work to stop, the Jews started rebuilding their own homes instead. That left the house of the Lord unfinished. The Lord sent the prophet Haggai with a message for the Jews. He said, "Is it really time for you to live in your paneled houses while God's house lies in ruins?" The Lord also sent the prophet Zechariah to encourage the Jews to strengthen their hands so the temple might be built (Zechariah 8:9). Two brave men, Zerubbabel and Jeshua, started rebuilding again, even though the governor of the land tried to stop them. But the Lord was with them and the work continued.

Still the surrounding people tried to make trouble. Their governor wrote a letter to the new king, whose name was Darius, telling him that the Jews were rebuilding the temple. He wrote, "The Jews say that King Cyrus gave them permission to do this. Can you see if that is really true?" Darius ordered his servants to search for the decree from Cyrus. When the servants found it, everything was just as the Jews had said. What happened next was a surprise for the governor. King Darius ordered him to let the Jews keep working on the temple. Not only that, Darius ordered the governor to pay for the work with money from the royal treasury! He even ordered him to provide the animals for the offerings, and everything else the Jews needed to worship God each day. Finally, the king said that anyone who tried to change his decree would have his house destroyed.

When the governor received the king's decree, he had to obey it in full. Instead of causing trouble for the Jews, he supplied everything needed to complete the temple. Things went well for the Jews, and God used the Persian kings to make sure that the temple was finished. When the day came that the temple was ready, the people had a dedication celebration. They sacrificed one hundred bulls, two hundred rams, four hundred lambs, and twelve male goats as a sin offering, one goat for each of the tribes of Israel. They also celebrated the Passover and killed Passover lambs for all the people, the exiles, and everyone who joined them to worship the Lord.

Did you know that Jesus once called his body the temple? When he chased the money-changers out of the temple in Jerusalem, the people asked him to do a miracle to prove he had the right to do it. Jesus answered, "Destroy this temple, and in three days I will raise it up." The Jews replied, "It has taken forty-six years to build this temple, and will you raise it up in three days?" But Jesus wasn't speaking about the stone temple; he was speaking about the temple of his body (John 2:19–21). Today everyone who believes in Jesus' death and resurrection becomes a part of God's new, living temple because the Holy Spirit lives in them. Now that God's presence can live with us, we don't need the temple building anymore. Now that Jesus has died as the perfect sacrifice for our sins, no more sacrifices are needed.

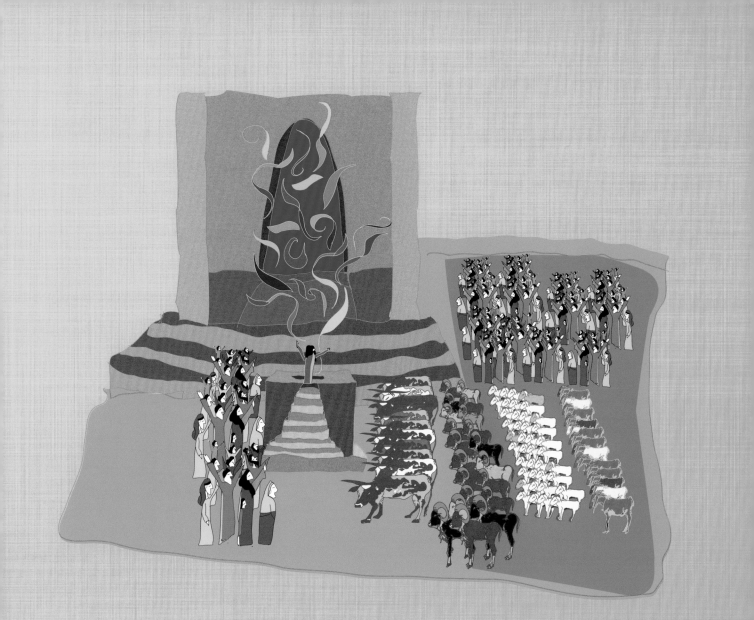

Let's Talk About It!

What kind of animals do you see in the picture?

What are the people going to do with them?

Why don't we need to sacrifice animals for our sin anymore?

Let's Talk About It!

What is the name of the city in the picture?

Why are guards posted around the wall of the city?

Why is rebuilding the wall so important for Israel?

Nehemiah

NEHEMIAH 1–6

Even though Jerusalem's temple was now complete, the walls around the city were still broken down and the gates had been burned, making it easy for anyone to attack it. A Jewish man named Nehemiah lived in Babylon and served as cupbearer for the Persian king. One day, Nehemiah asked a traveler from Judah how things were going in Jerusalem. When the traveler told him that the walls were broken down and the gates were burned, Nehemiah was very sad. He asked the Lord to forgive his people's sins and to work in the king's heart so that he would allow Nehemiah to help his people.

The king saw that Nehemiah was sad and he asked him why. When he heard that the walls of Jerusalem were broken down, he asked Nehemiah what he could do. This was just what Nehemiah had prayed for! He asked the king to send him to Jerusalem to help rebuild its walls. Amazingly, the king agreed! He gave Nehemiah letters that allowed him to travel through the land under the king's protection, and he wrote orders to the keeper of the king's forest to give Nehemiah whatever he needed for the work.

So Nehemiah returned to the city of Jerusalem. One night Nehemiah went out to inspect the broken walls and make a plan. Then he gathered the officials, priests, nobles, and those who would do the work and said, "You see the trouble we are in. Jerusalem lies in ruins with its gates burned. Let's join together to rebuild the walls, so that the people around us will no longer make fun of us and our God." Nehemiah told the people how God had answered his prayers and brought him—with the king's blessing—to help them. The people were so encouraged by Nehemiah's report that they said, "Let us rise up and build!" (Nehemiah 2:18). And they got ready to rebuild the walls.

Even though the king was helping Nehemiah, the enemies of Israel stirred up trouble. A man named Sanballat tried to discourage the people by making fun of them and accusing the Jews of rebelling against the king. But the people kept working, with each family rebuilding the wall closest to their home. As the broken places in the wall started to close, Sanballat planned an attack against Jerusalem. But Nehemiah posted guards and men with swords stood in the gaps. When Sanballat received word of the guards, he called off his attack and Nehemiah got the work started again. Half the people worked on the walls while the other half guarded the work with spears, shields, bows, and armor. When the gaps were almost filled, Sanballat again tried to stir up trouble by saying that Nehemiah was rebelling against the king. But Nehemiah did not stop the work, and when the wall was finished, the enemies of Jerusalem were afraid. They knew God had helped his people finish the work.

God first worked in King Cyrus's heart to rebuild God's temple, and then the Lord worked in the heart of Nehemiah's king to restore Jerusalem's walls. God did this because Jerusalem was an important part of God's saving plan. Jesus would one day be put on trial inside the city and crucified just outside its walls. God also worked in Nehemiah's heart to restore Jerusalem's walls. All of this was a part of his larger plan to save us.

The Birth of Jesus Foretold

LUKE 1

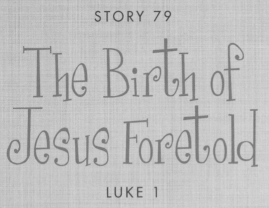

When we go from the Old Testament to the New Testament, we just have to turn a page or two in our Bibles. But there were almost four hundred years between Nehemiah and the birth of Jesus. In Jesus' day, Israel was once again ruled by foreigners. Now it was the Romans instead of the Persians. And the people of Israel were waiting for the Messiah. Would he ever come? The answer was on the way!

The first step of God's plan to send the Messiah was about to unfold with a man named Zechariah. Zechariah served God as a priest in the temple. He and his wife Elizabeth followed the Lord and obeyed his commands, but one thing made them sad: they had no children and they were getting old. One day Zechariah was chosen to burn incense in the Most Holy Place of the temple. While he was there the angel Gabriel appeared to him.

This certainly didn't happen every day! Zechariah was afraid. But Gabriel said, "Don't be afraid, Zechariah. God has heard your prayers and he is going to give you a son. You are to name him John. The Holy Spirit will be with him before he is even born. When he grows up he will bring many people back to the Lord. And he will prepare the way for God to come to his people."

This was a lot for Zechariah to understand. He didn't know what to think. "How can I be sure of this?" he asked. "My wife and I are very old." That was true, but Zechariah forgot that God can do anything. Gabriel told Zecha-

riah that because he didn't believe God's word, he wouldn't be able to speak until everything God had told him came true. At that moment, Zechariah discovered that he couldn't speak. He had a lot of time to think about what the angel had said, especially when Elizabeth discovered that she was going to have a baby at long last!

Six months later, something even more amazing happened. This time the angel Gabriel came to a young woman named Mary, who was Elizabeth's cousin. She was engaged to marry a man named Joseph, but she wasn't married yet. When Mary saw the angel she was afraid too. But Gabriel said to her, "Don't be afraid, Mary. God is very pleased with you. You are going to have a baby son, and you are to call him 'Jesus.' He will be the most special baby that has ever been born, because God himself is going to be his father. God will make him a king in the family line of David and he will reign over a kingdom that will never end." Mary had questions too: "How will this happen, since I am not married yet?" "The Holy Spirit will come upon you," Gabriel said, "and because of this, Jesus will be the Son of God." Mary believed the angel and agreed to be part of God's plan. Before he left, Gabriel told Mary that Elizabeth was also having a baby—because nothing is impossible for God.

Soon everything happened just as Gabriel had said. Mary went to visit Elizabeth and, as soon as Elizabeth saw her, Elizabeth's baby jumped inside her. Elizabeth said Mary was blessed to be the mother of her Lord and Mary praised God too. Zechariah couldn't say a word, but when his son was born, Zechariah told the family in writing to name his son John, and at once he could speak again!

Did you know that Mary's son Jesus was both man and God at the same time? That is very important. As a man, Jesus carried our sins for us on the cross and took our punishment. He lived a perfectly holy life without ever sinning. And because he was God, he grew up to heal the sick and raise the dead. Death could not win over him. Jesus came back to life on the third day so that some day we can rise and be with him in heaven.

Let's Talk About It!

According to the angel, who is going to give Mary a baby?

What name is Mary to give her baby?

What special things does the angel say about Jesus?

The Birth of Jesus

MATTHEW 1:18—2:15; LUKE 2:1—21

When Joseph found out that Mary was having a baby, he was confused and upset. He knew he wasn't the father, so he planned to end their engagement. But before that could happen, an angel came to him in a dream. The angel told him, "The baby growing inside Mary is from the Holy Spirit. Don't be afraid to marry her. She will give birth to a son and you are to give him the name 'Jesus,' because he will save his people from their sins." Joseph listened to the angel and obeyed the Lord.

After they were married, Caesar, the Roman ruler, commanded every man to register his name in his hometown so all the people could be counted. Since Joseph was a descendant of King David, he had to travel to Bethlehem. When Mary and Joseph arrived, it was so filled with travelers that there was no place to stay, even though it was time for her baby to be born. So Mary gave birth to Jesus in a stable, where animals were kept. She wrapped him in swaddling cloths and laid him in a manger, where animals ate their food. It didn't seem like a special beginning, but it was.

Outside the city that night, some shepherds were watching their sheep. Suddenly, an angel appeared to them. The shepherds were terrified, but the angel said, "Fear not! I bring you good news of great joy for all people.

Today the Savior has been born in the city of David. He is Christ the Lord! This is how you will know him: you will find a baby wrapped in swaddling cloths and lying in a manger" (Luke 2:8–12). Then angel after angel filled the sky, praising God. The shepherds could hardly breathe after seeing all the heavenly glory. Most people ignored shepherds, but angels had come to visit them! When the angels left, the shepherds went to see Jesus. They told Mary what the angel had said, and Mary tucked their words away in her heart. Some time later, three wise men came to Jerusalem, asking everyone if they knew where the king of the Jews had been born. King Herod the Great was the ruler over Jerusalem and he wasn't happy to hear that kind of talk. He asked the scribes and chief priests what the wise men might be talking about. They told him about an Old Testament prophecy that said a ruler would come from Bethlehem. So Herod sent the wise men off to seek the child. He said, "Please be sure to come back and tell me where you find him, so I can worship him too."

But that was a lie. Herod really planned to kill him. He didn't want to share his throne with anyone. After the wise men left, they saw the star they had been following and it led them to Jesus. When they found him, they fell down and worshiped him and gave him gifts of gold, frankincense, and myrrh. An angel warned the wise men not to return to Herod, so they went home another way. But when Herod realized he had been tricked, he ordered all the babies in Bethlehem to be killed. It was a terrible, evil plan, but God protected Jesus. An angel earlier warned Joseph about Herod, and Joseph and Mary fled to Egypt, where they were safe.

Did you know God planned the exact moment when Jesus would come into the world to save us from our sins? Paul tells us that "when the fullness of time had come," God sent his Son to redeem us so we could be brought into God's family (Galatians 4:4). God had our salvation all planned out even before he made the world (Ephesians 1:4). So it was easy for God to tell Joseph that Jesus was the one to "save his people from their sins" (Matthew 1:21).

Let's Talk About It!

Who came to visit the newborn baby Jesus?

How many animals are in the picture?

How do the wise men know where to find Jesus?

Let's Talk About It!

Who is holding Jesus in the picture?

What did God promise him?

What did he say about Jesus?

Jesus Presented in the Temple

MATTHEW 2:16—23; LUKE 2:22—52

Before Mary and Joseph fled to Egypt, they took Jesus to the temple in Jerusalem to present him to the Lord. They wanted to offer a sacrifice for him as the firstborn son, just as the law of Moses told them to. Long ago, God had told Moses that every firstborn son belonged to God and must be redeemed with a sacrifice. Many parents went to the temple to make this sacrifice, but something special happened when Mary and Joseph arrived at the temple. They were greeted by an old man named Simeon who loved God very much. The Holy Spirit had told Simeon that he would live to see the Messiah—he would not die until the Messiah had arrived! When Simeon saw Jesus, he knew the wait was over. Simeon took Jesus in his arms, thanked God and said, "Lord, now you are letting your servant depart this life in peace. Just as you promised, my eyes have seen your salvation come in this little boy. You are preparing him to be a light of truth to the Gentiles [which is what non-Jewish people were called], and a glory to your people Israel." Mary and Joseph marveled at his words. There was also a prophetess at the temple named Anna. Anna was also very old, and she worshiped the Lord night and day. When she saw all that was going on, she too gave thanks to God for the salvation Jesus was going to bring.

After staying some time in Egypt, Joseph was visited in a dream by an angel, who told him it was safe to take Jesus back to Israel because the wicked King Herod had died. So Joseph took Mary and Jesus back to a little town called Nazareth. Mary and Joseph raised Jesus in Nazareth, where the little boy grew and became strong. The Bible says he was filled with wisdom and God's special blessing was upon him.

Every year while Jesus was growing up, Mary and Joseph took him back to the temple in Jerusalem to celebrate the Passover. On one of those trips, when Jesus was twelve, he went to the temple and spoke with the teachers there. The people who listened were amazed at how much he understood and how wise his questions were. But Mary and Joseph left for home without Jesus. When they realized he was missing, they hurried back to Jerusalem to look for him. When they found him, they said, "Son, why did you treat us like this? We have been so worried, looking for you." Jesus said something surprising. "Why were you looking for me? Didn't you know that I had to be in my Father's house?" Then Jesus went home with them. As the years passed, he grew in wisdom. He was respected by people and specially loved by God.

Did you know that Jesus never sinned (Hebrews 4:15), not even once? He kept God's law perfectly, even as a child. Jesus obeyed the law to honor God and so that one day he could trade his obedience for our sin. Can you imagine that? Even though we do bad things, God is willing to take our sins and give us his sinless life! Jesus took the punishment we deserve when he died on the cross so we can be forgiven. He took the list of our sins and nailed them to the cross (Colossians 2:14). They are gone forever.

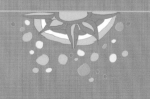

The Ministry of John the Baptist

MATTHEW 3:1–10; 14:1–12;
LUKE 3:1–20

John the Baptist, the son of Zechariah and Elizabeth, grew up around the same time Jesus did. When he became a man, God called him to be a prophet. He sent John to live in the Judean wilderness to proclaim a special message for God. John was different from the average Judean man. He ate locusts and wild honey and wore clothes made out of camel's hair, with a leather belt around his waist. People came from miles around to hear his preaching. John reminded everyone of God's law and told them God's kingdom would come soon. This made people think about their sins. John told them to repent, which means to turn away from your sin and ask God to forgive you. Then John would baptize the people who wanted to follow God. That is how he got the name John the Baptist.

John wasn't interested in baptizing people who didn't really want to repent. When religious leaders like the Pharisees and Sadducees came out with the crowd to be baptized, John wouldn't do it! He had only harsh words for them. He told them they shouldn't just say good things about repentance; they should live a life that matched the words they spoke. He finally called them a bunch of poisonous snakes!

He warned them, "Don't think you are safe with God just because you were born into Abraham's family. God could turn stones into children of Abraham! You must have a life that honors God the way it should, just like a tree is supposed to grow good fruit. Every tree that does not bear good fruit will be cut down and thrown into the fire."

All of this was so different and so powerful that people began to ask themselves if John was the promised Messiah. But John knew he was not the one. He was only a messenger, the one the prophet Isaiah spoke of when he said God would send a man into the wilderness to "prepare the way of the LORD" (Isaiah 40:3). So John told the people that one day soon another man would come. He would be the Messiah they were waiting for. This is how God used John to announce Jesus' coming. Later John would even baptize Jesus.

The very last words of the Old Testament talk about God's promise to send the prophet Elijah back to Israel. He would speak a message that would turn the hearts of the fathers to their children and the hearts of the children to their fathers. Yet for hundreds of years, no prophet came until John, who was the one who fulfilled God's promise. Jesus said John was the Elijah who was to come (Matthew 11:14).

John told everyone they needed to turn from sin and follow God. It was this courageous faith that cost John his life. Herod Antipas, the king after Herod the Great, threw John in prison because John told him it was sinful to take his brother's wife Herodias for himself. At a party some time later the daughter of Herodias came in to dance for Herod. Herod was so pleased that he offered to give her anything she wanted. Directed by her sinful mother Herodias, she asked Herod to kill John the Baptist. King Herod really didn't want to kill John, but felt he had to keep the promise he made in front of everyone. He ordered John the Baptist killed, and John became the first to die for believing in Jesus.

Let's Talk About It!

What is John the Baptist wearing?

What special job does God give John?

What does John tell the people to do?

Let's Talk About It!

What is John doing to Jesus?

Why is there a dove in the picture?

Who calls out from heaven, and what does he say?

The Baptism of Jesus

MATTHEW 3:11–17; JOHN 1:29–34

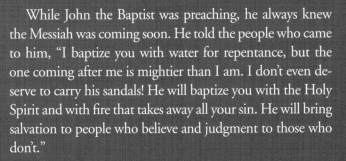

While John the Baptist was preaching, he always knew the Messiah was coming soon. He told the people who came to him, "I baptize you with water for repentance, but the one coming after me is mightier than I am. I don't even deserve to carry his sandals! He will baptize you with the Holy Spirit and with fire that takes away all your sin. He will bring salvation to people who believe and judgment to those who don't."

John's mother Elizabeth and Jesus' mother Mary were cousins. John might have known Jesus as they grew up. But John still needed a sign from God to know who the Messiah was. God told him that he would recognize the Messiah when he saw the Holy Spirit come down and remain on him (John 1:33). John kept watching for God's sign so he could announce the Messiah's coming. Meanwhile he preached repentance and told people the Messiah was on his way.

Then Jesus came to the Jordan River to be baptized by John. When John saw Jesus, he didn't want to baptize him. He said Jesus should be the one baptizing him! But Jesus answered, "You should do this for me, because this is part of how I will fulfill all righteousness." John agreed and baptized Jesus in the Jordan. As Jesus came up out of the water, John suddenly saw the Spirit of God coming down from heaven like a dove to rest upon Jesus. Then a voice from heaven said, "This is my beloved Son, with whom I am well pleased" (Matthew 3:17). John knew Jesus was the Messiah.

Do you wonder why John didn't want to baptize Jesus? We know Jesus never sinned. Maybe John, because they were related as family, knew that Jesus had never done anything wrong and had nothing to repent of like other people. John called Jesus the "Lamb of God" because Jesus would become a sacrifice for sin, like the lambs offered at the temple. But unlike the lambs that were sacrificed at the temple over and over again, Jesus' one death was all that was needed to take away the sins of everyone who trusts in him.

The Temptation of Jesus

MATTHEW 4:1—11

After Jesus was baptized he left the Jordan River, full of the Holy Spirit. You might be surprised to know where the Holy Spirit sent Jesus next. He sent him into the wilderness where Jesus fasted, which means he did not eat, for forty days. While he was there the devil tried to tempt him. Satan knew Jesus was hungry so he said to him, "If you are the Son of God, command these stones to become loaves of bread" (Matthew 4:3). Jesus certainly had the power to turn a stone into bread, but he wasn't going to obey the devil! Instead he answered with a verse from the Old Testament, "Man does not live by bread alone. He needs God's Word for life."

Then Satan tempted Jesus again. He took him up to the very top of the temple. He dared Jesus to prove he was the Son of God by throwing himself down to the ground. Satan tried to use God's Word to get Jesus to obey him. He quoted Psalm 91 and said that if Jesus really was the Son of God, the angels would protect him from any harm caused by the fall. But Jesus knew what Satan was doing. He answered him with another verse from the Old Testament, "It is written, 'You shall not put the Lord your God to the test'" (Matthew 4:7).

Satan was still not ready to give up. He tempted Jesus a third time by showing him all the kingdoms of the world. Then he said to Jesus, "If you will worship me, all of this will be yours." Again, Jesus gave his answer from God's Word. He said, "Be gone, Satan! For it is written, 'You shall worship the Lord your God and him only shall you serve'" (Matthew 4:10). Finally, Satan gave up. He left Jesus, but planned to return when the time was right (Luke 4:13). After the devil left, angels came to comfort and strengthen Jesus.

Did you know that every time Jesus answered the devil he quoted from the book of Deuteronomy? If you look up Jesus' first answer, you will see that it was Moses who told Israel they needed more than bread to live; they needed God's Word. You see, God led Israel in the desert for forty years to test their obedience and to teach them that they needed more than food to survive; they also need God's Word to feed their hearts (Deuteronomy 8:3). That was an important lesson for Israel because they were constantly putting their desires for food above their love and obedience to God. Israel failed to follow God in the wilderness, but Jesus succeeded. Unlike Israel, Jesus didn't complain that he didn't have food. He found his strength in the promises of God, and when he was tempted, he relied on God's Word. The book of Hebrews tells us that even though Jesus was tempted like us in every way, he didn't sin (Hebrews 4:15). That's really important! Jesus did what we could not do. He kept God's law and lived a perfect life. Now he offers his perfect record of righteousness as a gift to anyone who trusts in him.

Let's Talk About It!

Where did Jesus go to fast and pray?

What did Satan try to get Jesus to do?

How did Jesus answer him?

Let's Talk About It!

How do the three servants in the pictures tell the story by what they are doing?

How does Jesus turn the water into wine?

What does this story teach us about Jesus?

The Wedding Feast

In the days following his baptism and temptation in the wilderness, Jesus began to choose men who would follow and learn from him. He called them his disciples. One day Jesus took these men with him to a wedding celebration. Jesus' mother Mary was there too. Everything was going fine until they ran out of wine right in the middle of the wedding feast! When Mary found out she went to Jesus and told him about the problem. Jesus asked his mother, "What does this have to do with me? My time hasn't come yet." But Jesus' answer didn't discourage his mother. She told the servants, "Do whatever he tells you" (John 2:5).

Sitting in the house were six stone jars as big as barrels. They could hold thirty gallons each. When Jesus saw these jars, he told the servants to fill them with water. So the servants filled them to the very top. Then Jesus told the servants to pour some of what was in the jars and take it to the master of the banquet. Imagine how confused the servants were—why should they take water to the master of the banquet? But they listened to Jesus and did what he said. Soon they discovered that the water had miraculously been turned to wine.

The master of the banquet had no idea what had just happened. But when he tasted the water that had been turned to wine, he said to the bridegroom, "Everyone else serves the good wine first. Then, when people have had a lot to drink, they bring out the poor wine. But you have kept the good wine until now." This was the first miracle Jesus performed to show who he was. The disciples who came with Jesus believed in him when they saw what he did.

Jesus didn't perform this miracle just to help out at a wedding. He was showing that he was no ordinary man. Jesus was God! A short time later at another feast in the temple, Jesus stood up and called out in a loud voice, "If anyone thirsts, let him come to me and drink. Whoever believes in me, as the Scripture has said, 'Out of his heart will flow rivers of living water'" (John 7:37–38). Jesus also told a woman he met at a well, "Whoever drinks of the water that I will give him will never be thirsty forever. The water that I will give him will become in him a spring of water welling up to eternal life" (John 4:14). Isn't it interesting that the One who can help us with the things we need began by providing drink for a wedding? But that was only the beginning. When he died on the cross, Jesus provided what we need the most—salvation for all who believe. When we trust in Jesus, our thirst is satisfied forever.

Jesus Cleanses the Temple

JOHN 2:12—25

After the wedding feast where he turned water into wine, it was almost time for Passover so Jesus and his disciples traveled to Jerusalem. Soon they were at the temple. It was full of people buying and selling as if they were in a market. Some were selling animals to be used in sacrifices, like pigeons, sheep, and cattle. Others set up tables to exchange Roman money for temple money, right in the temple courts. When Jesus saw this he was not happy. In fact, he made a whip out of cords and chased those people out of the temple!

Jesus dumped out the boxes of coins and turned over the tables of the money-changers. But he didn't let the animals go. Instead he told the people who sold them: "Take these things away. Do not make my Father's house a marketplace." As the disciples watched, they remembered Psalm 69 where David talked about his strong desire to care for God's house. It was the same with Jesus.

The religious leaders were upset by what Jesus did. So they asked Jesus to give them a sign to prove he had the right to chase the people away. Jesus didn't give them a sign. Instead he simply said, "Destroy this temple, and in three days I will raise it up" (John 2:19). When the Jews heard this, they were astonished. What was Jesus talking about? It had taken forty-six years to build the temple! The leaders mocked Jesus for saying he could raise it up in three days. But that was because they didn't understand what he meant. Jesus wasn't talking about the temple building made of stone. He was talking about the temple of his body—the place where God was really living! Jesus didn't give them the sign they asked for but soon after, during Passover, Jesus performed other signs and many believed in him.

A few years later, when Jesus was arrested, some people tried to get Jesus into trouble by using his words against him. They told the high priest, "We heard him say, 'I will destroy this temple that is made with hands, and in three days I will build another, not made with hands'" (Mark 14:58). And when Jesus was on the cross, some people made fun of him for what he had said: "Aha! You who would destroy the temple and rebuild it in three days, save yourself, and come down from the cross!" (Mark 15:29–30). It wasn't until Jesus rose from the dead that the disciples remembered his words and finally understood that they had pointed to his death and resurrection all along.

Let's Talk About It!

What is Jesus doing in the picture?

Why did he do this?

When Jesus said he could rebuild the temple in three days, what was he really talking about?

Let's Talk About It!

Why do you think Nicodemus came to see Jesus after dark?

What Old Testament story does Jesus tell Nicodemus?

How is Jesus like the snake on a pole?

Nicodemus

JOHN 3:1 – 21

One evening a Pharisee named Nicodemus went to visit Jesus. Nighttime was a good time to go if you didn't want anyone to see you. And for a religious leader like Nicodemus, spending time with Jesus could cause problems, since the other leaders didn't like Jesus much. But Nicodemus had been thinking about Jesus. He wanted to talk with him. Perhaps he had heard about or even seen the signs and wonders Jesus was doing. Nicodemus thought Jesus must have been sent by God. No one could heal the sick unless God was with him. So when he got the chance, he went to share his thoughts with Jesus. "I know you are a teacher sent from God," Nicodemus said.

Jesus listened to Nicodemus. When he answered him, he said something very interesting. "Unless you are born again, you cannot see the kingdom of God." This must have sounded like a riddle to Nicodemus. After all, nobody can force themselves to be born—it is something that happens to you. How could God expect us to do something beyond our control if we wanted to enter his kingdom? Nicodemus had other questions too. How could a man be born twice? And how could an old man be born like a baby? Jesus told Nicodemus he was not talking about what happens to a person's body. Jesus said a person must be born of water and the Spirit to enter into the kingdom of God. "The Spirit is like the wind," Jesus said. "You can hear its sound, but you can't see it, and the wind goes wherever it wants." Jesus was teaching Nicodemus that you need God's Spirit to change your heart. Nicodemus marveled at Jesus' words but he still asked, "How can these things be?"

Jesus scolded Nicodemus (and the rest of the Pharisees) for not believing what he said. They were teachers of God's law and they should have recognized who Jesus was. But Jesus wanted to help Nicodemus understand. He reminded him of the Old Testament story where Moses lifted up a bronze snake in the wilderness. Everyone who looked up at it was healed of their poisonous snakebites. Jesus said he was like the bronze serpent on the pole. "Just as Moses lifted up the serpent in the wilderness, it will be the same for me. I must be lifted up so that whoever believes in me may have eternal life." Then Jesus spoke words that are some of the best known verses in the New Testament. See if you recognize them. He told Nicodemus, "For God so loved the world, that he gave his only Son, that whoever believes in him should not perish but have eternal life. For God did not send his Son into the world to condemn the world, but in order that the world might be saved through him" (John 3:16–17).

Do you wonder what happened to Nicodemus after his nighttime meeting with Jesus? The Bible gives us some clues. Later on, when the other Pharisees wanted to arrest Jesus without a good reason, Nicodemus stood up for Jesus and got in trouble for it (John 7:50–52). After Jesus died it was Nicodemus who brought seventy-five pounds of spices to prepare Jesus' body for burial. Then he helped Joseph of Arimathea wrap Jesus' body and carry it to the tomb (John 19:38–42). Nicodemus would never have done all that if he had rejected Jesus. Perhaps he listened to the words Jesus spoke that evening and believed. We just might meet him in heaven some day.

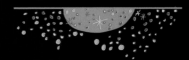

Good News

LUKE 4:16—44

One day when Jesus was just beginning the work God had sent him to do, he went back to Nazareth, the town he grew up in as a boy. On the Sabbath day he went into the synagogue and stood up to read something from God's Word. The attendant handed Jesus the scroll that had the book of Isaiah written on it. Jesus found the place (Isaiah 61) where Isaiah wrote, "The Spirit of the Lord God is upon me, because the Lord has chosen me to bring good news to the poor; he has sent me to care for those who are hurt and bring freedom to those who are bound." He read the verse and then he rolled up the scroll and said to the people, "Today this scripture has come true as you have listened to me read it."

At first the people marveled at Jesus' words. They said nice things about him. They remembered he was Joseph's son. Some of them may have remembered Jesus as a boy, growing up in their town. But Jesus knew their hearts. He knew some things were not right. He challenged them and hinted that they would reject him. He reminded them of times in the past when God chose to bless Gentiles instead of Jews. When the people heard this, all their kind words suddenly turned into terrible anger. In fact, they chased Jesus to the top of a hill where they intended to throw him off the cliff to kill him. But that didn't happen. Somehow, Jesus just passed through the crowd and went away. No one could kill Jesus before his work on earth was complete.

After that Jesus traveled to Capernaum. Again one Sabbath day he began teaching the people there. One person had an unclean spirit—a demon—living in him. This demon shouted out that Jesus was the Holy One of God. This was true, but Jesus knew the demon had an evil reason for saying it. Jesus knew when the time was right for people to be told who he was, and that time hadn't come yet. So Jesus rebuked the demon and told him to come out of the man. Right away, the demon left. He had to obey Jesus whether he liked him or not. When the people saw what happened, the news that Jesus had power over demons spread like wildfire. No one had ever seen anything like this!

After Jesus left the synagogue he went to Simon's house to spend the night and found Simon's mother-in-law there, sick with a high fever. So Jesus healed her. As evening came people who had heard what Jesus had done for the demon-possessed man began to bring other sick and demon-possessed people to him, hoping he would help them too. Jesus laid his hands on them, healed them, and cast out many demons. Some of these demons also shouted out that Jesus was the Son of God, but Jesus silenced them. The next morning the people tried to keep Jesus from leaving, but Jesus reminded them of Isaiah's prophecy: "I must preach the good news of the kingdom of God to the other towns as well, for I was sent for this purpose" (Luke 4:43).

The Bible gives the name "gospel" to the life and work of Jesus. Did you know the word "gospel" means "good news"? It's called the good news because it answers the question, "How can I be saved from my sins?" When Jesus died for our sins and rose from the grave three days later, he made a way for everyone who believes in him to be forgiven and go to heaven. Jesus took the punishment we deserved for our sin. Now we can have peace with God instead of punishment. That is really good news!

Let's Talk About It!

How did Jesus help the woman in the picture?

Why are all the people lined up outside the house?

If Jesus was physically here today, what would you ask him to do for you?

Let's Talk About It!

How many fish do the men catch before Jesus speaks to them?

How many fish do they catch after Jesus tells them to try again?

What special fish does Jesus tell them they will be catching from now on?

The Miraculous Catch

LUKE 5:1—11

As word spread about the signs and wonders Jesus was doing, more and more people came to see him and listen to his teaching. Sometimes the crowds got very large. One time this happened when Jesus was near the Sea of Galilee. The people began to crowd Jesus so much that he knew he wouldn't be able to teach. Looking around, Jesus saw two empty boats on shore and fishermen washing their nets. One boat was Simon's. Jesus asked Simon to take him out on the lake, a little bit from the shore. The people, who did not want to get wet, spread out across the shoreline, and up the hilly bank. After rowing a little way off shore, Jesus spoke to the crowd.

When Jesus was finished teaching, he told Simon to row out to deeper water and put out his nets to catch fish. Simon replied, "Master, we worked all night and didn't catch a thing. But if you say so, I will let down the nets." The tired fisherman lowered his heavy nets into the sea. What do you think happened? Not what Simon expected. When Simon began dragging the nets back into the boat, there were so many fish that the nets began to break!

Simon signaled to James and John, his partners in the other boat, to come and help. When they arrived, they began throwing the fish into their boat. But the fish just kept coming and coming until both boats were so full they began to sink under the weight! When Simon saw all this, he realized that Jesus was no ordinary man. He fell down at Jesus' knees and said, "O Lord, you shouldn't be here with me, because I am a sinful man." James and John stood in their boats, as surprised as they could be at the fish they had caught. Jesus looked down at Simon and said, "Do not be afraid; from now on you will be catching men" (Luke 5:10). The men were so affected by Jesus and what he had done that when they reached the shore, they left everything to follow him.

Did you know that Jesus is still calling people to become fishers of men? Today, when we hear about Jesus' amazing life and how he died on the cross, the Holy Spirit helps us to see our sin as Simon did. And like Simon, God calls us to leave our sinful lives behind and follow Jesus. God changes our hearts so that we want to tell others about Jesus. That is how we become fishers of men. When we believe, our job is to "cast the net" of the gospel to "catch" as many unbelievers as we can and bring them in to follow Jesus.

Jesus Heals the Paralyzed Man

LUKE 5:17—26

More and more people were talking about Jesus and the amazing signs and wonders that followed his teaching. No wonder the religious rulers became more interested in him too. One day the Pharisees and teachers of the law came from Jerusalem and every village in Galilee and Judea to listen to his teaching. Everyone crowded into one building—and all around it outside—to see him.

At the edge of the crowd was a paralyzed man, carried by a few of his friends on a stretcher. These men were desperate to get inside the house so they could lay the crippled man before Jesus, but there was no way to get through the door. Then one man had an idea. They climbed up on the roof and took the stretcher with them. They tore off the roof tiles, broke a hole through the ceiling, and lowered their friend down in front of Jesus. When Jesus saw their faith and what they had done to get the man in the room, he said to the crippled man, "Man, your sins are forgiven you" (Luke 5:20).

When the scribes and Pharisees heard that, they didn't like it at all! They started talking among themselves. "Who does this man think he is? Only God can forgive sins. Jesus is blaspheming against God!" They believed that Jesus was only a man—and it is a sin for any human being to say he is equal to God.

Jesus knew what they were thinking and he said to them "Why are you asking these questions in your hearts? Which is easier, to say, 'Your sins are forgiven,' or to say, 'Rise and walk'? To prove to you that I—the Son of Man—have the right and the power to forgive sins"—he turned to the man who was paralyzed and said—"I say to you, get up, pick up your bed, and go home." As soon as Jesus said this, the crippled man stood up, picked up his stretcher and went home, glorifying God as he left. When the religious leaders saw this, they were filled with awe. They glorified God and talked about the extraordinary miracle Jesus performed.

The religious rulers were wrong to be critical of Jesus, but they were right to say that only God can forgive someone's sins. You and I can forgive people when they sin against us, but we can't forgive a person for their sin against God. Only God can do that. Jesus wasn't forgiving the crippled man for breaking through the roof; he was forgiving him for his sins against God. That is why the Pharisees and the teachers of the law were so upset. They didn't realize that Jesus was God. They didn't know that Jesus would die on the cross to take the punishment for the crippled man's sins so he could be forgiven. Jesus knew their questions needed answers, and he used the healing to teach them. But, in the end, many of them rejected Jesus' teaching and refused to believe in him. Sadly, in a few years it would be the religious rulers who would plan Jesus' arrest and crucifixion.

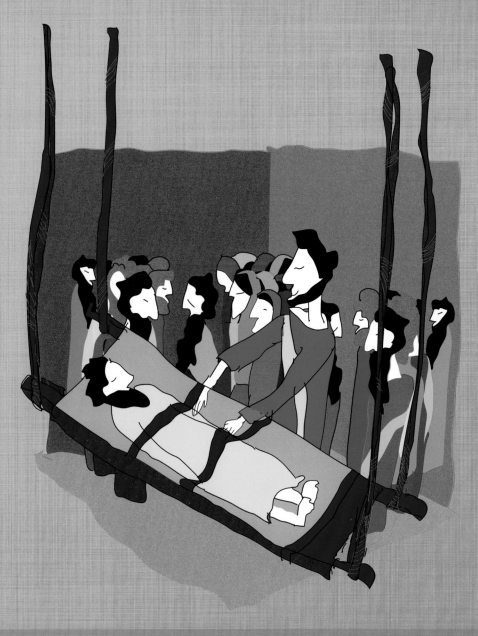

Let's Talk About It!

What is wrong with the man on the stretcher?

How do his friends get him through the crowd to see Jesus?

What two things does Jesus do for the crippled man?

Let's Talk About It!

What is Jesus doing in the picture?

Why do you think he is high on a hill?

What is one thing Jesus teaches the people?

The Sermon on the Mount— The Beatitudes

MATTHEW 4:23 – 5:16

As Jesus traveled through Galilee he healed people with every kind of disease and sickness. Stories about him spread as far as Syria, and big crowds began to follow him everywhere he went. People came from Jerusalem and Judea, but others came from much greater distances, even beyond the Jordan River. One day, seeing the large crowds that were following him, Jesus hiked to the top of a mountain and sat down with his disciples. Then he began to teach the disciples the Beatitudes as the crowd listened in. Each of the nine Beatitudes begins with the words "Blessed are." Each one describes a group of people who are blessed by God and then explains why they are blessed.

Blessed are the poor in spirit, for theirs is the kingdom of heaven.

Blessed are those who mourn, for they shall be comforted.

Blessed are the meek, for they shall inherit the earth.

Blessed are those who hunger and thirst for righteousness, for they shall be satisfied.

Blessed are the merciful, for they shall receive mercy.

Blessed are the pure in heart, for they shall see God.

Blessed are the peacemakers, for they shall be called sons of God.

Blessed are those who are persecuted for righteousness' sake, for theirs is the kingdom of heaven.

Blessed are you when others revile you and persecute you and utter all kinds of evil against you falsely on my account. Rejoice and be glad, for your reward is great in heaven, for so they persecuted the prophets who were before you. (Matthew 5:3–12)

Jesus had other things to teach his disciples too. "You are the light of the world," he said, and then he used a parable to explain what he meant. "When people light a lamp at night, they don't hide it under a big basket that would hide its light. Instead, they put the light on a stand to light up the whole house. Just like that, you should let your light shine so that other people can see it and give glory to God." The light Jesus talked about doesn't come from the people themselves but from God's presence in their lives. Jesus also said, "I am the light of the world. Whoever follows me will not walk in darkness, but will have the light of life" (John 8:12). We are the light of the world when Jesus, the Light of Life, lives in us.

The Beatitudes can seem like a difficult list to follow. If God requires us to have a pure heart, how could we, who are sinners, ever see God? The gospel provides the answer. Even though we are sinners—spiritually poor and not pure in heart—we can inherit the kingdom of heaven because Jesus lived a righteous (sinless) life. He gives us his sinless life for our sinful life when we believe and trust in him. Once we believe, we have a new desire to follow Jesus. Because of Jesus' mercy to us we want to be merciful to others. Because Jesus made peace with God for us we want to make peace with others. If we didn't have the gospel, the Beatitudes would just be a list of good deeds we could never do. With the gospel this list becomes a pattern for living and following Jesus!

The Sermon on the Mount—Love Your Enemies

MATTHEW 5:17—48

The day Jesus taught the Beatitudes he also explained many other things about life in his kingdom. Jesus wanted people to know that everything in the law of Moses pointed forward to him! Jesus was the one—the only one—who could obey God's law perfectly and fulfill everything the law of Moses required. But he warned the people that unless their righteousness was greater than the scribes and Pharisees, they would not go to heaven.

The Pharisees talked a lot about obeying God's law. They added strict, extra rules to protect them from breaking God's laws. But the Pharisees were only thinking about sinning on the outside. They forgot they were still sinful inside, in their hearts, which was the biggest problem of all. To help the crowd understand how sin works in our hearts, Jesus reminded them that anyone who murdered another person was guilty of breaking God's law. But then Jesus went on to explain that even a person who gets angry with his brother is guilty of the same sin of murder! Jesus taught that becoming angry with someone is like murdering that person in your heart. This was a sin that needed forgiveness too.

Jesus reminded them that the law required that they love their neighbor (Leviticus 19:18). But then he explained what that looks like in a very surprising way. "Love your enemies," he said. "Pray for the people who are cruel and hurtful to you." It's easy to love people who love you, but it's hard to love people who don't. But that's what God's law asks of us. In fact, Jesus said, "You therefore must be perfect, as your heavenly Father is perfect" (Matthew 5:48). That is what God's law really teaches.

When Jesus taught the people to love their enemies and pray for them, he was teaching them the core of the gospel. The apostle Paul tells us that Christ died for us while we were his enemies. When the disciples deserted him and his own people, the Jews, had the Romans crucify him, Jesus still prayed, "Father, forgive them, for they know not what they do" (Luke 23:34). He did everything God's law could ask of anyone. And when he rose again, Jesus offered his perfect life to anyone who trusts him to keep God's law in their place.

Remember, perfect means you don't make any mistakes at all! The only way we can be perfect is through Jesus, who kept the law on the outside and inside, in his heart. He did what we could not do. He lived a perfect life and then, while we were his enemies, he took our place to die for our sins. We can get to heaven if we repent of our sins and trust in Jesus. He offers salvation to everyone who trusts in him.

Let's Talk About It!

Who is the man kneeling down praying for?

What do you think he is asking God to do for his enemy?

Do you have any enemies you could pray for?

Let's Talk About It!

Who is Jesus teaching to pray The Lord's Prayer?
If God already knows what we need, why pray?
Repeat The Lord's Prayer.

The Lord's Prayer

MATTHEW 6:1–18

Jesus had many things to teach his disciples the day he gave the "Sermon on the Mount." After he taught them to love their enemies, he taught them not to live their lives like hypocrites do. A hypocrite is someone who acts one way when everyone is watching but another way when no one is around to see. A hypocrite wants people to think he is good and loves God, but inside he really just loves himself.

Jesus said, "Don't do good things in front of other people just to impress them. That doesn't please your Father in heaven. When you give to someone in need, don't try to make sure everyone else knows about it. That's what the hypocrites do—they want other people to praise them. But they will get no reward in heaven because they have chosen praise from people instead. If you give in secret you will be rewarded in heaven—and God is very eager to reward you. He loves to give his children treasure in heaven."

It's the same with praying, Jesus said. "The hypocrites like to stand and pray where everyone can see them, in the synagogues and on the street corners. But people who pray to impress others have already received their reward. Those who pray in secret will be rewarded by God, who can see what they are doing."

Jesus also explained that we don't need to pray out loud with a lot of words that impress other people. God our Father already knows what we need, even before we start to pray.

Instead, Jesus taught his disciples a short prayer we call The Lord's Prayer. The words to this prayer are: "Our Father in heaven, hallowed be your name. Your kingdom come, your will be done, on earth as it is in heaven. Give us this day our daily bread, and forgive us our debts, as we also have forgiven our debtors. And lead us not into temptation, but deliver us from evil" (Matthew 6:9–13).

Finally, Jesus talked about fasting. "When the hypocrites give up food and drink to fast," Jesus said, "they walk around with long faces so people will notice what they are doing. Those who try to look sad while fasting want others to praise them. They have received all the reward they are going to get. They will not get a heavenly reward. But those who fast in secret, where only God can see, will be rewarded by him in heaven."

Jesus taught these things because it is so easy to pretend to be good on the outside when we are really sinful on the inside. The only real way to cover up our sin is to cover it with the blood of Jesus, who died on the cross to take our sin away. For when we trust in Jesus, he covers our sin with his perfect record of obedience. Then he changes our desire to impress others to a desire to live for God—on the inside and the outside.

Treasure in Heaven

MATTHEW 6:19–34

Jesus spoke about the kingdom of God and heavenly treasure when he taught the people. Heavenly treasure is the treasure God gives us in heaven for obeying him while we live on earth. "Treasure in heaven never wears out," Jesus said. "That is why you should store up treasures there. Earthly treasure doesn't last. The things we buy wear out. Rust and decay destroy them. Robbers can come and steal them if we don't lock them away. But in heaven there is no rust or decay." And any treasure God gives us there is safe because there are no robbers in heaven! It will last for ever and ever.

Jesus talked a lot about treasure and money because he knew they often make us forget about God. Jesus said, "No one can serve two masters, for either he will hate the one and love the other, or he will be devoted to the one and despise the other. You cannot serve God and money" (Matthew 6:24). Jesus knew that we worry about our

lives and, instead of trusting God for help, we try to solve our problems with money.

Jesus wasn't saying that money is bad, but he wanted people to trust the Lord for what they need. God owns everything! He can provide for all our needs every day. We don't need to worry. To teach people how God provides, Jesus said, "Look up at all the birds around you. They don't plant crops or harvest their own food. God provides food for them. If God does all that for the birds, shouldn't we trust God for what we need? We are much more valuable to God! Anyway," Jesus said, "worrying about what you need won't add a single day to your life. It doesn't do any good."

Jesus looked around the hillside and pointed to the flowers. "Look at these flowers," he said. "They don't work to buy clothing or spin thread to weave their dress, but look at how beautiful they are! They are more beautiful than even King Solomon, dressed in his finest royal robes. If God provides beauty for the flowers, don't you think he will provide what we need to wear? And don't worry about what you will eat either. Your Father in heaven knows everything you need. Instead of worrying about these earthly things," Jesus said, "make following God the most important thing in your life. God promises to give us all the other things we need."

We might think food and clothing are our most important needs, but we have a bigger need: we all need to be forgiven for our sins. Jesus died on the cross so we can be forgiven. He took care of our biggest need. If God was willing to give up his only Son to take our sins away, we can be sure he will give us the little things we need, like food and clothing.

Let's Talk About It!

Who gives the flowers their beautiful colors and cares for the birds?

What can we learn from the way God cares for the flowers and the birds?

Name one way God provides for you.

Let's Talk About It!

Who built his house on the sand?

What did the wise man build his house on?

Why is trusting in Jesus like building your house on the rock?

The Wise & Foolish Builders

MATTHEW 7:15—27

Near the end of his teaching on the mountain, Jesus told stories called parables and used word pictures that would help people remember what he said. For example, Jesus said that false prophets—people who didn't tell the truth about God—were like wolves who try to sneak their way into God's flock of sheep. They dress up like sheep so they look like sheep on the outside, but inside they are wolves who want to attack the sheep and kill them. Jesus used another word picture to explain how God's people could recognize these wolves. Jesus said that every tree bears its own special kind of fruit. If you have an apple tree, you get apples, but you won't get apples from a grapevine. If you have a healthy tree, you will get good fruit, but the fruit from a diseased tree will be bad. If you see a tree and don't know what kind it is, you can look at its fruit and you will know. And you will be able to tell if the fruit is good or bad.

People don't bear fruit like trees, of course, but Jesus was saying you can tell a lot about people by their "fruit"—the things they do and say. If a person tells you he is a Christian but he does things that are sinful, he may not be a Christian at all. Just because someone says he is a Christian doesn't mean God has changed him on the inside, in his heart. That's why we compare the words someone says with the fruit of his life, his words and actions.

Jesus also taught a parable about two builders. He said, "Everyone who hears my words and obeys them will be like a wise man who built his house on a rock. When the rains fell, and the floods came, and the winds blew and beat on that house, it did not fall because it had been built on the rock. But a man who does not obey my teaching is like a man who builds his house on sand. When the wind and rains come to his house, the water will carry away the sand from under his house. It will crash to the ground because its foundation has been washed away."

When Jesus finished teaching these parables, the crowds were amazed at what he had said. They had never heard anyone talk about God and sound so sure about what he was saying. Of course, we know that Jesus is no ordinary man; he is also the Son of God.

The warnings Jesus gave the crowd are written in the Bible for us too. We need to build our house—our life—on the rock. That means we need to put our trust in Jesus, the Rock of our salvation. Jesus warned people that not everyone goes to heaven. Even if we try really, really hard to be good, one sin ruins our perfect record and makes us God's enemies. And no one can be that good—no one but Jesus. Jesus said that only those who do his Father's will go to heaven. God the Father sent his Son Jesus to die on the cross for all the sinful things we do. If we trust in God the Father's plan, we are doing the Father's will. That's building your house on the rock!

The Four Soils

MATTHEW 13:1–23

SEED

One day Jesus was in a house teaching for a long time. After awhile he walked down to the sea and sat down. Right away, great crowds began to gather, coming very close to him so they wouldn't miss anything he might say or do. So that everyone could hear him, Jesus got into a boat and went out a little distance from shore, just as he had before. The crowd spread out along the beach so that everyone could see and hear. And there from the boat, Jesus taught one of his most famous stories, the parable of the sower and the seeds.

A sower is someone who "sows" or plants seeds into a field so they will grow into a crop. Some larger seeds, like corn, are carefully planted in rows, one by one. The seeds of other plants, like wheat and barley, are often scattered on a field by the handful. In Jesus' story, the sower was scattering those kinds of seeds. As he did, some seeds fell along the path, where birds could easily see them. They flew right over and ate them up. Other seeds fell on ground with a lot of rocks. There wasn't much soil for the seeds to grow in. They sprouted quickly but they were weak. When the sun rose up in the sky, these plants withered away without deep roots. A third group of seeds fell among thorns. Those plants had enough soil to grow in, but when the thorny weeds grew up around them, the weeds choked them out. Finally, some of the seeds fell into good soil. These seeds sprouted quickly, grew strong, and weren't choked out by weeds. They gave the sower a great

harvest—as much as one hundred times the amount of seeds used to plant the field.

When Jesus finished the parable, the disciples didn't understand its meaning. Later Jesus told them what the parable meant. The seeds in the story are God's Word, and God is the sower who sows the seeds in the earth. The birds represent Satan, who quickly snatches God's Word away from some people. They forget about it right away and it does them no good. Some people are like the soil with all the rocks in it. At first they are happy to hear God's Word and believe it, but when hard times come upon their lives, they give up and walk away from God. Other people are like the soil with all the weeds and thorns. They hear God's Word but then start thinking about money and other things that crowd out their thoughts about God. Finally, some people's hearts are like good soil. When God's Word is sown into their hearts, they understand it and believe it. It bears good fruit in their lives.

Jesus told the disciples something else very interesting that day. He said, "Many prophets and righteous people longed to see what you see, and did not see it, and to hear what you hear, and did not hear it" (Matthew 13.17). Even as they wrote about God's future promises, the Old Testament prophets knew they would not live to see them fulfilled. But they longed to understand how God would save his people and who would be the one to do it (1 Peter 1:10–12). Jesus was the promised Savior the prophets spoke about. The disciples had him right in front of their eyes and didn't even know it!

Let's Talk About It!

What do the seeds in the story represent?

What are the weeds doing in the picture?

Which plants are growing healthy and strong?

The Hidden Treasure

MATTHEW 13:31—46

Jesus told many stories or parables to explain what the kingdom of heaven is like. Did you know that by teaching with parables, Jesus fulfilled a prophecy from long ago? Asaph, the psalm writer and musician who served King David, spoke about Jesus when he wrote, "I will open my mouth in parables; I will utter what has been hidden since the foundation of the world" (Matthew 13:35 and Psalm 78:2).

In one parable Jesus said that a man was sowing seed in his field, but an enemy came one night and sowed weeds in the same field. The weeds grew up alongside the wheat, but at harvest time the Master commanded that the weeds be separated out and burned. Jesus said, "I am the one who is sowing the good seed, the children of the kingdom who believe in me. The enemy is Satan, who sows the weeds, which are people who refuse to believe in me. The harvest is the Judgment at the end of the world. Then those who followed Satan and refused to believe in me will be thrown into a fiery furnace. But the good seed, those who believe, will live in the kingdom with God their Father." Jesus also said that God's judgment was like a fishing net that caught all kinds of fish.

The good fish were saved, but the bad were thrown into a fiery furnace.

In another parable Jesus explained that his kingdom would grow very big and bless many. He said, "A mustard seed starts out very tiny, the smallest of all the seeds. But it grows into a tree so big that birds can build nests in its branches." Just like that tree, God's kingdom was going to reach a lot of people even though Jesus had only twelve disciples at the start. Jesus also said that God's kingdom is like the tiny bit of yeast a person uses to make bread. When the yeast is mixed into the dough, it affects every part and causes it to grow. Like yeast in bread, the kingdom of God starts small but will grow and be spread into the whole world.

Jesus also told two parables about treasure to explain how valuable God's kingdom is. He said, "A man was traveling across a field when he noticed something sticking out of the ground. When he looked more closely, he discovered it was a hidden treasure. *The treasure must belong to the owner of the field,* he thought. So he sold everything he had to buy the field, and the treasure became his. Another man was a merchant looking for pearls. One day he found a special pearl that was very valuable. He wanted it so much that he sold everything he had to buy it."

Did you know that these parables are all about Jesus? There is nothing in this world more valuable than he is! Jesus wants us to know that so we will be willing to give up the whole world to follow him. Although Jesus started with just a few followers, his kingdom grew as he said it would. Today millions of people around the world love Jesus. But mixed in with real believers are people who don't really love the Lord. When Jesus comes back, there will be a great judgment. Those who trust in Jesus and what he did on the cross will be saved, like the wheat and the good fish. But those who don't trust in the Lord will be sent to the place of fire the Bible calls hell. No wonder Jesus was so careful to teach us and warn us!

Let's Talk About It!

Point to the treasure.

What is the man who found the treasure selling to buy the field?

What does the treasure represent?

Let's Talk About It!

Why are the men in the boat afraid?
Point to Jesus and tell what he is doing.
How can this story help you when you feel afraid?

Jesus Calms the Storm

MARK 4:35 — 5:20; LUKE 8:22 — 39

After finishing a long day of teaching from on a boat, Jesus told his disciples to row to the other side of the lake. As they set off Jesus laid down in the boat to rest and soon fell asleep on a cushion. Suddenly, a terrible windstorm blew in. Without any warning the wind began churning up the water, creating waves so high that they crashed over the boat, which started to fill with water. The disciples were afraid so they woke Jesus up. "We are going to die, Jesus! Don't you even care?" they cried.

Right away Jesus stood up and rebuked the wind and said to the sea, "Peace! Be still!" As soon as Jesus spoke those words, the storm stopped and the fierce winds were gone. There wasn't the slightest breath of a breeze, and the sea was as calm and quiet as a mirror. Then Jesus turned to the disciples. "Where is your faith?" he asked (Luke 8:25). The disciples had been afraid of the wind but now they were in awe of Jesus. They were experiencing what the Bible calls the fear of the Lord. They asked each other, "Who is this? Even the winds and water obey him!"

The disciples would see Jesus do even more that day. After rowing across the lake they landed in the country of the Gerasenes. As soon as Jesus stepped out of the boat, a demon-possessed man came to him. What a terrible life this

The man couldn't even live in a house. Instead he wandered around people's tombs and cried out at night. When people tried to chain him up, he tore the chains apart. No one was strong enough to control him or rescue him from his suffering. But that was about to change.

When the man saw Jesus, he fell down and a demon inside him spoke. "What do you want with me, Jesus, Son of the Most High God? Please don't torment me," he said even though he had been cruel to the suffering man. "What is your name?" Jesus asked the demon. "My name is Legion because there are many of us inside this man," he answered. The demons knew Jesus would not allow them to keep hurting the man. They begged Jesus not to send them into the bottomless pit where they can never escape. They asked if they could go into a large herd of pigs on a hillside nearby. Jesus gave them permission, so they left the man and entered the pigs. As soon as they did, the pigs rushed down a steep bank into the lake and drowned. The herdsman ran and told everyone the story and people soon came to see it for themselves. But when they saw the man, now healed of the demons, calm and quiet and able to talk with people, they were filled with fear. In fact, they asked Jesus to leave. The man who had been healed wanted to go with Jesus, but Jesus said, "Go home to your friends and tell them how much the Lord has done for you." And that is what he did.

The disciples saw our Lord's awesome power that day and that he was no ordinary man. Only God could command the wind and the waves like Jesus did. The demons knew who Jesus was and called him the "Son of the Most High God" (Luke 8:28). You see, Jesus was a man, but he was also God. Because he was a man, he could die in our place. But because he was God, death could not defeat him. Jesus died for us as a man but rose again with the power of God. As a man, Jesus got tired just like we do and slept in the boat during the storm. But when the disciples woke him, he showed his power as God over all things by commanding the wind and the waves.

Jesus Feeds the Multitude

MATTHEW 14:13—21; LUKE 9:10—17; JOHN 6:1—15

No one had ever seen anyone do the miracles Jesus was doing, and no one had ever heard anyone talk about God and his kingdom the way Jesus did. No wonder people followed him everywhere he went! Even when Jesus sat down somewhere just to talk with his disciples, the news would spread: "Jesus is here! Jesus is here! Let's go hear what he has to say!" Soon the crowds would surround him again, eager to hear every word and hoping to see a miracle.

This happened one day when Jesus climbed a mountain to talk with his disciples. Soon the whole mountain was covered with people, so Jesus taught them too. At the end of the day the disciples asked Jesus to send the people home. "They haven't had anything to eat all day and there is no place for them to spend the night," they said. To test their faith, Jesus said, "You give them something to eat" (Luke 9:13). Philip replied, "How can we do that? Even if we had 200 denarii (which was about 200 days' wages), we wouldn't have enough money to buy food for all these people!" There were about five thousand men in the crowd and even more women and children.

Then Andrew spoke up. "There is a little boy here with five barley loaves and two fish, but that is not nearly enough." Normally, that would have been true, but not this time! The little boy's lunch was part of God's bigger plan.

Jesus asked his disciples to have everyone sit down in groups of fifty. Then Jesus took the boy's bread and fish and thanked God for it. He broke the fish and the loaves into small pieces and gave them to the disciples to share with the crowd. The Bible doesn't tell us exactly how it happened, but sometime between the time Jesus broke up the food and the disciples passed it out, more and more food grew from those first, small pieces. The disciples passed out the fish and loaves to every person in the crowd, and everyone ate all they wanted.

Afterward, Jesus sent the disciples to gather the leftovers. They came back with twelve baskets full of food—more than twelve times what Jesus started with! Everyone who was there that day knew they had seen a miracle. They said, "This has to be the Prophet we have been waiting for God to send!" Jesus knew what they were thinking. He also knew they desired to make him their king, but that was not why he had come. So he sent the crowds away and slipped away by himself to another part of the mountain.

The Jews wanted a king like David, who would fight and conquer Rome, the country that ruled over them. But Jesus didn't come to start a war against Rome. He didn't come to free the people from their earthly enemies. Jesus came to fight against the kingdom of Satan and to free us from our enemies of sin and death. Jesus could have defeated the Romans in a second, but he had a bigger plan—to save us from our sins. That's why he did not let the people make him their king.

Let's Talk About It!

Look at the picture. Has the crowd eaten yet?

What part in the story does the little boy play?

How can so much food be left over from five loaves and two fish?

Let's Talk About It!

Point to Peter and explain the trouble he's in.
What is Jesus doing in the picture?
What are some ways we need to trust God in our lives?

Jesus Walks on Water

MATTHEW 14:22–36

It had been an amazing day. Jesus had fed five thousand people with one little boy's lunch! Some people were so excited that they were ready to make Jesus their king. But that wasn't Jesus' plan. He sent the crowd away and told his disciples to get into their boat and row across the lake. Jesus didn't go with them. He wanted time by himself to pray. As the day passed into evening, Jesus was alone with his heavenly Father. Times like that were the best times for him.

Things in the boat were not going well. The disciples started strong, but a wind blew in against them and waves crashed against the boat. Hard as they tried, they made little progress. This time Jesus was not with them to calm the storm. They were on their own.

When Jesus finished praying, it was the middle of the night. He walked down to the water's edge—and then he kept right on walking. He walked on top of the water and, even though it was dark, he headed towards the disciples' boat. After awhile, Jesus came close to their little boat, as the disciples fought against the waves.

Do you think the disciples were glad to see Jesus as he walked across the water? Now they wouldn't be alone in the boat! Now Jesus was here to help them! But that isn't what happened. When the disciples saw Jesus walking on the water, they got really scared. They told each other, "It's a ghost!" and they began to cry out in fear.

Jesus said, "Don't be afraid. It's me." Peter burst out, "Lord, if it is you, tell me to come to you on the water." Jesus said, "Come." So Peter stepped out of the boat onto the waves. Just like Jesus, his feet stayed on top of the waves and he didn't sink.

But then Peter started looking around at the wind and the waves. What was he doing out there? He became afraid again and right away he started sinking. "Lord, save me," he cried. Jesus grabbed Peter's hand and said, "You have so little faith. Why did you doubt?" Jesus took Peter back to the boat, and as soon as they got in, the wind stopped and the water became calm. The disciples in the boat worshiped Jesus and said, "Truly you are the Son of God" (Matthew 14:33).

When you read a story this exciting, it is easy to miss one of the most important parts. Here it is: the disciples worshiped Jesus! They were beginning to see that Jesus was not just an ordinary man; they were starting to realize he was God! Jesus didn't boast about who he was. He didn't go around telling everyone he was God. But that night in the boat, when the disciples worshiped Jesus as God, he didn't stop them. They had seen Jesus' miracle of the fishes and loaves; they had watched him command the wind and the waves and heal the sick. Now they had seen him walk on water. Jesus was more than a prophet, a great teacher, and an ordinary man. Jesus was God, and he deserved to be worshiped. Peter didn't realize it at the time, but when he called out to Jesus, "Lord, save me," he was saying the words everyone needs to say to Jesus, the Son of God.

Take Up Your Cross

MATTHEW 16:16—28; MARK 8:27—38; LUKE 9:18—27

Once when Jesus was walking with his disciples, he asked them a question. "Who do the crowds say that I am?" (Luke 9:18). "Some people think you are John the Baptist," they answered. "Others say you are Elijah or one of the prophets who has come back from the dead." But then Jesus asked them, "But who do you say that I am?" (Luke 9:20).

Peter had the answer right away. "You are the Christ, the Son of the living God" (Matthew 16:16). When Jesus heard Peter's answer, he said, "You are blessed to know that, Peter! No one could have helped you know that except my Father in heaven." But Jesus told the disciples not to tell anyone else who he really was.

From then on Jesus began to tell his disciples what was going to happen to him. Even though he was the Son of God, he was going to die. He would go to Jerusalem, where the religious leaders—the elders, chief priests, and scribes—would turn against him and plan to have him killed. Their plan would succeed, but that would not be the end, Jesus told them. "I will come back to life after three days. I will rise again from the dead." After hearing that Jesus would die, Peter pulled him aside. "Don't say such things, Jesus! This will never happen to you!" This time Jesus did not praise Peter for what he said. Instead, he spoke very strong words against him. "You are a stumbling block to me, Peter. You are standing in the way of what God wants me to do. You are not thinking about things the way God does; you are thinking the way people on earth think."

By this time a crowd was forming. Jesus called out to them and said, "If anyone wants to follow me, he must take up his cross every day and live for me, not for himself. Whoever loves the world more than me will lose his life. But whoever gives up loving the world for me will be saved. What good is it to have the whole world if you lose your life and never go to heaven to be with God?" Jesus warned the people that someday he would come from heaven with his angels, and everyone would be judged according to what they had done.

Isn't it interesting that Peter could say something so true and right about Jesus one moment and then say something so terribly wrong the next? God had helped Peter see that Jesus was the Messiah, but Peter probably thought this meant that Jesus would defeat the Romans and rule over an earthly kingdom. Jesus didn't come to do that. He came to give up his life for us and win the battle over sin and death. He took our sin to the cross and died. But Jesus didn't stay dead. He won the greatest victory of all, over death, when on the third day he rose from the dead!

Let's Talk About It!

What is an idol?

Why are idols at the foot of the cross in this picture?

What does God want us to do with our idols?

Let's Talk About It!

Who is with Jesus on the mountain?

What do you think it was like to watch Jesus transfigured?

What does this tell us about Jesus?

The Transfiguration

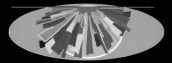

When Jesus told the disciples that he must suffer and die and then would be raised from the dead, the disciples did not understand what Jesus was talking about. Jesus also told them, "Some of you who are standing here will not die before you see the kingdom of God as it comes with power." The disciples didn't understand that either! But about a week later, Jesus took Peter, James, and John up onto a high mountain and gave them a taste of the power and the glory of the kingdom that was coming. There on the mountain Jesus was suddenly transformed from a normal looking man, revealing the brightness of his glory. His face shown like the sun and his clothes were as dazzling white as light.

All of a sudden Elijah and Moses appeared out of nowhere and began to talk with Jesus. Peter, James, and John were terrified. No one had ever seen anything like this before! Then a cloud drifted down and surrounded them. They heard a voice from inside the cloud saying, "This is my beloved Son; listen to him" (Mark 9:7). When the disciples heard God's voice (because that is who it was), they fell down with their faces on the ground to worship God. Then Jesus came over to them, touched them, and told them to get up. When they did, no one was there but Jesus.

On their way down the mountain, Jesus told them, "Don't tell anyone what you have seen until I have risen from the dead." The three disciples kept it to themselves, but they still wondered what Jesus meant by being raised from the dead. They asked Jesus why the religious leaders taught that Elijah had to come first, before the Messiah. Jesus answered, "Elijah does come first to make things ready. And Elijah has already come, and he has suffered just as the Son of Man [one of the names Jesus called himself] is going to suffer." That is when they realized that John the Baptist was the Elijah Jesus was talking about.

Can you imagine what it must have been like to see Jesus radiant in glory, shining like the sun in dazzling white? For just a few moments the three disciples had that chance. They got a glimpse of the holiness, glory, and power of Jesus as God—something no one had seen outside heaven. No wonder they were terrified! They knew Jesus, the man who did and said extraordinary things. But nothing could really prepare them to see Jesus, the Son of God, shining with heavenly glory. And yet the transfiguration the disciples saw was only a tiny hint of the power Jesus would show in his resurrection. That is when his words about the kingdom of God coming in power would come true.

STORY 103

Jesus Cleanses Ten Lepers

LUKE 17:11—19

As Jesus traveled about he performed signs and wonders and healed the sick. When people heard that Jesus was coming, they gathered on the road ahead and waited for him to arrive. One day on his way to Jerusalem, somewhere between Samaria and Galilee, ten lepers waited outside a village, hoping to see Jesus. Leprosy was a terrible, incurable disease back then. Once a person got leprosy he was required to leave his home and family and live outside the city, away from other people. The Jewish law said a leper had to call out "Unclean, unclean!" to warn people who got near him to stay away.

When the lepers saw Jesus outside the village they stayed at a distance, but instead of calling out "Unclean! Unclean!" they called out, "Jesus, Master, have mercy on us" (Luke 17:13). When Jesus saw the lepers and heard their request, he said, "Go and show yourselves to the priests" (Luke 17:14). That was what the law told a leper to do if he was healed. If the priest agreed that the leprosy was gone, the person could go back to his home and family. When the lepers heard Jesus' command, they hoped he had healed them, and they hurried to obey.

As they went on their way to the priests, all ten were healed! How happy they must have been! But do you know what happened next? Only one of them turned around to thank Jesus for what he had done. That man praised God loudly, at the top of his lungs, and when he reached Jesus, he fell at his feet and thanked him over and over. The leper who returned was a Samaritan, a group of people the Jews didn't like. Jews and Samaritans didn't usually like to be together. Jesus looked down at the thankful man and said, "Didn't I heal ten lepers? Where are the other nine? Didn't anyone come back to thank God except this foreigner?" Then Jesus said to the thankful man, "Get up and go your way. Your faith has made you well."

Were you surprised that the lepers who were Jewish did not stop to thank Jesus, but the Samaritan leper did? In the end, many Jews rejected Jesus as the Messiah. In this story the Samaritan who knelt at Jesus' feet got more than his leprosy healed; God touched his heart as well. The other nine found healing for their leprosy, but this man found Jesus and forgiveness for his sin. Jesus praised him for his faith. You and I might not have leprosy, but our hearts are sick with sin just like this man's heart and body was. When Jesus died on the cross he made a way for all of us to have our sins removed. That is something worth thanking God for!

Let's Talk About It!

How many lepers did Jesus heal?
How many lepers returned to thank him?
Where did the others go?

Jesus Claims to Be God

JOHN 10

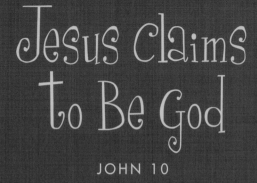

The Bible tells us that God is a shepherd and he takes care of his people like a shepherd cares for his sheep. That is why King David said, "The LORD is my shepherd" in Psalm 23. God called Israel's leaders shepherds too, but they didn't lead, feed, or protect their flock as God wanted them to. Because of that God punished them and promised to someday send a shepherd who would not fail. In the book of Ezekiel, God said that he would give his people one shepherd like his servant David who would feed his sheep and be their shepherd (Ezekiel 34:23).

One day while he was teaching, Jesus said he was the shepherd God promised long ago. He said to the people, "I am the good shepherd. The good shepherd lays down his life for the sheep" (John 10:11). "I will not desert my sheep if a wolf comes to attack them. A hired man might run away, but my sheep belong to me. I will stay to protect them," he promised. Again Jesus told the people, "I am the good shepherd. I know the ones who belong to me and they know me, just as my heavenly Father knows me and I know him. I will give my life for the sheep." Jesus also said he had the power

to take up his life again if he died. That was not something most people had heard Jesus say before. Some people said he must have a demon to say such things. Others said he was crazy. But still others disagreed and said, "Jesus has healed the blind. He doesn't talk like someone who has a demon."

A little later they asked Jesus, "If you are the Messiah, would you please just say so?" But Jesus didn't answer their question the way they wanted. Instead, he called himself a shepherd again. He said, "My sheep hear my voice, and I know them, and they follow me. I give them eternal life, and they will never perish, and no one will snatch them out of my hand. My Father, who has given them to me, is greater than all, and no one is able to snatch them out of the Father's hand. I and the Father are one" (John 10:27–30).

Then the people who had been listening picked up stones to throw at Jesus. They wanted to kill him! But Jesus calmly asked them why. "Because," they answered, "you are just a man, but you are saying you are God. That is the sin of blasphemy!" Jesus did not run away from them but tried to explain. "I am doing the works God my Father has given me to do. You have seen them and that is why you should believe my words. What you have seen should show you that the Father is in me and I am in the Father," he said. But the people, especially the religious leaders, did not want to believe him. They wanted to arrest him! But Jesus escaped and went away, across the Jordan River.

When Jesus said he gives eternal life and is one with his Father, it made the Jews angry. They knew Jesus was claiming to be God and they didn't believe he was. That is why they tried to kill him. In the end Jesus did give his life on the cross, and he took it up again when he rose from the dead. Today Jesus the Good Shepherd is calling all of us to do what the people in this story refused to do: believe and follow him.

Let's Talk About It!

What do the men intend to do with the stones they are holding?

What does Jesus' reflection say about him?

Who do the sheep in the story represent?

Let's Talk About It!

What is the Pharisee (the man in front) praying?
How is the tax collector's prayer different?
What sin do you need to ask God's forgiveness for today?

The Pharisee & the Tax Collector

LUKE 18:9—17

One day while Jesus was teaching his disciples, others gathered around to listen. Jesus knew that some of them thought they could get into heaven by the good works they did. They also looked down on others they didn't think were good enough. But Jesus knew they were not nearly as good as they thought they were and no one is good enough to earn their way into heaven. To help them, Jesus told the parable of the Pharisee and the tax collector.

"There were two men who went up to the temple to pray," Jesus said. "One was a Pharisee." Pharisees were religious rulers who added many of their own strict rules to God's law. They thought these extra laws would keep them from breaking God's laws. But after awhile those extra rules just made the Pharisees proud. The Pharisee in Jesus' story was like that. He stood by himself at the temple and prayed, "God, I thank you that I am not like other sinful men I see around here, especially that tax collector over there." The Pharisee kept praying, but really he was just boasting to God about all the good things he thought he had done.

"The other man," Jesus explained, "was a tax collector." The people in Jesus' day looked down on tax collectors because they took the people's money and gave it to the Romans. That was bad enough, but often the tax collectors took extra money to keep for themselves. They got rich by stealing from their own people. But the tax collector in Jesus' story was sorry about what he had done. He stood far away from everyone and couldn't even lift up his head when he prayed. He beat on his chest to show how sorry he was and said, "God, be merciful to me, a sinner!" (Luke 18:13). Jesus said, "The tax collector is the one who went home that day forgiven by God, not the Pharisee. People who praise themselves will be humbled. But those who humble themselves and admit their sins will be lifted up by God."

While Jesus was teaching, some people began disturbing the crowd. They were trying to get their children close enough for Jesus to touch. This annoyed the disciples. They tried to stop the parents, but Jesus stopped the disciples instead. He said, "Let the children come to me. Don't make it hard for them, because the kingdom of God belongs to people like them. Unless a person receives God's kingdom like a child, he will not be able to go to heaven."

What does it mean to come to God like a child? Children depend on their parents to give them food, clothes, and everything they need. That is how we are to trust in God, especially for our righteousness and salvation. The Pharisee in Jesus' parable thought he was righteous because of the good things he did on his own. But the tax collector knew there was nothing he could do to make up for his sin by himself. Like a little child, all he could do was trust that God would forgive him if he asked. You and I are sinners too. Jesus offers his righteousness to us. If we trust in him, our sins will be forgiven like the tax collector's were.

Lazarus

Lots of people knew about Jesus, but there were a few who became his close friends. A man named Lazarus and his sisters, Mary and Martha, were people Jesus liked to visit. They lived just a few miles from Jerusalem in a little village called Bethany.

One day Lazarus got very sick. Mary and Martha sent a message to Jesus, hoping he would come and help. But when Jesus got the message, he did not go to help Lazarus. Instead he said, "This illness does not lead to death. God is going to use it to show the glory of the Son of God." Jesus could have healed Lazarus without even going to Bethany, but he had a bigger plan. Jesus stayed where he was for two more days and during that time Lazarus died. Then Jesus said to the disciples, "Lazarus has died and I need to go wake him. For your sake I'm glad I was not there, because it will help you to believe in me."

As Jesus traveled to Lazarus's home, Martha met him on the road a few miles away. "Lord, if you had been here, my brother would not have died," she said (John 11:21). "But I know that even now God will give you whatever you ask." "Your brother will rise again," Jesus told her. Martha replied, "I know he will rise again on the last day." But Jesus had something more in mind. He said to her, "I am the resurrection and the life. Whoever believes in me, though he die, yet shall he live, and everyone who lives and believes in me shall never die. Do you believe this?" (John 11:25–26). "Yes, Lord," she said. "I believe you are the Son of God, the Messiah God promised to send into the world."

Martha left and brought her sister Mary to Jesus. When Mary saw Jesus she fell at his feet and said, "Lord, if you had been here, my brother would not have died" (John 11:32). Mary was crying and soon Jesus was weeping too, as he saw how sad people were over the death of the friend he loved. Mary and Martha took Jesus to the cave where Lazarus's body lay. The entrance was closed off with a large stone. "Take the stone away," Jesus said. Martha did not think this was a good idea. "After four days, there will be a terrible smell," she warned him. But Jesus said to her, "Did I not tell you that if you believed you would see the glory of God?" (John 11:40). So they took away the stone and Jesus prayed to his Father in heaven. Then he called out with a loud voice, "Lazarus, come out" (John 11:43). Suddenly, out of the tomb came Lazarus! He stood in front of them all, still wrapped in the linen strips he had been buried in. Now everyone's tears were tears of happiness!

When Jesus said, "I am the resurrection and the life," he was telling Martha that he is the one who gives life. When Martha heard those words, she knew just what to say: "I believe." These are the same two words God wants us to say. When Jesus raised Lazarus from the dead, it gave us a picture of what Jesus does for anyone who trusts in him. Because of sin death comes to everyone, but Jesus conquered death and sin when he died on the cross. And just as he raised Lazarus, Jesus himself rose again, winning a battle over death forever for everyone who believes.

Let's Talk About It!

Name the three people standing with Jesus in the picture.

What does this story tell us about Jesus?

What does the crowd, gathered for the funeral, think about what Jesus did?

Let's Talk About It!

Point to Zacchaeus.

What does Jesus say to Zacchaeus?

Why don't the people want Jesus to go home with Zacchaeus?

Jesus & Zacchaeus

LUKE 18:18 — 19:10

Jesus often talked about money because he knew how easily money could take God's place in people's hearts. Once a rich young ruler asked Jesus, "What do I need to do to have eternal life?" Jesus told him, "Sell everything you have and give the money to the poor. Then come and follow me." Instead of following Jesus, the man sadly walked away. He was very rich and wanted his money more than he wanted Jesus. Jesus was sad to see the young man go. "How hard it is for rich people to enter the kingdom of God!" he said. In fact, Jesus told his disciples it is easier for a camel to go through the small hole in a sewing needle than it is for a rich person to enter into the kingdom of God. But anyone who gives up something for God will be richly rewarded in heaven.

Not long after this, Jesus told his disciples that they were going to travel to Jerusalem so that "everything that is written about the Son of Man by the prophets will be accomplished" (Luke 18:31). Jesus was using the name "the Son of Man" for himself. He wanted the disciples to know that he was the one the prophets were talking about. Jesus explained that he would be arrested, beaten, and killed, and rise again on the third day. Even though the disciples had heard this before, they still didn't understand what Jesus meant.

On their way to Jerusalem, Jesus and the disciples met another rich man named Zacchaeus. Zacchaeus was a tax collector and became rich by cheating people. He was not a good man, but he wanted to see Jesus. There was just one problem: Zacchaeus was too short to see over the crowd! So he ran ahead and climbed a sycamore tree along the path Jesus was walking.

When Jesus reached the sycamore tree, he stopped. He looked up at Zacchaeus and said, "Zacchaeus, hurry up and come down because I am going to stay at your house today." Zacchaeus could hardly believe it! He quickly climbed out of the tree and welcomed Jesus to his home. But the people in the crowd grumbled about Jesus' plan. "Why is he going to his house? Doesn't he know what a sinner Zacchaeus is?" Jesus did know, and that is exactly why he went. Zacchaeus stood before Jesus and promised to give half of all he owned to the poor. "And if I have cheated anyone," he said, "I will give them four times what I took from them." Jesus replied to Zacchaeus, "Today salvation has come to this house….For the Son of Man came to seek and to save the lost" (Luke 19:9–10).

The rich young ruler did not want to give up all he had to follow Jesus, but Zacchaeus didn't even wait to be asked! Not only did he promise to give away half his money to the poor, he also promised to repay everyone he had cheated. God surely worked in Zacchaeus's heart. When salvation came to him, it changed his whole life. Did you know this is true for us today too? When God opens our eyes to see how wonderful Jesus is, the treasures of the world fade away.

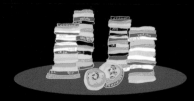

Triumphal Entry

LUKE 19:28—44; JOHN 12:12—19

Jesus and his disciples were on their way to Jerusalem. There were a lot of people on the road with them because it was almost time for Passover, the feast that celebrated God's rescue of Israel from slavery in Egypt hundreds of years before. Each year thousands of people went to Jerusalem to celebrate Passover.

When they reached Bethany, Jesus sent two of his disciples into the village to pick up a young donkey they would find in a certain place. "Untie the colt and bring it here," Jesus said. "If anyone asks you what you are doing, tell him, 'The Lord needs it.'" Sure enough, they found the colt tied up just as Jesus described. As the disciples began to untie it the owners asked what they were doing. The disciples said the Lord needed it, and the owners let them go.

The disciples took the donkey to Jesus and threw their cloaks on it to make a saddle. Jesus climbed onto the donkey and rode it into Jerusalem. This fulfilled the words of the prophet Zechariah, who said the King of Jerusalem would come riding the colt of a donkey (Zechariah 9:9). Zechariah's prophecy was coming true right before their eyes! But the disciples didn't realize that Jesus was fulfilling Zechariah's word until after he rose from the dead and was glorified. Then they remembered what had happened that day and finally understood it.

It was about two miles from Bethany to Jerusalem, and as Jesus rode past the Mount of Olives a great crowd of people gathered along the road. Some of them had seen

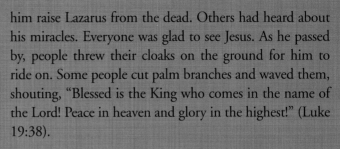

him raise Lazarus from the dead. Others had heard about his miracles. Everyone was glad to see Jesus. As he passed by, people threw their cloaks on the ground for him to ride on. Some people cut palm branches and waved them, shouting, "Blessed is the King who comes in the name of the Lord! Peace in heaven and glory in the highest!" (Luke 19:38).

Everyone was happy and excited about Jesus. What would he do next? Maybe he was coming to Jerusalem to solve all their problems!

But not everyone was happy. The Pharisees did not like what they were seeing at all. The people loved Jesus but didn't pay much attention to the Pharisees. They complained, "Look, the world has gone after him" (John 12:19). When they heard the people call Jesus a king, they told him to tell his disciples to stop. But Jesus answered, "I tell you, if these people were silent, the stones themselves would call out the same thing."

When Jesus got close to Jerusalem he cried. He knew that the people who were celebrating his arrival didn't understand who he really was or why he came to Jerusalem. They wanted an earthly king to save them from Rome, not a heavenly king to save them from sin. Jesus knew that some of the very same people who shouted "Hosanna!" would be shouting "Crucify him!" in just a few days.

Let's Talk About It!

What are the people doing in the picture?
What will soon happen to Jesus in Jerusalem?
What terrible thing will these same people be shouting?

The Widow's Offering

MARK 12:41–13:2;
LUKE 20:1–21:9

While Jesus was in Jerusalem he taught in the temple. Lots of people were listening to him there, but not all of them were his friends. Religious leaders—the scribes, chief priests, elders, and Sadducees—took turns questioning him. They wanted to trick him into saying something that would get him into trouble, but Jesus could not be trapped. The more they tried to catch Jesus in a mistake, the more people saw how wise he was and how different his words were from everyone else's. Finally, in a voice loud enough for everyone to hear, Jesus warned his disciples against these religious rulers. "Beware of the scribes who love to look good on the outside where everyone can see them," he said. "Secretly they take advantage of widows and poor people by taking their money. They will be punished for their evil deeds."

Jesus walked over and sat down where he could see people drop their offerings into the temple treasury box. Many rich people were giving large amounts. Then a poor widow came over to the offering box. Jesus watched her put in two small copper coins. He pointed out the woman to the disciples and said, "Truly, I tell you, this poor widow has given more than all the rest of them. The people who gave large amounts of money still had plenty left over for themselves. But this poor widow gave God everything. Those two coins were all she had left to live on."

As Jesus left the temple one of his disciples talked about how beautiful it was. "Look, Teacher, what wonderful stones and what wonderful buildings!" (Mark 13:1). And the buildings were beautiful, because King Herod had decorated them with gold and marble. But Jesus looked at the temple and said, "A day is coming when all this will be destroyed. Not even one stone will be left standing on top of another." Jesus was right. A few years later, while many of those men were still alive, the temple was completely destroyed.

This story talks about two very different ways to live. The religious rulers wanted to look good on the outside. So did the rich people who gave large amounts of money so people would be impressed. But it was the widow who trusted the Lord. Her beauty was on the inside, where God could see it. In the same way, the temple building looked good on the outside with its beautiful decorations, but it was only a building. Jesus, our Savior, walked among the crowd in the temple but few recognized how beautiful he was. What about us? Will we live for God's glory and trust in Jesus, or will we live to impress others? Like the Pharisees, we are all sinners on the inside. We need Jesus to open our eyes to see his beauty and take away our sin.

Let's Talk About It!

Who is putting more money in the offering, the man or the woman?

Who has more money left at home, the man or the woman?

Why does Jesus say the woman gave more than everyone else?

Let's Talk About It!

What is Jesus doing and why?

Who should have been the ones to wash feet?

How is Jesus still at work washing us today?

Jesus Washes the Disciples' Feet

JOHN 13:1—15

Now that they were in Jerusalem, Jesus and his disciples made plans to celebrate the Passover. Jesus told two of the disciples, "Go into the city and a man with a water jar will meet you. Follow him into the house he enters and say to the owner, 'The Teacher says to you, "Where is the guest room I may use to eat the Passover with my disciples?"'" The disciples left and, sure enough, everything happened just the way Jesus had said. The disciples gathered in an upstairs room large enough for all of them to eat together.

In those days when people gathered for a meal, a servant would wash the dirty feet of all the guests. People wore sandals, not shoes, back then, and the dirt roads they walked on were muddy and dusty. Pretty soon their feet were muddy and dusty too. People felt welcomed when they came to someone's house and a servant washed their feet.

That night there was no servant in the room to do the job. And none of the disciples wanted to do it. They were busy arguing about which one of them was the greatest! Even though Jesus had taught that someone who wanted to be great should be the servant of all, his friends still did not understand his message. Jesus decided to show them instead.

Jesus was thinking about many things as he got up from the table. He knew that in just a few hours he would be arrested and killed. He knew he would soon be returning to his Father in heaven, and there was still so much he wanted his friends to understand. So to help teach them, Jesus picked up a towel and tied it around his waist like an apron. He found a basin and filled it with water and, one by one, he went to each disciple to wash his feet. There were the disciples, watching their Master do the job they didn't want to do—the job they should have done for him. The room must have gotten very quiet as Jesus went from one man to the next.

Finally, it was Peter's turn, but Peter couldn't stand it. He burst out, "Lord, you shouldn't be washing my feet!" Jesus knew Peter's heart was just as dirty with sin as his feet were with mud. But Peter was proud and didn't want Jesus to wash his feet. Jesus said to Peter, "If I do not wash you, you won't share in what I am doing." Peter knew he wanted to be with Jesus. "Then, Lord, wash my hands and face too!" he said. That was a much better answer.

When Jesus was finished, he took off the towel and went back to the table. "Do you understand why I washed your feet?" he asked. "If I am your Lord and Teacher and I can wash your feet, you should follow my example and wash each other's feet."

Peter was surprised that Jesus would do a servant's work and wash their feet. He didn't know Jesus had already given up much, much more. Before Jesus was born he lived in heaven as God the Son in magnificent splendor and glory. Jesus set aside his glory to be born as a baby in a manger. The apostle Paul tells us that when Jesus humbled himself to become a man, he "made himself nothing, taking the form of a servant" (Philippians 2:7). Soon after this Passover meal Jesus would be arrested, mocked, lied about, beaten, and killed. It was by his death that Jesus did far more than wash feet. It was there he washed our sins away.

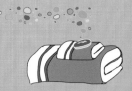

The Last Supper

MATTHEW 26:14—30; LUKE 22:1—34

When the religious leaders watched Jesus ride into Jerusalem before the Passover and saw the crowds ready to make him king, they decided to kill him. So the chief priests and other leaders started looking for a way to get rid of Jesus. This wasn't easy because of the crowds that followed him everywhere. But then something unexpected happened. Judas Iscariot, a disciple of Jesus, came to the leaders offering to do a terrible thing. He would lead them to Jesus when no crowds were around. They could capture him, arrest him, and do whatever they wanted with him. The chief priests were very happy. They gave Judas thirty silver coins to pay him for betraying Jesus. Then they just had to wait until the time was right.

As Judas and the rest of the disciples began the Passover meal with Jesus, this plan was in Judas's mind. Imagine how he felt as everyone gathered around the low table for their meal, reclining on cushions on the floor. Would anyone find out? Would anyone notice how different he was feeling? Then Jesus took bread from the table and gave thanks to God. He broke the bread and gave it to his disciples. "Take this bread and eat it," Jesus said. "It is my body, given for you. Do this to remember me." Then Jesus took the cup of wine from the table. He gave thanks to God and offered it to them saying, "Drink of it, all of you, for this is my blood of the covenant, which is poured out for many for the forgiveness of sins" (Matthew 26:27–28).

Then Jesus said something shocking. "One of you—someone sitting at the table with me right now—is going to betray me." The disciples (except for Judas) could hardly believe such a terrible thing! *Who could it be?* they wondered. One of them asked Jesus who he meant. "I am going to dip this bit of bread into the bowl. The one I give it to is the one," Jesus said. Jesus dipped the bread and handed it to Judas. Judas took the bread from Jesus' hand and, at that moment, Satan entered into him. Jesus said to Judas, "What you are going to do, do quickly" (John 13:27). So Judas got up and left. He went out into the dark night to betray his Master to his enemies.

Did you know that when Christians take communion at church on Sundays they are remembering the special meal Jesus shared with his disciples the night he was betrayed? We call it the Lord's Supper. The apostle Paul said that when we celebrate the Lord's Supper, we are remembering Jesus' death on the cross until he comes back again. Each time Christians take Communion together, they are looking back, not just to the last Passover supper Jesus shared with his disciples, but to Jesus' sacrifice on the cross. The cross is where Jesus' body was broken for us and his blood was shed for our sins. The disciples didn't realize it at the time, but when Jesus broke the bread and shared the cup, he was pointing to his death on the cross.

Let's Talk About It!

What did Jesus say the bread and wine represent?

Point to Judas. What is he about to do?

How do we remember this special meal today?

Let's Talk About It!

How is this picture different from the one in Story 111? (Hint: Count the disciples.)

What does Jesus teach his disciples after that last supper?

Who will Jesus send to be with his disciples—and with us—forever?

Jesus Promises to Send the Holy Spirit

JOHN 14

After Judas left to betray Jesus, Jesus took time to encourage and comfort and teach the friends he loved. He started by saying, "Don't let your hearts be troubled and worried. Believe in God and believe in me." Then he talked about heaven, since that was where he was going and where he wanted to take them too. "In my Father's house [that's what Jesus called heaven], there are many rooms," Jesus said. "You can be sure I am going to prepare a place for you there. Someday I will come back to take you there with me so we can be together. You know the way to where I am going."

Thomas didn't understand and said, "Lord, we don't know where you are going! How can we know the way?" Jesus answered, "I am the way, and the truth, and the life. No one comes to the Father except through me" (John 14:6).

When Philip heard Jesus talk about the Father, he spoke up. "Lord, show us the Father. That will be enough for us." But Jesus said to Philip, "Do you still not know who I am even though I have been with you so long? If you have seen me, you have seen the Father. The Father and I are one. He is in me and I am in him."

Jesus knew how hard it was for the disciples to understand the things he taught them, so next he made a wonderful promise. "I am going to ask the Father to send you a Helper, the Holy Spirit, who will be with you forever. The Holy Spirit will teach you and help you to remember everything I have taught you." Jesus continued, "I will not leave you as orphans; I will come to you. Yet a little while and the world will see me no more, but you will see me" (John 14:18–19). One disciple asked, "How will we know you are with us, Lord?" Jesus answered, "If anyone loves me, he will obey what I say. My Father will love him and we will come and make our home with him."

Jesus knew his death was just hours away, and he wanted to comfort his disciples and strengthen their faith. He said, "I leave my peace with you. Don't let your hearts be sad or afraid. I have told you what's about to happen ahead of time so that when it does, you can believe and have faith in me." They sang a hymn and then Jesus said, "It's time to go." And they left the room to pray on the Mount of Olives.

The things Jesus taught his disciples must have sounded confusing. First Jesus said he was going away but the Father would send the Holy Spirit to be with them. Then Jesus said he wouldn't leave them, but he would come to them. Jesus also said that he and the Father would make their home with the disciples. There is only one way all these things could be true at the same time! Jesus, the Holy Spirit, and the Father are all one and the same God—one God in three distinct persons. We call this the Trinity, and it is hard to understand. On a night when the disciples were afraid and sad, it must have been extra hard to understand what Jesus was saying.

Jesus Is Arrested

MATTHEW 26:36—56;
MARK 14:32—65;
LUKE 22:39—54; JOHN 18:1—12

Jesus and his disciples walked to a large grove of olive trees on top of the mountain called the Mount of Olives to pray. Judas, the disciple who planned to betray Jesus, knew that was where they would be. So while Jesus and the disciples were talking and praying, Judas met up with some soldiers preparing to arrest Jesus. He was ready to lead the way.

Jesus warned the disciples of the hard things that were ahead. "You are all going to fall away because of me," he said. But Peter didn't want to hear that. He was going to be different! "That might happen with everyone else, but I will never fall away," he boasted. Jesus knew differently. He told Peter, "Satan has already asked to test you, Peter. I have prayed that your faith would not fail." But Peter didn't want to listen. "I am ready to go to prison and to death for you, Lord!" he said. Jesus quietly replied, "I tell you the truth, Peter. Tonight, before the rooster crows, you will deny me three times." Again Peter told Jesus that he would not deny him. The other disciples said the same thing.

When they came to a place called the Garden of Gethsemane, Jesus asked the disciples to sit down and pray. Then he took Peter, James, and John deeper into the grove with him and said, "My heart is filled with sorrow. Please keep watch and pray with me." Then Jesus went on a bit further, knelt down and prayed to his heavenly Father. "My Father, if it is possible, please take this cup away from me, but only if it is your will." The "cup" Jesus was talking about was the cup of God's wrath, filled with God's punishment for our sins. He knew how great the punishment for those sins would be. It was hard to face, even for Jesus. He prayed this prayer three times. Then God sent an angel to strengthen him. Each time Jesus prayed he walked back to the disciples. Each time he found them asleep, unable to stay awake and pray.

The third time Jesus woke them up and said, "The time has come. My betrayer is here." And there came Judas, with soldiers and officials. "Who are you looking for?" Jesus asked the soldiers. "Jesus of Nazareth," they said. "I am he," Jesus said.

When Jesus said "I am he," the soldiers stepped back and fell to the ground. When the soldiers stood back up, Judas went to Jesus and kissed him. That was the signal Judas had arranged to betray the Lord. The soldiers and officials then stepped forward to arrest Jesus, but Peter took out his sword and cut off the ear of the high priest's servant. "Put your sword away," Jesus told Peter as he healed the man's ear. "Don't you realize that my Father would at once send me more than twelve legions of angels if I asked? But that would not fulfill God's Word." Jesus turned to the crowd. "Why do you come with clubs and swords? You have seen me in the temple many times. But this has happened so that God's Word through the prophets would come true." The soldiers grabbed Jesus and led him away. And, just as Jesus warned, the disciples ran away.

Terrible things were happening to Jesus and the worst was yet to come. But it is important to remember that his suffering was all part of God's plan. Hundreds of years earlier, Isaiah wrote about Jesus' arrest, saying that even though he would be treated cruelly, Jesus would not fight back or say anything to stop the people arresting him (Isaiah 53:7–8). Jesus could have called down angels from heaven to rescue him, but he didn't. He let the soldiers take him without fighting so he could die on the cross for our sins.

Let's Talk About It!

What is happening to Jesus?
Why doesn't he fight back and use his angels to destroy the soldiers?
Where are his disciples?

Let's Talk About It!

Point to the rooster in the picture.
What part does it play in the story?
How does Peter sin that night?

Peter Denies Jesus

MATTHEW 26:57–75;
MARK 14:43–72; LUKE 22:54–71; JOHN 18:15–27

After arresting Jesus, the soldiers tied his hands together and led him away to the high priest. John and Peter followed a little way behind. John knew the high priest so he was able to walk into the courtyard, but Peter remained outside the walls until John came back for him. It was chilly that night, so some people had started a fire in the middle of the courtyard to warm themselves. A servant girl looked at Peter's face in the flickering firelight. "You were with Jesus the Galilean," she said. "I don't know what you are talking about!" Peter lied. That was the first time he denied knowing Christ. A little bit later another servant told the crowd, "This man was with Jesus of Nazareth!" "I do not know the man, I swear it!" Peter said, denying Jesus a second time.

Meanwhile, inside, Annas the high priest asked Jesus questions about his teaching. "Many people have heard me teach in the temple. Why don't you ask them?" Jesus said. That made the people so angry that they struck Jesus in the face. Then Annas sent him to Caiaphas, the high priest. There Jesus listened as different people told Caiaphas lies about Jesus. The problem was that everyone who spoke had a different story—no one could agree! Jesus didn't say a word. Finally the high priest asked him, "Tell us if you are the Son of God, the Messiah!" Jesus answered, "You have said so. But I tell you, from now on you will see the Son of Man seated at the right hand of Power and coming on the clouds of heaven" (Matthew 26:64). When he heard that, the high priest tore his robes saying, "That is blasphemy! He deserves to die for what he has said." Other people blindfolded Jesus and spat in his face. They slapped him, made fun of him, and hit him with their fists.

Out in the courtyard Peter sat by the fire. A servant of the high priest, a relative of the man whose ear Peter had cut off, asked, "Didn't I see you in the garden with Jesus?" Peter lied again, saying, "I don't know the man you are talking about!" But just at that moment, a rooster crowed and Jesus turned and looked right at Peter. Peter remembered what Jesus had said—he would deny him three times before the rooster crowed. Peter ran out of the courtyard and cried as though his heart would break. And while he wept the Jewish leaders took Jesus to the palace of the Roman Governor, Pontius Pilate. They had made their decision: Jesus should be killed, and they wanted Pilate to order it.

Before Jesus was arrested Peter was very sure of himself. In the garden he brought a sword and even cut off a man's ear to fight for Jesus. But when Jesus didn't fight back and was arrested, Peter grew afraid. He lost his courage and he denied knowing Jesus three times. What went wrong? Peter's confidence was in himself, not in Jesus. Peter was a sinner. But the good news is that Jesus would die on the cross for Peter. He took the punishment Peter deserved for denying him. Like Peter, we often trust in our own strength, but we need to trust in Jesus. That is important because, like Peter, we can't win the battle with sin on our own.

The Crucifixion & the Criminals

MATTHEW 27:1—38; MARK 15:1—22;
LUKE 23:1—43; JOHN 18:28—19:22

All through the night after Jesus was arrested, the high priest questioned him and people told lies about him. Early the next morning, he was led away to the governor's palace, where Pontius Pilate ruled. The Jews told Pilate that Jesus had committed crimes against Rome by claiming to be a king, but Pilate didn't want to get involved. When he heard that Jesus was from Galilee, he sent him to King Herod, who was in Jerusalem at the time. Pilate hoped Herod would fix the problem. When they stood before Herod, the Jewish leaders accused Jesus again, but Herod didn't think Jesus had done anything wrong, so he sent him back to Pilate. Pilate questioned Jesus a second time, but he still didn't think Jesus was guilty of anything. He knew the religious leaders were jealous of Jesus. He just wanted to let him go.

Each year at Passover the Romans had a tradition to allow one prisoner to go free. Pilate asked the crowd, "Do you want me to free Jesus, the King of the Jews?" "No!" the crowd shouted. "Give us

Barabbas!" (Barabbas was another prisoner.) "What should I do with Jesus, then?" Pilate asked. "Crucify him!" the leaders and the people said. "But why?" Pilate asked. "What evil has he done? He hasn't done anything to deserve death." But the people only shouted more loudly, "Crucify him! Crucify him!"

So Pilate gave up. He sent Jesus away to be beaten by the Roman soldiers. After whipping Jesus until he bled, the soldiers twisted a crown of thorns and placed it on his head.

THE KING OF THE JEWS

They put a purple robe on him and made fun of him and struck him on the face. But when Jesus came out wearing the crown of thorns and the purple robe, the chief priests and officers shouted, "Crucify him! Crucify him!" Still Pilate looked for a way to set Jesus free. But the Jews shouted to Pilate, "If you let him go, you are no friend of Caesar." Finally Pilate released Jesus to be crucified.

The soldiers led Jesus up a hill to be crucified. They nailed him to a wooden cross and lifted him up to hang there until he died. Pilate ordered a sign to be attached to the cross that said, "Jesus of Nazareth, the King of the Jews" (John 19:19). Two robbers were crucified with Jesus, one on each side. One of them mocked Jesus and said, "If you are Christ the Messiah, save yourself and us!" But the other robber said, "You and I deserve our punishment but Jesus has done nothing wrong." He called out to Jesus, "Remember me when you come into your kingdom" (Luke 23:42). Jesus answered with these amazing words: "Today you will be with me in Paradise" (Luke 23:43).

Two robbers hung on crosses with Jesus. One believed while the other mocked. The Bible tells us that God's arm is not too short to save anyone (Isaiah 59:1). Even the thief in this story, who led a sinful life all the way to the end, was saved from his sin on his very last day. We all have the same choice to make as these two robbers. We can reject Jesus, like the thief who made fun of him; or we can put our faith in him, like the one who asked Jesus to remember him. Those are our choices: We either believe in Jesus or we reject him. If we put our faith in Jesus, no sin is too great to be forgiven. Like the robber who repented, we all start out as God's enemies in our sin. But Jesus' death on the cross brings us back into a good relationship with God (Romans 5:10–11).

Let's Talk About It!

How many robbers are crucified with Jesus?

Why does one robber have his face turned away from Jesus?

How are we like the robbers?

The Death of Christ

MATTHEW 27:33—66;
MARK 15:23—47; LUKE 23:33—56;
JOHN 19:23—42

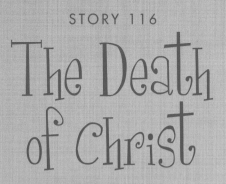

As Jesus hung on the cross, many people thought he was just another criminal getting what he deserved. The soldiers took his clothes for themselves. While Jesus suffered on the cross above them, he prayed aloud, "Father, forgive them, for they know not what they do" (Luke 23:34). Jesus' mother, Mary, and some friends were there watching, along with Jesus' disciple John. When Jesus saw them there, he told Mary to think of John as her son, and he told John to care for Mary as his own mother. From that time on John took Mary into his home.

The people mocked Jesus. They said, "Why don't you come down from the cross if you are the Son of God?" "You trust in God—why doesn't he help you now?" "You saved other people—why can't you save yourself?" "If you are the King of Israel, come down from the cross. If we see it, we'll believe." Because Jesus was dying, they didn't think he was the Messiah anymore. Jesus said nothing in return.

As hours passed, God caused the sun's light to disappear and darkness fell on everything. In the middle of the after-noon, Jesus called out in a loud voice, "My God, my God, why have you forsaken me?" (Matthew 27:46). Finally the time came when his terrible suffering was over. Jesus called out, "It is finished (John 19:30). Father, I give my spirit into your hands." With that, Jesus bowed his head and died. At that moment, an earthquake shook the land and rocks split open. The curtain in the temple was torn in half from top to bottom. Tombs opened and people were raised from the dead. When the Roman centurion standing at the cross felt the earthquake and saw all that happened, he said, "Truly this was the Son of God" (Matthew 27:54).

Later some soldiers were sent to see if the crucified men were still alive. If they were still alive, they were going to break their legs so they would die more quickly. But when they saw that Jesus was already dead, they pierced his side with a spear, just to make sure. Blood and water poured out. Jesus had died.

Joseph of Arimathea, a disciple of Jesus, asked Pilate for permission to take his body and bury it. Joseph and Nicodemus, the Pharisee who visited Jesus at night, took Jesus down from the cross. They wrapped his body with spices and cloth strips and buried him in Joseph's new tomb. Then a large rock was rolled in front of the entrance. The world's saddest, darkest day was over.

The three most important words Jesus spoke on the cross are, "It is finished." The terrible pain of crucifixion made it a horrible way to die. But the suffering Jesus experienced was much worse. While he hung on the cross, God the Father turned his back on him. The Father poured out his anger for our sin upon his Son. Though Jesus was sinless he became sin for us. He took the punishment for our sin as our substitute. When Jesus said, "It is finished," he was saying that the punishment was over, the penalty had been paid, and God's anger over the sins of those who believe in his Son Jesus was all gone.

Let's Talk About It!

Why is Jesus' death so important?

What does God the Father do when Jesus hangs on the cross?

Where do Jesus' friends put his body?

Let's Talk About It!

What do you see going on in the picture?

What happened to the soldiers who had been guarding the tomb?

Why is Jesus' resurrection so important?

The Resurrection

MATTHEW 27:62—28:16;
MARK 16:1—13; LUKE 24:1—12; JOHN
20:1—18

Jesus was dead and buried in a tomb, but that wasn't enough for the Pharisees and chief priests. They went back to Pilate and said, "This man was a fake. When he was still alive, he told people he would rise from the dead after three days. If his disciples get into his tomb and steal his body, they will tell everyone that Jesus has risen from the dead. You have to keep that from happening!" So Pilate sent some soldiers to make sure the tomb was closed up tightly so no one could get in. While the religious leaders watched, they put a Roman seal on the stone that closed up the tomb and posted their soldiers to guard it.

It was early in the morning the third day after Jesus died. Some women who loved Jesus were taking spices to the tomb to anoint his body. On their way they asked each other, "Who will roll the stone away for us so we can get inside the tomb?" But they didn't have to worry! For moments earlier, while the guards stood watch, two angels came down from heaven. Their bodies shined like lightning and their clothes were as white as snow. The guards were so afraid that they were shaking. They fell down on the ground as though they were dead. One angel rolled back the stone and sat on it, as a great earthquake shook the ground. Soon the women arrived and saw the angels with the stone rolled away! What had happened? One angel said to the women, "Do not be afraid, for I know that you seek Jesus who was crucified. He is not here, for he

has risen, as he said! Come, see the place where he lay" (Matthew 28:5–6). Then the angels instructed the women to tell his disciples that Jesus would meet them in Galilee.

When the women went into the tomb, Jesus' body was gone! Quickly they ran to tell the disciples. But the disciples found their story hard to believe. Peter and John ran to the tomb to see for themselves. They went inside and saw Jesus' grave clothes lying there, but Jesus himself was gone! That's when they believed what the women had told them. After the disciples went home, Mary Magdalene, one of the women, stayed outside the tomb, crying. Two angels came to her and asked, "Why are you crying?" "Someone has taken my Lord away," Mary said, "and I don't know where they have laid him." She had taken the disciples the message, but she hadn't understood it herself. Then Mary turned and noticed a third man standing there. She thought he was the gardener, but then he called her name, "Mary." At once she knew it was the Lord Jesus. She fell at his feet and worshiped him. "Jesus said to her, 'Do not hold onto me, because I have not yet ascended to the Father. But go to my brothers and say to them, 'I am ascending to my Father and your Father, to my God and your God'" (John 20:17). So Mary returned to the disciples and told them she had seen the Lord.

Did you know that Jesus' death and resurrection is the most important part of the whole Bible? Every story in the Bible that took place before Jesus looks forward to his death and resurrection. Every story after Jesus' death and resurrection looks back upon those days to celebrate the good news of the gospel! The apostle Paul said the resurrection is so important that we are lost without it (1 Corinthians 15:14–17).

Doubting Thomas

JOHN 20:19-29

It was evening on the day of the resurrection. Two of Jesus' disciples were walking along the road, talking about all the things that had happened. Jesus came up to them and started walking with them, but they did not recognize him. "What are you talking about?" he asked. The disciple named Cleopas answered sadly, "Are you the only one in Jerusalem who doesn't know what has been happening the past few days? Jesus, the man of God we hoped would save Israel, was crucified because of the evil plans of our chief priests and rulers. And now, three days later, some women have reported that his tomb is empty and angels have said he is alive! Some other disciples went to the tomb and found it was empty, but they didn't see Jesus."

Jesus said, "O foolish ones, your hearts are so slow to believe what the prophets spoke about long ago! Don't you realize that Christ had to suffer these things to come into his glory?" The time flew by as Jesus explained how all of God's promises in the Bible led up to his life, death, and resurrection. As the disciples came to a village, they begged their newfound traveling companion to stay with them. They sat down for supper and as Jesus blessed the bread, their eyes were opened. This was Jesus! Just then Jesus vanished, disappearing from their sight. The disciples hurried back to Jerusalem to tell the others the wonderful news.

They found the other disciples huddled together behind locked doors because they were afraid of the Jewish leaders. As they talked excitedly about what they had seen, suddenly Jesus was in the room with them! "Peace be with you," he said (John 20:19). The disciples were so startled they didn't know what to think. "Maybe he is a spirit," some said. But

Jesus said, "Why do you doubt? Look at my hands and my feet—it's really me! Touch me and see, because a spirit doesn't have flesh and bones like I do." The disciples were amazed—and so happy! Jesus said, "Do you have anything to eat?" They gave him some broiled fish and he ate it in front of them. There was no question about it—Jesus had really come back from the dead. He was alive again!

Jesus reminded them of all the things he had taught them. He showed them how his death and resurrection made all the promises of the Bible come true. Before, it had often been hard for the disciples to understand the things Jesus taught, but now he opened up their minds to understand God's Word. Then Jesus said to them, "Peace be with you. As the Father has sent me, even so I am sending you" (John 2:21). He breathed on them and said to them, "Receive the Holy Spirit" (John 20:22).

Thomas was not with the disciples that night. When the others told him what had happened, Thomas did not believe them. "I won't believe unless I see the nail marks and put my fingers in his hands and side," he said stubbornly. Eight days later Thomas was with the disciples in a locked room when Jesus appeared again. Jesus said to Thomas, "Put your finger here and see my hands and put your hand in my side. Don't doubt; believe!" Now all Thomas's demands seemed so foolish to him. All he could say was, "My Lord and my God!" (John 20:28). Jesus said, "You have believed because you have seen me. Blessed are those who believe even though they haven't seen me."

Many people today still don't believe that Jesus is God. They say he was just a good teacher. But if that was true, Jesus would have corrected Thomas by saying, "Thomas, don't call me God." But Jesus didn't say that—because he is God! It was right for Thomas to worship him. Thomas believed when he saw Jesus face-to-face. But Jesus said, "Blessed are those who have not seen and yet have believed" (John 20:29). We are the ones who haven't seen him but believe in Jesus by faith in God's Word.

Let's Talk About It!

Why is Thomas called "Doubting Thomas"?
In the picture, what is Thomas saying to Jesus?
According to Jesus, who is blessed?

Let's Talk About It!

What is Peter thinking as he runs through the water towards shore?

What does Jesus later say to Peter?

Who are the lambs in the story?

Another Miraculous Catch

JOHN 21

The disciples were full of joy after they saw Jesus arisen from the dead. Now they understood many things they hadn't understood before. But they still had lots of questions. When would they see Jesus again? No one knew. How should they spend their time now that Jesus was no longer teaching the crowds every day? They didn't know that either. So one day Peter decided to go fishing, doing what he'd always done until Jesus had said, "Come, follow me." He invited some other disciples to come along. Thomas, Nathanael, James, John, and a couple of others got into the boat and went out to fish. All night long they fished, but they caught nothing.

It was almost dawn when they saw a man on shore. It was Jesus but they did not recognize him. They were not very far out from land and Jesus called out, "Friends, do you have any fish?" "No," they answered. "Throw your net on the right side of the boat and you will find some," Jesus called back. The disciples did what Jesus said, but when they started to pull the net back into the boat, it was so heavy with fish that they couldn't pull it in! "It is the Lord!" John realized. He told Peter, and Peter didn't waste a moment. He jumped into the water and swam to Jesus while the others tried to pull the net full of fish to shore.

When the boat finally landed, the disciples got out and saw Jesus next to a charcoal fire. There were some fish laid out on it and some bread. "Bring a few of the fish you just caught," Jesus suggested. Peter dragged the net onto the beach and the disciples counted the fish. There were 153 large fish, yet the net had not torn. Jesus and the disciples ate their breakfast of bread and fish together. This was the third time Jesus had appeared to them after rising from the dead. Although Jesus never said who he was, they knew it was the Lord.

After breakfast, Jesus spoke to Peter as they sat with the other disciples. "Simon, son of John, do you love me more than these?" Peter answered, "Yes, Lord, you know that I love you." Then Jesus told him, "Feed my lambs." Again Jesus asked if Peter loved him. "Yes, Lord, you know that I love you," Peter replied. Jesus told him, "Take care of my sheep." Then Jesus asked a third time, "Do you love me, Peter?" Peter was sad that Jesus had asked a third time. "Lord, you know all things. You know that I love you," he said. Again Jesus replied, "Feed my sheep." Then Jesus told Peter that he would die serving God. And once again, just as he had in the beginning, Jesus said to Peter, "Follow me."

Do you remember when Peter told Jesus he was willing to follow him to prison and to death? As soon as Jesus was arrested, Peter's confidence melted into fear. Before the night was over and the rooster crowed, Peter denied knowing Jesus three times. Then, after the resurrection, Jesus asked Peter three times if he loved him. It was no accident that Jesus asked the question three times—the same number as Peter's denials. This was Jesus' way of restoring his relationship with Peter and calling him to the work of feeding and caring for the people of God, his sheep. In that meeting Peter was forgiven and restored to Christ. Jesus erased any lingering doubts Peter might have had by repeating two special words: "Follow me" (John 21:19). Jesus' sacrifice on the cross made a way for Peter to be forgiven, and the cross provides for our forgiveness as well. The question for us is the same question Jesus asked Peter: "Do you love me?" Do we love Jesus?

The Great Commission

MATTHEW 28:11—20; LUKE 24:45—49

When the Roman soldiers guarding Jesus' tomb were knocked to the ground by the earthquake and the blinding light at the resurrection, some of them went back to the chief priests and told them what had happened. The chief priests quickly called for the elders and came up with a plan.

They paid the soldiers to spread a rumor that Jesus' disciples had stolen his body from the tomb while they fell asleep. The chief priests promised that the soldiers would not get in trouble for sleeping on the job if Pilate heard the story. So the soldiers agreed, took the money, and spread the false story among the Jewish people. But those who saw Jesus after he rose from the dead knew it was a lie.

One day the disciples headed to a mountain in Galilee to meet Jesus again. When Jesus appeared they worshiped him. But not all of them believed; some still doubted. Jesus gave his followers a command we now call the Great Commission. He said, "Go and tell people from every nation about me, so they can believe and become my disciples too. Baptize those who believe in the name of the Father and of the Son and of the Holy Spirit. Teach them everything I have taught you. And be sure of this: I will always be with you." The disciples followed these instructions for the rest of their lives.

Do you see God's promise to Abraham in Jesus' words? Look again if you don't. Jesus commanded the disciples to go and tell people from every nation about him. God promised that Abraham's family would be a blessing to all nations (Genesis 18:18). Jesus, the far-off great-grandson of Abraham, is the one God planned to keep this wonderful promise. Jesus didn't die on the cross only for the Jews. He died on the cross for people from every nation. Jesus' sacrifice on the cross didn't just bring salvation for the Jews, but for the Gentiles too. Because of Jesus, people from every tribe, language, and nation can worship the Lord together. Many Jews didn't like this teaching. They were afraid that their religion was in danger. But no false rumor about the resurrection, the ministry of Jesus, or the early church would ever stop the gospel from reaching people and changing hearts.

Let's Talk About It!

Who is Jesus meeting with in the picture?

Point to the arrows in the picture and explain why they are flowing out from the disciples to the world.

What message does Jesus tell his disciples to share?

Let's Talk About It!

What is happening to Jesus in the picture?

How can Jesus fly up into the sky?

What does the angel exhort the disciples to remember?

The Ascension

LUKE 24:50—53; ACTS 1:1—11

During the forty days after he rose from the dead, Jesus appeared many times to the disciples. He taught them about the kingdom of God and explained how the Old Testament pointed to his death and resurrection. Now it was time for them to share this good news of salvation with the world. So Jesus commanded his disciples—who had seen it all with their own eyes—to preach the gospel to everyone. But Jesus didn't send the disciples out right away. He told them to wait for the promised Holy Spirit to come and they would receive power from heaven. Jesus said, "John baptized with water, but you will be baptized with the Holy Spirit not many days from now" (Acts 1:5). Then Jesus led them on a walk to Bethany, the little village near the Mount of Olives.

The disciples asked, "Lord, is this the time when you are going to make Israel its own kingdom again?" Jesus told them they were not allowed to know the days his Father set for such things, and then he said, "But you will receive power when the Holy Spirit has come upon you, and you will be my witnesses in Jerusalem and in all Judea and Samaria, and to the end of the earth" (Acts 1:8).

Then Jesus raised his hands and blessed his disciples. As he did he began to lift from the ground. The disciples watched as Jesus rose up to heaven. Finally, far up in the sky, a cloud hid him from their sight. While they were still watching, two men in white robes appeared. "Men of Galilee," they said, "why are you standing there looking up into heaven? This Jesus, who was taken up from you into heaven, will someday come back in the same way you saw him go." Then the disciples worshiped Jesus and returned to Jerusalem full of joy. They spent much of their time in the temple, praising and thanking God for all they had seen.

Did you notice something different about the disciples in this story? Not one of them doubted! At first after Jesus' resurrection the disciples doubted and didn't believe Jesus rose from the dead. But over time they all came to believe. Finally, after watching Jesus return to heaven, they worshiped him and were filled with joy. We might have expected them to be sad about losing Jesus, but they weren't. Jesus had promised to prepare a place for them in heaven and come back to take them there. The two men in white robes also reminded the disciples that Jesus would come back someday. Today, we are still waiting for the glorious day when Jesus will return. One day he will come back on the clouds to the sound of a loud trumpet. Christians who are alive on that day will be gathered up to meet him in the sky (Matthew 24:30–31).

Pentecost

After Jesus ascended into heaven the eleven remaining apostles returned to Jerusalem. They gathered in the upper room with Jesus' mother Mary, his brothers, and his other followers. Together they spent time praying while they waited for the coming of the Holy Spirit. During this time Peter said they should choose a replacement for Judas, who had betrayed the Lord. "This man," Peter said, "must be one of the men who were with the Lord the whole time since John's baptism." Two men were suggested: Joseph called Barsabbas and Matthias. The apostles prayed and asked the Lord to guide their choice. Then they cast lots, which is like drawing straws to see who got the shorter straw. That man would be God's choice. Matthias was chosen, so he became the twelfth apostle from that day on.

The group patiently waited and prayed for Jesus' promise to come true. Then on the day of the feast of Pentecost, their wait was over. A great sound filled the room like a mighty, rushing wind from heaven. Then small flames, like tongues of fire, appeared above each person, and they were all filled with the Holy Spirit. In that moment the Holy Spirit gave each of them the ability to speak in other languages. The Spirit Jesus promised had come!

Meanwhile, people from many countries had gathered in Jerusalem for the feast. They heard the sound coming from the house and came closer. But as they listened more carefully, they were bewildered—each one could hear his own language being spoken! "Aren't all these people from Galilee?" they asked each other. "How can they be speaking to us in our own languages?" The people in the crowd were from all the surrounding lands—Medes and Parthians, Elamites, people from Mesopotamia, Judea, Cappadocia, Pontus and Asia, Phrygia and Pamphylia, Egypt and Libya, Cyrene, visitors from Rome, Cretans, Arabians, and of course Jews. All of them heard the apostles talking about God's mighty works in their own languages. How had this happened?

Most of the people were amazed at what they were hearing and wondered what it might mean. But a few had their own idea of what was going on. "They are drunk," they said. "They are filled with new wine" (Acts 2:13), even though it was still early in the morning. Of course, those people couldn't have been more wrong.

The outpouring of the Holy Spirit at Pentecost marked the beginning of God's plan to reach the nations with the gospel. The book of Acts tells us that people from at least fifteen different countries were there that day. Jesus came to fulfill the promise God made to Abraham centuries before, that he would be a blessing to the nations. With the coming of the Holy Spirit, the fulfillment of that promise—to reach the nations with the good news of salvation—had begun!

Let's Talk About It!

What is happening to the disciples in the picture?

Who is the Holy Spirit and why did Jesus send him for all of us?

What amazing thing do the disciples do next?

Let's Talk About It!

What is Peter telling everyone about?

How has the Holy Spirit changed Peter since the night the rooster crowed?

How can the Holy Spirit change us?

Peter & the Prophet Joel

ACTS 2:14–36

Once the Holy Spirit fell upon the Christians at Pentecost, he gave them courage to tell others about Jesus and share the gospel story of his death and resurrection. This was especially true of Peter. Remember, after cutting off the ear of the high priest's servant, Peter's bravery melted into fear at the arrest of Jesus. Peter became so afraid for his own safety that he denied knowing the Lord three times. Without the Holy Spirit, his courage didn't last.

But now, filled with the Holy Spirit, Peter's courage was strengthened and he was ready to tell everyone about Jesus! So right there, in the midst of all the excitement and confusion, while the disciples were speaking in different languages, Peter stood up and spoke to the crowd. "Listen carefully to me," Peter said. "These men are not drunk, as you suppose. It is only nine o'clock in the morning! What is happening in front of you is what the prophet Joel spoke about."

Then Peter quoted from the book of Joel and said, "In the last days, God will pour out his Spirit on all people. Sons and daughters will prophesy, young men will see visions, and old men will receive dreams. God's Spirit will be poured out on all people, even servants. God will do great wonders on the earth and everyone who calls on the name of the Lord will be saved." Peter boldly proclaimed the gospel. He said, "You remember the miracles Jesus performed while he lived among you. You saw them! It was God's plan to give up his Son to die, but wicked men nailed him to the cross and killed the Lord of glory. But that was not the end." Peter shared, "Death could not hold Jesus in the grave because it had no power over him. God raised Jesus from the dead!"

Peter quoted Psalm 16 and told the crowd, "When David said God would not allow his 'holy one to see corruption,' he was talking about Jesus. King David died, but he saw ahead to the day when God would set one of his descendants on the throne. David foresaw the resurrection of Christ. And this Jesus—the one you crucified—is the fulfillment of all God's promises."

What a difference the Holy Spirit made in Peter's life! He went from being afraid of a servant girl at Jesus' arrest to fearlessly challenging the men who helped put Jesus to death! It happened just as Jesus said when he told the disciples to wait and they would receive power from heaven to be his witnesses, first in Jerusalem and then to the rest of the world. We can see that Peter certainly received that power as he talked about the good news of Jesus' life, death, and resurrection to the crowd. Peter's fear was gone, replaced by courage from the Holy Spirit to tell everyone about Jesus.

New Believers

ACTS 2:36—47

After the Holy Spirit filled Peter, he stood up in front of the crowd and challenged them: "Let all Israel know that God has made Jesus, the one you crucified, both Lord and Christ!" As Peter shared the gospel, the Holy Spirit began to work in the lives of the people listening. Suddenly they realized the sinful thing they had done to crucify Jesus, God's Son. Convicted of their sin, they called out to Peter and the rest of the apostles, "Brothers, what shall we do?" (Acts 2:37).

"Turn away from your wickedness and be baptized in the name of Jesus Christ for the forgiveness of your sins," Peter said. "Then you too will receive the gift of the Holy Spirit." He continued, "The promise is for you and for your children and for all who are far off, everyone whom the Lord our God calls to himself" (Acts 2:39). Peter continued preaching, calling on people to trust in Jesus and be saved from their sin. Three thousand people believed the good news of the gospel that day. They were baptized and became part of the very first Christian church.

Hundreds of years before, the prophet Joel wrote down these words from God: "I will show wonders in the heavens above and…the earth below….And it shall come to pass that everyone who calls upon the name of the Lord shall be saved" (Acts 2:19, 21). These words came true as many trusted in Jesus and were saved. Afterward the apostles performed many signs and wonders among the people. And as God worked in their hearts the new believers wanted to learn more about Jesus. They spent their days praying, listening to the apostles' teaching, and having fellowship with other believers.

These new Christians shared what they had with one another. Some sold their belongings and gave the money to those in need. They gathered at the temple and met in homes to worship the Lord. They ate together and shared their food with glad and generous hearts. And every day more and more people were saved. These new believers formed the very first local church. Their worship and their love for one another helped the people around them see what a wonderful difference God can make in a person's life.

Isn't it amazing how God's power changes people? All of us are born selfish sinners who want to keep what we have for ourselves. Even little children don't like to share their toys. But this story shows us that God could change even the hearts of the people who crucified Jesus! Did you know that God's Spirit works in us the same way today? First, God helps us see how sinful we are. Then he helps us believe that Jesus died for us to take away our sins. When we believe, we are changed by God's Spirit. Our hearts fill with the joy of being forgiven. Once we come to understand that our real treasure is found in Jesus, it's easy to share our things with the needy.

Let's Talk About It!

What is happening in the left picture?

How is the right picture different from the left one?

What do you think happened?

The Lame Beggar Walks

ACTS 3:1 — 4:22

One day Peter and John went up to the temple to pray. As they neared the entrance, along came a crippled man carried on a stretcher. This man had been crippled since he was born. He had never been able to walk. Every day he was brought to the temple gate so he could ask people for money as they passed by. When he saw Peter and John, he did what he always did. He asked them for money too.

Peter and John stopped and went over to the man. "Look at us," Peter said to him. The man looked up, expecting to receive some money. Instead Peter said to him, "I have no silver and gold, but what I do have I give to you. In the name of Jesus Christ of Nazareth, rise up and walk!" (Acts 3:6). Taking the man by the hand, Peter helped him to his feet. As the man stood, his ankles and feet became strong. Then the three of them entered the temple, with the man walking and leaping and praising God! The people who saw it were amazed. They recognized him as the crippled man who begged at the temple gate. Now he was healed, jumping around as though he had never had a problem.

Peter saw their reaction and challenged them. "Why are you so surprised at this, as though it was our power that made this man walk? This was the power of Jesus at work—the one you handed over to Pilate to be killed. You turned your back on God's Holy and Righteous One and asked for a murderer to be set free instead. You killed the Author of life, but God raised him from the dead. We are witnesses to this—we saw the risen Jesus. And it is Jesus' name—and faith in it—that has healed the man you now see before you." Peter called the people to turn away from their sin and trust in Jesus. He taught them how the prophets of the Old Testament pointed to Jesus. Many of the people who heard them believed.

But not everyone was happy. This teaching greatly annoyed the priests and Sadducees, who came with the temple guard to arrest Peter and John and put them in jail. The next day the religious leaders questioned Peter and John. They asked them, "What name or power did you use to heal that beggar?" Peter, filled with the Holy Spirit, answered them, "I want you and all of Israel to know that it was by the name of Jesus Christ of Nazareth—the man you crucified and whom God raised from the dead—that this man is standing before you, completely well." That was not the answer the religious leaders wanted. They hoped to scare Peter and John into being quiet. They threatened them and ordered them not to tell anyone about Jesus. But Peter and John refused. "We can't help but talk about what we have seen and heard," they said. The religious leaders let them go because everyone else was praising God for healing the crippled man.

Peter had one more challenge for the leaders that day. He told them, "Jesus is the stone that you, the builders, rejected. He is now the cornerstone. Salvation comes from no one else. There is no other name under heaven that can save us." Peter's words are as true today as they were then. Believing in Jesus and his death for our sin is the only way anyone can be saved.

Let's Talk About It!

Who are the two men in the front of the picture?

Why does the man on the left have his hands up in the air?

What do the people in the crowd think about what happened?

Let's Talk About It!

What did Ananias and his wife say they would do with the money they got from the sale of their land?

How did they lie?

Who did Peter say they lied to?

Ananias & Sapphira

ACTS 4:32 — 5:16

As the gospel spread through Jerusalem and the first church grew and grew, God's work in the believers' hearts could be seen in the wonderful things they did. Many who owned houses or land sold their property and gave the money to the apostles. They wanted it to be used to help anyone who had a need. Joseph, who was also called Barnabas, was one man who sold a field and brought the money to the apostles as an offering for the poor.

But there was one couple, Ananias and Sapphira, who had something else in mind. They wanted everyone to see them sell their property and give the money to the poor, but they didn't actually want to give all the money. When Ananias got the money from the sale of their land, he kept part of it for himself and gave what was left to the apostles. He pretended he had given everything, but he and Sapphira knew that was a lie.

God knew it too, of course, and he led Peter to say, "Ananias, why has Satan filled your heart to lie to the Holy Spirit and to keep for yourself some of the money from the land?" Ananias had no answer to that. Peter spoke sternly to Ananias. "No one forced you to sell it, and no one forced you to give away any of the money after it was sold. You could have kept it all! It was a sin for you to do what you have done.

You have not lied to men but to God." When Ananias heard Peter's words, he fell to the floor, dead. Everyone who heard this was filled with fear at the seriousness of sin and God's judgment. Some of the younger men wrapped up Ananias's body and carried him away for burial.

Three hours later Sapphira came into the room where the apostles were gathered. She had not heard what had happened to her husband. Peter asked her, "Did you sell the land for this much money?" He was giving Sapphira a chance to tell the truth. But, like her husband, Sapphira lied. Instead of saying, "No, we got more than that when we sold the land," she told Peter they had given all the money. Peter said to her, "How could you and your husband have agreed together to test the Spirit of the Lord? The men who have buried your husband are at the door and they will carry you out next." At that moment Sapphira fell to the floor. When the young men came back in, they found her dead, just like her husband. They took her body away and buried her next to Ananias. Great fear fell on the church and everyone who heard the story.

Peter said that when Ananias and Sapphira lied, they were sinning against God. Ananias and Sapphira lied to Peter, but it was much more serious that they lied to God. While Jesus was still on earth, he told Peter he would build his church and the gates of hell would not stand against it. Ananias and Sapphira's lie threatened the spread of the gospel and the health and strength of the new church. The Lord was not going to allow anything to hurt his church. God's judgment on Ananias and Sapphira helped the new believers to see how serious it was to sin against God. That helped them to follow and obey the Lord.

The Death of Stephen

ACTS 6–7

As the church in Jerusalem grew, more and more poor people, especially widows, needed help with food and the daily things of life. The apostles knew the Lord wanted them to spend their time praying and teaching God's Word, so they asked the church to choose seven men to take care of the widows and make sure everyone was treated fairly. "Choose men who are full of the Holy Spirit and wisdom," they said. One of the men chosen was Stephen, a man full of the Holy Spirit and faith.

The Holy Spirit was also using Stephen to preach the gospel with great signs and wonders. More and more people were paying attention to what Stephen said and did. The Jewish religious leaders didn't like that. They asked him hard, tricky questions as he spoke in public, hoping to make him look foolish. But Stephen's wisdom was too great for them because the Holy Spirit was helping him.

So this group tried another plan. They persuaded some men to say that Stephen was speaking against Moses and God. Though they knew this was a lie, they brought the story to the elders and scribes and stirred up the people against Stephen. Before long, Stephen was arrested and brought before the Jewish council. The false witnesses told their stories and said that Stephen was preaching against the temple and trying to change the customs Moses had given them. Stephen knew he was only preaching the good news about Jesus. Despite all the things these men said, Stephen trusted the Lord. People watching him saw that his face looked like the face of an angel.

When it came time for Stephen to defend himself, he answered by preaching the gospel to everyone gathered there. He began with Abraham and went on to talk about Joseph, Moses, David, and Solomon. Stephen reminded his listeners of God's promises, Israel's sin, and their slowness to believe and trust God. Finally Stephen said, "Just like your fathers before you, you are stubborn, stiff-necked people. You always resist the Holy Spirit. And you have betrayed and murdered Jesus, the Righteous One of God!"

The people were furious! But Stephen had even more to say as God gave him a vision. "I see the heavens opened and the glory of God. I see Jesus standing at God's right hand." With that, the people grabbed Stephen and dragged him out of the city. There they stoned him to death while a Pharisee named Saul stood by, pleased with what he saw. From that day on things were hard for the church in Jerusalem. Stephen's death marked the start of a great persecution, a time when Christians were mistreated, captured, and even killed by their enemies. Many Christians had to run away from Jerusalem. They were scattered throughout the countryside because it wasn't safe to stay together anymore.

When you first read about Stephen's death and the persecution of the church, it can seem like a total defeat. But God always works everything according to his master plan. The Christians who were scattered because of the persecution started preaching the gospel in the countryside. Because of that, many people outside Jerusalem heard the gospel and were saved. Luke reported, "The hand of the Lord was with them, and a great number who believed turned to the Lord" (Acts 11:21). From that day until now, no one has ever been able to stop the advance of the gospel!

Let's Talk About It!

What are the people doing and why?

What happened to the other Christians?

How does God use persecution to spread the good news about Jesus?

Let's Talk About It!

What is happening to Saul in the picture?
Why is Ananias afraid of Saul?
How does God change Saul?

Saul Is Knocked to the Ground

ACTS 8:1—8, 26—40; 9:1—28;
22:4—21; 26:9—18

After Stephen's death Saul the Pharisee took the lead in punishing Christians for believing in Jesus. He did all he could to destroy the new church. He went from house to house, looking for men and women who were Jesus' followers. He would drag them off to prison, where they stayed locked up until they went on trial for believing in Jesus. When they were found guilty, Saul would vote for their death as punishment.

Despite all this, the good news about Jesus was shared with more and more people. As Christians ran away from the persecution in Jerusalem, they shared the gospel with the people they met. A man named Philip preached in Samaria and many people believed God's message. Later he met an Ethiopian official on the road and shared the good news about Jesus with him. The Ethiopian believed and commanded his chariot driver to stop so he could be baptized right away. From there, Philip preached the gospel all the way to Caesarea.

Even while the good news spread, Saul chased after Jesus' disciples. He wanted nothing less than to kill them all. He received the high priest's permission to arrest Christians in Damascus, and he planned to bring them back to Jerusalem in chains. But God had a different plan for Saul. As he got closer to Damascus, ready to carry out his evil scheme, a bright light from heaven flashed around him. Saul fell to the ground and a voice called out, "Saul,

Saul, why are you persecuting me?" (Acts 9:4). Saul called out, "Who are you, Lord?" He did not realize it was Jesus. The Lord replied, "I am Jesus, whom you are persecuting" (Acts 9:5). "Stand on your feet. I am sending you as my witness to the Gentiles, so they can turn from darkness to light, be forgiven of their sins, and believe in me." Jesus told Saul to go into the city, but when Saul opened his eyes he was blind. His friends had to lead him by the hand into the city.

Inside Damascus, the Lord gave a Christian named Ananias a vision. In it Jesus said, "Go and find a man named Saul. He is praying and he has seen a vision that a man named Ananias will lay hands on him so he can receive his sight." But Ananias was afraid of Saul. "I have heard about all the evil he has done to the Christians in Jerusalem." The Lord comforted Ananias and said, "He is the person I have chosen to carry my name to the Gentiles. He will suffer many things for my sake." Ananias obeyed the Lord and went to the house where Saul was staying. He laid hands on him and said, "Brother Saul, the Lord Jesus who appeared to you on the road…has sent me so that you may regain your sight and be filled with the Holy Spirit" (Acts 9:17). At that moment something like scales fell from Saul's eyes and he could see again. Right away Saul got up and was baptized as a Christian.

Instead of capturing Christians to take them to jail, Saul began to preach the gospel to anyone who would listen. Now the Jews made plans to kill him! But Saul escaped during the night, lowered in a basket through an opening in the city wall.

Did you know that Saul is the same person as the apostle Paul? After he became a Christian, Saul used the name Paul. And just as Jesus foretold, the Lord used Paul to spread the gospel to Gentiles all over the world. Saul's conversion shows us that God can save anyone, no matter how sinful. Saul had planned to destroy the church but he was no match for Jesus. No one can stop the spread of the gospel. Often when Christians are persecuted, God's

The Gentiles Are Converted

ACTS 10:1—11:18

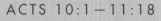

When the persecution broke out against the Christians in Jerusalem they were scattered all around. These Jewish Christians shared the good news of Jesus with the people they met. That is how Gentiles— non-Jewish people—began to hear the gospel. But now there was a problem: many Jewish Christians didn't want anything to do with Gentiles. They thought Gentiles were unclean, and some didn't think Gentiles should be part of God's people at all!

In a seaport town called Caesarea, about sixty miles from Jerusalem, lived a soldier named Cornelius. He was a Gentile, but he worshiped the God of the Jews

and prayed to him faithfully. One day an angel of God came to him in a vision. "Your prayers have been heard, Cornelius. I want you to send men to Joppa to find a man named Peter and bring him back to you. He is staying with Simon the tanner." (A tanner is a leather maker.) Right away Cornelius sent two servants along with a soldier to bring Peter back.

The next day, while these men were on their way, Peter went to pray on the roof of Simon's house. God gave him a vision of a large sheet coming down from heaven. The sheet was full of unclean animals that God's law said his people should not eat. But a voice said, "Rise, Peter; kill and eat" (Acts 10:13). "No, Lord," Peter answered, "I have never eaten anything that is common or unclean" (10:14). But the voice called out again and said, "What God has made clean, do not call common" (10:15). This happened three times before the sheet was taken back up to heaven.

While Peter was still thinking about the vision, the three men arrived at Simon's house and asked for Peter. Back up on the roof, God's Spirit spoke to Peter, "Three men are looking for you. Go with them because I

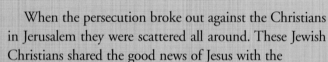

have sent them." Peter went downstairs and heard their story about Cornelius's vision. The next day Peter traveled with them to Cornelius's house, where Cornelius, his family, and his close friends were waiting. When Peter saw them he said, "You know it is against God's law for a Jew to visit anyone of another nation." He continued, "But God has shown me that I should not call any person common or unclean" (Acts 10:28). That is what God's vision was meant to teach Peter.

Peter told the story of Jesus' death and resurrection to Cornelius, his friends, and his family. While Peter was still preaching, the Holy Spirit came down on everyone who was listening and they began to speak

that God had given the Gentiles eternal life through Jesus, just like he did the Jews.

Before Jesus came the Gentiles were not part of God's people. But the cross changed everything. The apostles were learning that the promise God first gave to Abraham to bless all nations was fulfilled through

the gospel of Jesus. That was a big change. Jesus, a far-off grandson of Abraham, didn't only die for the Jews. He came for people from every tribe, tongue, and nation. Jesus' blood was able to save everyone, both Jew and Gentile, from their sin. The door to salvation was opened for all through the blood of Christ.

in tongues. Some Christian brothers who had come with Peter from Joppa were amazed to see the Holy Spirit given to Gentiles, but there was no doubt about it! Peter saw that the Gentiles believed in Jesus and commanded them to be baptized. Later, when Peter returned to Jerusalem, some people criticized him for eating with Gentiles. But when Peter told the whole story, they praised God. They realized

Let's Talk About It!

What animals are in the picture?

Why doesn't Peter want to obey God and eat those kinds of animals?

What is God trying to teach Peter?

The Fruit of the Spirit

GALATIANS

As the good news about Jesus spread to the Gentiles, new churches began in Judea, Samaria, and Asia. The apostle Paul traveled through Asia, preaching the gospel wherever he went. Soon there were churches in cities all along the Mediterranean Sea. Paul also took the message of Jesus to inland areas like Galatia, Macedonia, and Rome. But Paul didn't stay in one place for long. Once a church began, Paul chose men he had taught and trained to be the pastors who would take care of the people. He also trained men like Titus and Timothy to help him care for the leaders in the churches he began. With churches spread all over the world, Paul could not easily return to visit them. Instead he wrote letters to teach, encourage, and help them grow.

Many of Paul's letters are now part of our Bible, like the one he sent to the churches in the cities of Galatia. The Holy Spirit guided Paul as he wrote these letters so they are more than Paul's words—they are God's words. Even though Paul often wrote to one particular group of believers, because his words were inspired by God they could help anyone. For example, in his letter to the Ga-

latians, Paul warned against false teachers who try to add to the gospel. These men told the Galatians that believing in Jesus was not enough, that they could not be saved unless they followed Jewish rules too. Paul knew that was not true. He said that if you add anything to the gospel, it becomes a different gospel. If you say, "I need Jesus to die for my sins *and* I need to keep Jewish rules to be a real Christian," you are not really trusting in Jesus at all. That good advice can help any Christian, not just the Galatians. That is why God made sure Paul's letter was preserved to be a part of our Bible as the book of Galatians.

In the letter, Paul teaches that our sins are not forgiven because of the good things we do for God. Our sins are forgiven because of the perfect thing God did for us when he sent Jesus to die on the cross for our sins. When we trust in Jesus, the Holy Spirit frees us from the power of sin and changes our lives in ways that everyone can see. When God saves an angry, impatient person, he or she starts to become loving, patient, and kind. Paul called these changes in a believer's life "the fruit of the Spirit," and he gave the Galatians a list of examples. He said, "The fruit of the Spirit is love, joy, peace, patience, kindness, goodness, faithfulness, gentleness, self-control; against such things there is no law" (Galatians 5:22–23). The fruit of the Spirit is very different from the acts of our sinful nature like anger and jealousy. When you see the fruit of the Spirit in someone, you can tell that God is at work in his life.

The fruit of the Spirit is not a list of things we need to do to earn God's love. After all, God loved us while we were his enemies! The fruit of the Spirit flows out of our lives as God changes our hearts and we live for him. In this life we still sin, but our aim is to be more like Jesus. So each time we fail to be patient, fail to be kind, fail to be good, or fail to have self-control, we don't give up. We remember that all our sins were paid for at the cross. When we do well, we thank God for the way his Holy Spirit has helped us. Paul ended his letter by telling the Galatians that the only thing we should boast about is what Jesus did for us on the cross.

Let's Talk About It!

Point to the fruit growing out of the heart and read each one.

Who causes a heart to grow fruit like this?

What does the cross have to do with the fruit?

The Body of Christ

ACTS 18:1—11; 1 CORINTHIANS 12

The apostle Paul took many missionary journeys to bring the good news about Jesus to people who had never heard it. On one trip Paul went to a Greek city called Corinth. He started by visiting the synagogue there each Sabbath to try to convince the Jews that Jesus was the Messiah. But the Jews in Corinth refused to believe. So Paul left the synagogue, shook the dust off his clothes and said to them, "If you refuse to believe, you have no one to blame but yourselves." He continued, "I am innocent. From now on I will go to the Gentiles" (Acts 18:6).

Paul was welcomed into the house of Justus, who lived next door to the synagogue. As Paul taught the Gentiles there, many believed.

And since he was preaching so close to the synagogue, some Jews became Christians as well. Even the ruler of the synagogue got saved as he listened to Paul preach. One night the Lord spoke to Paul in a vision. "Do not be afraid, but go on speaking and do not be silent, for I am with you, and no one will attack you to harm you, for I have many in this city who are my people" (Acts 18:9–10). Paul stayed and taught the Corinthians for a year and a half.

Years later, Paul got the news that the Corinthian church was struggling. There was a lot of sinning going on! The Corinthians had become proud of the many spiritual gifts God had given them instead of being humble and grateful. Husbands and wives were not faithful to each other, and there was a lot of arguing in the church as people took sides against each other. Some even took their arguments to court instead of making peace with each other in the church. Instead of being united in Christ, they were divided. Some said they followed Paul, while others said they followed Peter or Apollos. So Paul, guided by the Holy Spirit, wrote a letter to encourage and correct them. Because the Holy Spirit helped

Paul we say that his letter was inspired by God. His letter to the Corinthians helps us when we struggle with sin today too.

In the letter, God spoke through Paul about how his people should live together in unity. Paul said that the church is like a human body, which is made up of many parts like hands, arms, legs, and eyes. Paul wrote, "If the foot should say, 'Because I am not a hand, I do not belong to the body,' that would not make it any less a part of the body" (1 Corinthians 12:15). Paul wanted the Corinthians to see that even though we are different from one another with different spiritual gifts, we all belong to Christ and we're all part of his body, the church. Paul asked, "If a person's whole body were an eye, how could that person hear? Or if his whole body were an ear, how would he be able to smell?" Paul wanted them to see that we all need each other. The eye cannot say to the hand, "I don't need you," nor can the head say to the feet, "I don't need you." The body needs all its parts! All Christians are saved by Jesus' death on the cross. We are all called to spread the good news about Jesus and use our gifts to help others. But God gave each of us different gifts. He wants one person's strengths to serve another person's weakness. So instead of boasting about our strengths or fighting with each other, we should use our gifts to serve one another. Everyone's special gifts are meant to work together to build the church and spread the good news of the gospel. In fact, Jesus said that the way people will know we are his disciples is by our love for one another (John 13:34–35).

Let's Talk About It!

Why do the different people in the picture need each other?

What gifts has God given the different people in your family?

What gifts has God given you?

Let's Talk About It!

What is happening in the picture?

How is the woman in the picture showing love to the boy?

How has Jesus shown us God's love?

Love

1 CORINTHIANS 13

Everyone wants to be loved, but we don't always want to love others. That was the problem with the church in Corinth. They boasted about their spiritual gifts, but they were unkind to one another. So the apostle Paul took time to write them about the greatest spiritual gift of all—the gift of love.

The Corinthians thought that spiritual gifts like speaking in tongues were more important than love. Maybe they didn't even think love was a spiritual gift at all! But love is a wonderful gift. When you combine it with God's other gifts, it makes them better. And if you have all the other gifts but don't use them with love, they are worthless. God gave us spiritual gifts to bless others, not to puff ourselves up. Love makes sure that the gifts are doing what they should.

Inspired by the Holy Spirit, Paul wrote to his Corinthian friends, "If I speak in the tongues of men and of angels but I don't have love, I am nothing more than a noisy gong or a clanging cymbal. If a person has faith strong enough to move a mountain but doesn't have love, he is nothing. Even if someone gives away everything he has, nothing good comes of it without love." You can be the most gifted person in the world, but it doesn't mean anything if you use your gifts for yourself instead of others. That was the Corinthians' problem.

To make sure the Corinthians understood God's message, Paul gave them a long description of what love looks like. God wanted them to know that love is more than a feeling; it is something we do. When we are patient and kind to others, that is love. When we are proud and rude, that isn't love. We show love to others when we do what they want, not what we want. Love is not easily upset or hurt. It doesn't hold a grudge. It isn't happy when bad things happen to others; it is glad when the truth comes out. Paul said, "Love doesn't give up. It keeps on hoping and believing. It is willing to go through hard times along the way." When the Corinthians finished reading Paul's list, they must have been ashamed of all their fighting and arguing.

Love is the one gift that lasts forever. The other spiritual gifts like knowledge and tongues and prophecy will come to an end—we won't need them when we see God face-to-face in heaven. But even then, love will remain.

What do you think was the greatest display of love the world has ever seen? It was when God gave his only Son Jesus to die on the cross to take our sins away. God sent Jesus to die for us while we were his enemies—when we hated him. God was patient and kind to send us Jesus. Jesus did not think of himself—he thought of us. He didn't hold our sins against us. He even forgave the men who nailed him to the cross. That is love!

Paul's Work in Ephesus

ACTS 19:1—20:24

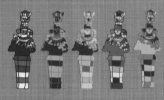

On another of Paul's missionary journeys, he traveled along the coastline of Asia and stopped at a city called Ephesus. He met a group of men who were followers of John the Baptist. Soon he discovered that they had not heard of the Holy Spirit and didn't know about Jesus. So Paul explained that John the Baptist was only the messenger God sent to prepare the way for Jesus. When these disciples heard about Jesus, they believed Paul's message. Paul baptized them in Jesus' name and, when he laid his hands on them, the Holy Spirit came to them. They began to prophesy and speak in tongues.

Paul decided to stay in Ephesus and preach the gospel there. For three months he taught at the synagogue, telling people about Jesus and trying to persuade them about the kingdom of God. But some of the people were stubborn; they did not want to believe. They said evil things about the Christians in front of everyone at the synagogue. So Paul stopped teaching there and found another place to teach his followers. For the next two years, God's word about Jesus spread to Greeks and Jews throughout Asia. People were healed of their diseases and evil spirits were cast out through Paul's ministry. As people were saved, they confessed their sins and turned away from false gods. People who had practiced magic arts burned their books and followed Jesus instead.

After those two years, the Holy Spirit told Paul to travel through Macedonia, where the Philippians and Corinthians lived. So Paul sent his helpers, Timothy and Erastus, ahead to Macedonia while he stayed in Ephesus to finish up his ministry.

Then, just when Paul was about to leave, a riot broke out against the Christians. It started with a silversmith named Demetrius. Demetrius made idols to sell to travelers who came to Ephesus to worship the goddess Artemis. He gathered the other craftsmen together and said, "Men, you know we make our money from the people who worship Artemis. But this man Paul is persuading them to turn away from all gods but Jesus. If we don't stop him, no one will buy from us anymore. Artemis and her beautiful temple will be forgotten. We must do something!" Demetrius's words threw the whole city into confusion. Two of Paul's friends were arrested and the people began to chant over and over, "Great is Artemis of the Ephesians!" (Acts 19:34). Finally, a man named Alexander took control. He calmed the crowd and convinced them to go home. "Otherwise we could all be arrested for rioting," he warned. After that, Paul was able to say goodbye to his disciples and leave for Macedonia.

Paul left the church in Ephesus to be cared for by the men he trained and prepared to lead it. Paul, as an apostle, was called to take the gospel to places where no one had ever heard about Jesus, and to start more local churches with those who believed. Paul spent his life sharing the gospel, often leaving behind people he loved. Paul did get a chance to visit the church in Ephesus again, and a letter he wrote to them is now in the Bible. It's called the book of Ephesians.

Let's Talk About It!

Who is preaching to the people?
What is Paul telling the people?
Point to Demetrius standing off by himself. Why is he frowning?

Let's Talk About It!

What happened to the hard heart of the man in the picture?

Who changed his heart?

Who do you know that God has made a "new creation"?

A New Creation

2 CORINTHIANS 5:11—6:2; 7:5—13

On Paul's second missionary journey, he traveled to a place called Troas. Troas was a city along the coast of the Aegean Sea. Paul hoped to meet Titus there and hear about his visit with the Corinthian church. But things did not go the way Paul hoped. First, he couldn't find Titus. Then, when he began to teach about Jesus, people didn't want to listen. So Paul kept traveling on to Macedonia, hoping to find Titus and hear about the Corinthians. When Paul finally arrived, he was tired from the journey and a little discouraged. But soon he found Titus, and his friend had good news about the Corinthian church.

Titus told Paul the Corinthians were doing well. That comforted Paul because he had earlier written them a letter to correct them about some serious sins. Titus was overjoyed to report that the Corinthians had turned away from their sin. Paul was so glad to hear the news! Paul had been very sad about writing the letter of correction. It wasn't something he enjoyed. Titus's good news made Paul want to write another, happier letter. In this letter (which is 2 Corinthians in our Bible), Paul encouraged his friends to keep following God.

As Paul wrote the Corinthians again, the Holy Spirit guided Paul to teach about Jesus. Paul knew that not everyone who read his letters was a Christian and that it was important for believers to always remember the gospel. So Paul reminded the Corinthians that Jesus died and rose again so people who believe in him would live for God instead of themselves. When people become Christians, Paul wrote, everything about their lives is changed into something new: "If anyone is in Christ, he is a new creation. The old has passed away; behold, the new has come" (2 Corinthians 5:17). And he said that everyone who becomes a Christian becomes an ambassador or messenger for Christ. God calls us all to tell others about Jesus. That is still true for Christians today. We are Christ's ambassadors, taking the good news of the gospel to others. God speaks to people through the message we share.

Did you know that amazing changes take place in people's lives when they become Christians? They might still look the same on the outside, but inside a whole lot is different. That's why the Holy Spirit inspired Paul to describe a Christian as a "new creation" (2 Corinthians 5:17), where the old is gone and the new has come. Every person starts out as a sinner inside—that's the old part Paul is talking about. We don't follow God or do what he wants us to do. Instead, we are slaves to sin and we can't change on our own. But when God makes us a new creation, he breaks the chains of our slavery to sin and sets us free. When God makes us a new creation, he brings us back to life, forgives our sin, and gives us Christ's righteousness so we are brand new inside. Then, day by day, God changes us on the outside too! We still sin, but we can confess our sin and God forgives us. Then we get back up and try again! Instead of living for sin, we start living for God. Instead of running after the pleasures of the world, we run to Jesus.

God Loves a Cheerful Giver

1 CORINTHIANS 16:1–4; 2 CORINTHIANS 8–9

More and more Gentiles were hearing the good news and following Jesus, but the Christians back in Jerusalem were having a hard time. The followers of Jesus were still treated badly by the Jews and many were poor. To help them, the apostle Paul decided to collect money from the Gentile churches in Asia, Macedonia, and Rome. In his first letter to the Corinthians, Paul said that each person should set aside some money each Sunday. Then, the next time Paul came to visit, the Corinthians could give him their gift for the suffering Christians in Jerusalem.

Paul told the other churches in Macedonia what the Corinthians were doing. When they heard the sad story they wanted to help too. In fact, even though these churches were very, very poor themselves, they begged Paul to let them have a part in the offering. When the money from these churches was collected, Paul was full of joy at how much they had given. It was more than Paul would ever have expected.

After that, the Holy Spirit guided Paul to write the Corinthians to tell them it was time to collect all the money they had saved over the past year. Paul told them that Titus would come soon to pick up their gift and take it to Jerusalem. Paul wanted them to be ready when Titus arrived, so they could give him the gift they had promised.

Paul knew God wanted people to give for the right reasons. He wanted their hearts to be filled with love as they shared what they had with others. So the Holy Spirit inspired Paul to say in his letter that each person should give what he has decided in his own mind to give. No one should feel forced to give, because "God loves a cheerful giver" (2 Corinthians 9:7). Their offering was important because it would help take care of the poor Christians in Jerusalem, and that would bring praise and glory to God.

Isn't it good to read about God's people sharing their money to help the poor? Paul tells us it was the gospel at work in their hearts that made them want to give. Before we know and love Jesus, we desire the treasures of the world. But when God helps us see how much Jesus has given us—forgiveness of sins and eternal life in heaven—the things of this world don't seem so important anymore. In 2 Corinthians 8:9 Paul reminded his readers that Jesus had done the same for them. "He was rich, but he became poor when he came to earth to die for our sins. Now we can be truly rich because of what he did." And when we understand that everything we have comes from God—including our money—it is easier to share it with others. We know God will supply all we need.

Let's Talk About It!

What is the man giving away in the picture?

How does he feel? Why is that?

When we give, what attitude should we have, according to the Bible?

Let's Talk About It!

Who is Paul writing to?

From the pictures in the small circles, tell what Paul is writing about.

Who helped Paul know just what to write?

A Gift of Righteousness

ROMANS 1–3

Paul's missionary work in Asia and Macedonia kept him from traveling to Rome, but now he was planning a visit. He wrote a letter to let them know he was coming. "I hope to see you on my way to Spain. I hope you can help me on my journey after 'I have enjoyed your company for a while'" (Romans 15:24). First, Paul was going to Jerusalem to deliver the gift the Gentile churches had collected for the poor Christians there. After that, Paul said, he would go to Rome.

Paul's letter to the Roman believers was much more than a note to announce his visit. Paul filled the letter with teaching about Jesus. Having never met Paul, the Romans only knew about him from the stories and reports they'd heard. And not all of the stories about Paul were good, so Paul wanted to tell them about his ministry. Even more important, Paul wanted to tell them about the gospel he was preaching. Once they heard his teaching, Paul was sure the Christians in Rome would welcome him. Paul first explained that it was Jesus who called him to be an apostle. Then, step-by-step, he taught how the gospel saves people from their sin. When the Romans finished reading Paul's letter, they would know exactly what he taught and believed.

Paul quoted from the Old Testament as he explained how everyone is a sinner and needs Jesus. He used the words of King David and said, "As it is written: 'None is righteous, no, not one; no one understands; no one seeks for God. All have turned aside; together they have become worthless; no one does good, not even one'" (Romans 3:10–12). Paul taught that we are all sinners and that none of us can please God on our own. One day everyone will stand before God as our judge who will know each law we have broken—every lie, every angry word, and every evil deed.

Paul's talk about sin must have sounded pretty hopeless. But Paul didn't end his letter there. He also shared the good news of the gospel. It's true that we are all sinners and can't earn forgiveness by doing good works, but God offers to give us his righteousness as a free gift! Jesus came to earth to live a sinless life so he could give his perfect righteous life as a gift to everyone who trusts in him. Then Jesus died in our place so we could be forgiven. That is the good news of the gospel!

Paul was eager to preach the gospel in Rome. But he couldn't wait to tell them about it! So he wrote it all down for them in his letter that they might believe in Jesus too. Paul wrote that he was not ashamed of the gospel, which he said is God's power to save everyone who believes (Romans 1:16). Did you know that God kept Paul's letter to the Romans safe and it is part of our Bible? Today we too can enjoy Paul's letter to the Romans and read his wonderful explanation of the gospel. Paul's letter is just as much God's letter to us as it was his letter to Rome!

Abraham: Father to All by Faith

ROMANS 4:1–25

As the Spirit of God was helping Paul write this letter to the Romans, he reminded Paul of the story of Abraham. Paul knew that false teachers were saying that a person could be saved by obeying the law, but Paul knew God planned to save all people by faith in Jesus. So he explained to the Romans that all the way back to Abraham, God called people to put their trust in what God did for them, not what they did for God. God called Abraham to follow him by faith long before God gave the Ten Commandments to Israel. That means Abraham couldn't have earned his way to heaven by obeying the law, because the law had not been written yet! Paul went on to explain that none of us can work our way to heaven by our good deeds anyway. Even if we tried to obey the Ten Commandments perfectly, we would still make mistakes and sin against God. It only takes one sin to keep us from God, and being sinless is impossible for everyone but Jesus.

If Abraham was saved by his good works, he could have boasted that he earned his own way to heaven. But that is

follow him; God is the one who gave Abraham a son when he was physically too old; and God is the one who promised that Abraham's descendants would be as many as the stars in the sky and the grains of sand on the seashore. If God did all that, what did Abraham do? The answer is very simple, and Paul explained it in Romans 4:3: Abraham believed God's promise and that is what made him right with God. God did all the work and all that Abraham did was put his trust in the work God did. When God saw that Abraham believed and had faith in him, he accepted Abraham into his family and his kingdom. For example, when Abraham was one hundred years old, way too old to have children, he believed God would keep his promise and give him a son. When God saw that Abraham trusted in his plan (which one day would lead to Jesus), God counted Abraham's faith as righteousness. That means that when Jesus died on the cross he died for Abraham's sins too.

The Jewish people say that Abraham is their spiritual father. Paul explained that Abraham was not just the father of the Jews—he is the father of everyone who believes God's plan and puts their faith in Jesus. Through faith in Jesus people from every nation can be accepted by God and is called a child of Abraham. That is how God kept his promise to make Abraham the father of many nations.

So what about us? Do we need to obey the law and try to earn our way to God? Do we work our way to heaven by keeping God's rules and never doing anything wrong? The answer to both is no. God wants us to follow in Abraham's footsteps and put our faith in God's plan of salvation in Christ! God used Paul's letter to the Romans to make it very clear: God accepts us the same way he accepted Abraham. We are saved when we put our faith in God's plan. When we believe that Jesus died on the cross for our sins and was raised from the dead to save us, God counts our faith as righteousness, just like he did with Abraham.

Let's Talk About It!

What Old Testament person was Paul writing about?

What do the stars in the picture represent?

What important word (beginning with the letter "F") was Paul teaching about?

Let's Talk About It!

What do you think the woman in the picture is doing?

Point to the cross.

Why is it important that the tomb behind the cross is empty?

STORY 138

Believe & Confess

ROMANS 9—10

In his letter to the Romans, God used Paul to explain something very important: the good news that we are saved by God's grace. This means salvation is a free gift from God, not something we earn by our good works. In many different ways, Paul showed the Romans that we are not saved by the good things we do; we are saved by the good things Jesus did for us. From the very beginning, it was God's plan to send his Son Jesus to die on the cross for our sins. And it was always God's plan for Gentiles and Jews—people from every nation—to be saved when they put their trust in what Jesus did for them. That is true for us today too.

To help the Romans understand, Paul reminded them of the story of Jacob and Esau. Even though Esau was born first, God told his mother Rebekah that the older son (Esau) would serve his younger brother, Jacob. That is exactly what happened. When the brothers grew up, Esau sold his birthright for a bowl of stew. Later, Jacob stole Esau's blessing by disguising himself as his brother. God passed on to Jacob—not Esau—the promises he had first given to Abraham. Jacob's sons were the ones whose families became the twelve tribes of Israel. And Jesus was born into the tribe of Jacob's son Judah. Paul said that God chose Jacob, not Esau, to carry on the promise so everyone would know that God's choices don't depend on man's traditions or on the good or bad things we do.

In Paul's letter to the Romans God teaches us that no one can be saved by obeying the law of Moses. If we tried

that, we would have to keep all the commandments perfectly, and no one has ever done that except Jesus. We are saved from our sin by trusting in Jesus and what he did for us. Through Paul's letter to the Romans, God still speaks to us, saying, "If you confess with your mouth that Jesus is Lord and believe in your heart that God raised him from the dead, you will be saved" (Romans 10:9). Everyone who asks the Lord to forgive their sins because of what Jesus did will be saved. It doesn't matter if they are Jews or Gentiles. When we hear the good news about Jesus and all he did for us, the Holy Spirit helps our hearts to believe.

That is why it is so important to tell everyone about Jesus. How can people believe in Jesus if they have never heard what he did on the cross and how he rose from the dead? Somebody has to tell them or they will never know. That is why the Holy Spirit guided Paul to quote Isaiah who said: "How beautiful are the feet of those who preach the good news!" (Romans 10:15).

Some people think the good news about Jesus is too good to be true. "It can't be that simple," they say. "How could I be saved just by believing in Jesus? Salvation can't be that easy!" But there is nothing easy about what Jesus did. Jesus gave up his glory in heaven to come to earth as a man. He died a terrible death on the cross when God's anger about our sin was poured out on him. The people he came to save turned their backs on him. None of that was easy. But everything changed when he rose again on the third day! Now Jesus offers us his victory over sin if we believe in him. It might seem easy to us when God gives us faith to believe, but it wasn't easy for Jesus to take the punishment our sins deserved.

Paul in Chains

ACTS 21–28

When the Christians in Jerusalem were persecuted for their faith and left poor, Christians in the churches in Asia heard about it and wanted to help. They collected money to send and gave it to Paul to take to Jerusalem. Now Jerusalem was a dangerous place at that time, but God told Paul he should be the one to present the gift. So he boarded a ship headed for Jerusalem. Along the way, Paul's ship stopped to make deliveries and trade with people in different cities. When the ship stopped at Tyre to unload cargo, the Christians there talked with Paul. They were worried about his safety and told him he shouldn't go on to Jerusalem. On another stop, the prophet Agabus told Paul he would be arrested, tied up, and handed over to the Gentiles by Jews. The Christians there begged Paul to turn back, but Paul knew he had to keep going. He said, "I am ready not only to be imprisoned but even to die in Jerusalem for the name of the Lord Jesus" (Acts 21:13).

When Paul arrived in Jerusalem, things seemed to go well—at first. Jesus' brother James and the other pastors of the church greeted him warmly. They enjoyed sharing what God was doing among them. Paul told how God used him to preach the gospel to the Gentiles, and the other men shared how God was saving thousands of Jews in their city. But those good times didn't last. Before long, unbelieving Jews saw Paul in the temple. They told lies about Paul, which made a crowd so angry that they came to capture and kill Paul. When the Roman guard heard about the riot, they rescued Paul from the angry crowd by arresting him. They would have beaten Paul for causing the disturbance, but when he told them he was a Roman citizen they had to stop. So they kept him under arrest until he could be taken to court.

Paul's arrest didn't satisfy the angry Jewish leaders. They wanted to kill Paul! In fact, more than forty men promised not to eat or drink until Paul was dead, and they hatched a plan to kill him. When Paul's nephew heard about it he warned the Roman soldiers, who sent Paul guarded by two hundred soldiers to the governor. When Paul stood before the Roman governor, the Jews accused him of stirring up riots. But Paul told the governor he had only come to Jerusalem to bring an offering for the poor. Still, the governor decided that Paul would remain in prison until his trial. Later, when the trial finally took place, the Romans were ready to set Paul free. But the Jews argued against this because they wanted Paul dead. Paul knew God wanted him to go to Rome, so he asked the governor for a trial in Rome before Caesar. Because he was a Roman citizen, the governor agreed. Paul was put on a ship as a prisoner to sail to Rome. It was a hard journey. There was even a shipwreck along the way. But three months later Paul arrived safely in Rome.

Once in Rome Paul told the Christians there that he was a prisoner for the Lord. Even then God still used Paul to spread the good news about Jesus. Do you know how? Instead of a prison cell, Paul was placed under house arrest. That meant he was allowed to stay in a home with a single guard to watch him. So even though Paul was in chains, he could still preach! The Romans allowed people to visit Paul, so from morning until night Paul explained the gospel to those who came to visit. Many put their trust in Jesus. The guards watching Paul heard the message too. So you see, even Paul's imprisonment was part of God's plan.

Let's Talk About It!

What does Paul have around his neck and wrist?

Why is Paul in trouble?

Do you think Paul is afraid? Why or why not?

Let's Talk About It!

Who are the two men in the picture?
Why are they in chains?
Why is Paul writing to the Colossians?

The Supremacy of Christ

COLOSSIANS 1—2

While Paul was in prison in Rome, he was joined by another prisoner named Epaphras. Epaphras was also a Christian, called by God to tell others about Jesus. He had started a small church in the city of Colossae after preaching the gospel there. Now that he was in prison with Paul, he told him all about his friends, the Colossians, and how God saved them. Paul and Epaphras prayed together for the Colossian church.

One day Paul decided to send them a letter. Even though he couldn't visit, he could still encourage them and teach them important truths about Jesus and the good news of salvation in his writing. Paul knew that good, solid teaching would help them if any false teaching came along.

Paul began his letter by telling the Colossians that he was praying that their church would learn more about God. Then he began to teach them all about Jesus. Paul taught them things he learned through the Holy Spirit, who helped Paul know what to write. Paul said that Jesus is God and that "all things were created through him and for him" (Colossians 1:16), and Jesus is the one who holds the whole creation together. He added that Jesus is the leader of the church.

Paul also talked a lot about the gospel, saying, "Jesus has rescued us from the kingdom of darkness and brought us into his kingdom." Paul explained that when Jesus died, he took the penalty we deserved for our sin. Because of that we have peace with God. We will not fall under God's judgment for our sin. Even though Paul had not met the Colossian Christians face-to-face, he wanted them to know how concerned he was about them. He wrote, "I am not with you physically, but I am with you in spirit. I am filled with joy about your strong faith in Jesus."

Paul warned the Colossians, "Don't be fooled by false teachers who want to lead you away from Christ. When they make you follow their traditions and keep their rules they are adding to Jesus' work—and no one can do that!" Paul explained, "You started out spiritually dead because of your sin. But God made you alive through Christ. He forgave all your sins by nailing them to the cross. That is all you need! You don't need to follow special laws about what foods to eat and things like that. Those old laws were only meant to point us to Jesus. Now that he has come, you don't need to listen to anyone who says you must follow those laws to be saved. That will never, ever work!"

Paul's letter to the Colossians was passed from church to church. Later, it became part of the Bible with many of Paul's other letters. Today we read these letters and see how Paul shared the gospel with different people. In this letter we see that even though Jesus created the world and holds it together by his power, he was willing to give up his glory to become a man and die on the cross to save us.

Chosen before the World Began

While Paul was in prison in Rome, he often thought about the church he had started in Ephesus. At its beginning God blessed the Ephesian church with great power. God did amazing miracles there: handkerchiefs and aprons that Paul touched were taken to the sick, who were healed and delivered from demons. Paul couldn't visit the Ephesian Christians now because he was in prison, but he prayed for them all the time. He wanted to make sure they were doing well and still trusting in Jesus.

One day Paul's friends brought him some news about the Ephesians. "The church is still strong in its faith," they told him. Paul was so encouraged by the good report that he decided to write them a letter. He wanted to be sure the church would continue trusting Jesus as the only way to be forgiven of their sin and accepted by God.

Paul began his letter with a long praise to God the Father, God the Son, and God the Holy Spirit. Once again, the Holy Spirit was speaking through Paul, showing him things he could never have known by himself. For example, Paul wrote that before the world began God the Father looked down through time and chose us to be his adopted children. Paul also made sure to share the gospel—that Jesus died on the cross to take the punishment for our sins so that we could be forgiven and welcomed into God's family. Paul said that God is able to work everything that happens, in heav-

en and earth, according to his plan. And he reminded the Ephesians that when they believed the gospel story, the Holy Spirit filled them and now lives with them as their guarantee that one day they will go to heaven to be with Jesus.

Paul wanted his friends to know how much he prayed for them. He said, "I never stop thanking God for you. I remember you in my prayers, and I ask our heavenly Father to work in your heart so that you can know him better and better." He encouraged his friends by reminding them that the same power that raised Jesus from the dead was now working in them to keep them close to God. Just thinking about that made Paul so happy that he began a wonderful praise to Jesus. He said God had given Jesus a seat in heaven at his right hand, with more power than any ruler the world has ever seen. God put Jesus in charge of everything and made him the head of the church (Ephesians 1:20–23).

Did you know that Paul lived with the Ephesians and taught them about Jesus for two years? Even so, Paul wanted to make sure they still believed the gospel truth he first shared with them. You see, the gospel is not something we hear once, believe, and never need to hear again. We need to hear the good news about Jesus over and over. Paul never tired of sharing the gospel and telling people about Jesus and how he died for our sins so that we could be forgiven.

Let's Talk About It!

When did Paul say God chose us?

Can you find the world in the picture?

How could God know who we were before we were born?

Let's Talk About It!

What choice do the people in the picture have before them?

What does the cross and the statue represent?

Can you remember having to make a choice like this in your own life?

From Death to Life

ACTS 19; EPHESIANS 2

When Paul first visited Ephesus he discovered that the Ephesian people worshiped idols. They worshiped the goddess Artemis and built a great temple for her. This temple was as big as a football field and over five stories tall. One hundred columns, fifty feet tall, lined the outside of the building, holding up its roof. Many people traveling through Ephesus stopped to visit the temple and worship Artemis. But Artemis was only an idol and could do nothing for the people. Unless they heard about Jesus and put their trust in him, they would die, lost in their sin.

As Paul wrote his letter to the Ephesians, he reminded his friends just how lost they were before they came to know Jesus. Paul said they were once dead in their sins, following the same path as the world and the devil. Paul didn't mean that their bodies were dead. He meant that they were dead spiritually, in their hearts. They couldn't ask the Lord to help them with their sin any more than a physically dead person can ask a doctor to help him with his sickness. They were happy with their idol worship, enjoying the pleasures of the world, doing whatever they wanted. They didn't pay attention to the true God of the Bible at all. Paul reminded them that they were "children of wrath, like the rest of mankind" (Ephesians 2:3). This means they deserved God's judgment and anger because of their sin.

Then Paul, inspired by the Holy Spirit, reminded them of the good news of the gospel. He said that God, who was rich in mercy, saved them from their sin. Even though they were dead in their sins and could not call out to God for help, God made them alive again in Christ so they could believe and be saved by his grace (Ephesians 2:4–5). "By grace" meant that God's salvation was a free gift. Paul explained it this way: "For by grace you have been saved through faith. And this is not your own doing; it is the gift of God, not a result of works, so that no one may boast" (Ephesians 2:8–9).

Paul reminded the Ephesians that, without Jesus, they would be separated from God's promises and God's people. The Ephesians were not part of Israel; they were Gentiles. But when Jesus died on the cross, the walls that separated Jews and the Gentiles tumbled down. Now all people, no matter what tribe or race they are from, are saved the same way—by trusting in Jesus. Jews and Gentiles that believe in Jesus are all part of the same family of faith, the church of Jesus Christ.

Did you know that before God touches our hearts we are spiritually dead and far away from God, just like the Ephesians were? Unless God makes our hearts come alive, we will never follow him. We will just do whatever we want, like the Ephesians once did. But because God loves us, he sends the Holy Spirit to make our hearts come alive and believe in Jesus. Then, like the Ephesians, step-by-step we turn away from our idols to follow the Lord. All this is possible because of the free gift of God's salvation through the death of his Son.

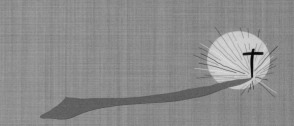

STORY 143

The Gift of Men

ACTS 20:17—38; EPHESIANS 4:1—24

Paul remained in Ephesus for two years, teaching the new Christians about Jesus and how to live for him. Later, Paul returned to the area on his way to Jerusalem, when he was delivering the money the Gentile churches had collected for the poor Christians in Jerusalem. His ship stopped in the city of Miletus. Since Ephesus was only three days away, Paul called for the Ephesian elders to meet him so they could spend time together.

When the Ephesian pastors arrived, Paul told them, "The Holy Spirit is sending me to Jerusalem, but I don't know what will happen to me there, only that prison and sufferings are ahead." Paul told the elders they would never see his face again. What a sad day that was for everyone! The Ephesian elders loved Paul. He was the one who had started their church, taught them the truth about Jesus, and trained them to lead the church after he was gone. Now it was time to say goodbye. But Paul wanted to make sure these men were ready for the challenges soon to come, and he left them some final instructions.

He warned them to be on their guard. "Pay careful attention to yourselves and to the flock God has given you to care for," he said, and continued, "Jesus shed his blood for each one." Then Paul warned the elders to watch out for false teachers. They were so dangerous that Paul called them "fierce wolves" (Acts 20:29). These men would come and try to persuade people to stop following Jesus and leave the church.

When Paul was finished teaching, he said his last goodbyes to his friends. They prayed together and then walked him back to the ship. Paul's words were true. He never saw the Ephesian elders again. But after he was arrested in Jerusalem and put in prison in Rome, Paul did write the Ephesians a letter, which became a part of our Bible. Now we can all learn and grow by reading it.

When you read Paul's letter you see that he wanted the people in Ephesus to know that their leaders were gifts from the Lord. He wrote that God gave his church apostles, prophets, evangelists, shepherds (pastors), and teachers to teach and train us to do the work God wants us to do. God gave the church these leaders, Paul said, to teach his people and to help us grow. That way the people of the church would not be confused and tricked by the false teachers—the fierce wolves Paul had warned their pastors about.

Did you know that the pastor of your church is a gift from God to you, just like the Ephesian pastors were a gift to them? Paul said God gave us these men so they could help us become more like Jesus. We live thousands of years after Paul lived, but God is still caring for his people by giving us leaders in our churches. Pastors are still called by God today to teach us about Jesus and his Word. That way we won't be fooled when we hear things about God that aren't true. If we listen carefully to what our pastors teach us from the Bible, our church can learn to follow Jesus more and more, just like the Ephesian church.

Let's Talk About It!

Who is Paul hugging in the picture?
What is sad in this story?
Who has God given us as gifts?

Putting Off the Old Self

EPHESIANS 4:1—6, 17—32; 5:1—2

As Paul wrote to the Ephesians, he reminded them of all God had done for them and urged them to live for God. Paul wrote, "I want you to live like people who were saved by Jesus. Follow him. Be humble, gentle, and patient with everyone, especially each other. Show love to each other because you aren't separate people, each going your own way anymore. You are part of one body of Christ, guided by one Holy Spirit. You share the same hope: 'one Lord, one faith, one baptism, one God and Father of all, who is over all and through all and in all'" (Ephesians 4:5–6).

This was very different from the way unbelieving Gentiles lived, Paul reminded them. Instead of trusting in Jesus, they hardened their hearts against him. They went their own way and did all kinds of bad, sinful things. Paul knew that many of the Ephesian Christians once lived the same way, but now God had rescued them from that life to follow Jesus. Paul said that becoming a Christian was like starting a whole new way of life. Once people are changed by Jesus, they need to "put off" their old way of life and "put on" a new way of life—to trade one way of living for another. Paul said the old way of life was our sinful life, with all our sinful thoughts. Now that they were following Jesus the Ephesians should "put on the new self" because God had changed their hearts to be like him. Now they could live righteous lives instead of sinning like they did before (Ephesians 4:24).

For example, Paul said, instead of lying—that's the old self—they should tell the truth. That's putting on the new self and living like Jesus. Instead of stealing—that's the old self—they should put on the new self and work for what they need, sharing with people who don't have enough. Instead of talking sinfully, like the old self does, they should put on the new self and use their words to encourage people. Instead of being unforgiving and angry, saying unkind things about people like the old self would, they should be kind, tenderhearted, and forgiving, just like God is when he forgives us. That is the new self.

Because the Holy Spirit inspired Paul's words, they are God's Word for us too. Just like the Ephesians, God wants us to "put off" the old self of sin and "put on" the new self to be more like Jesus. It is like having an old tattered coat and getting a brand-new one. Before you can wear the new one, you have to take the old one off and toss it aside. But that isn't something we just make up our minds to do. If God's Spirit isn't living in us we don't have the power to change. We can't just decide to live for God on our own. God changes our hearts first; only then will we follow him and want to live to please God and put off the old self. Paul encouraged the Ephesians to always remember the gospel. He said, "Walk in love, as Christ loved us and gave himself up for us, a fragrant offering and sacrifice to God" (Ephesians 5:2). Day by day as we remember what Jesus did for us, we put off the old self of sin and, with the Holy Spirit's help, we become more like Jesus, the one we love.

Let's Talk About It!

What has the man on the left taken off and tossed aside?

Can you list two things that are a part of the "old self"?

What does God want to help you leave behind to follow Jesus?

Let's Talk About It!

What is your favorite piece of God's armor?

Why is the sword different from the other pieces of armor?

Why do we need this armor?

The Armor of God

EPHESIANS 6:10–20

While Paul was waiting for his trial in Rome, he lived chained in a house, guarded by Roman soldiers. As the days passed different soldiers took turns guarding Paul morning, noon, and night. That meant Paul spent a lot of time around his Roman guards. He saw their armor and their swords at their sides. A soldier was probably with Paul the whole time he wrote his letter to the Ephesians. The Holy Spirit used the soldiers to give Paul an idea. Paul wanted to encourage the Ephesians in a way that even children could understand. So he talked about the armor of his Roman guards to teach the Ephesians how to fight their battles with sin and the devil.

Every Christian, Paul said, is in a battle with God's enemies. Paul wrote, "Be strong in the Lord and in the strength of his might. Put on the whole armor of God, that you may be able to stand against the schemes of the devil" (Ephesians 6:10–11). Then Paul named each part of the soldier's armor and used it to teach how the gospel protects us against our enemies.

Paul called the soldier's belt "the belt of truth." God's Word is our truth, and when we wrap it around our lives like a belt, it holds everything together. He called the breastplate that protects the soldier's chest "the breastplate of righteousness." Even though we are all sinners, Christians are protected and covered by the righteousness of Christ. Jesus' sinless life covers our sin so now we are forgiven. A Roman soldier's shoes were specially made to help him bravely run

into battle. They are like the gospel, Paul said. The good news gives us courage to run and tell everyone about Jesus because we know the gospel message can change the hearts of our enemies and bring peace.

The shield Christians hold up is "the shield of faith." When the devil shoots his fiery arrows of lies and accusations at us, we can hold up our faith in Jesus to keep from being hit. On our heads we wear the "helmet of salvation." When Satan wants to discourage us with the evil things he says and does, our salvation keeps us from believing his lies and giving up. Finally, God gives us a sword to go with our armor, a weapon we can use to go out and fight—and that is the Word of God. It is so powerful that nothing can win a battle against it, so we should never be without it.

Do you see how all the armor, even the sword, point back to the good news about Jesus? Paul learned he could trust the gospel to protect him and keep him strong even when he was suffering, beaten, and thrown in jail. When we "put on the armor," we are really putting on the gospel and believing what it says. The armor helps us remember we are well protected when we put our trust in Jesus. And with God's Word as our sword, we can cut down Satan's lies just like Jesus did when Satan tempted him in the wilderness.

The Humility of Christ

ACTS 16:6—15;
PHILIPPIANS 2:1—11

While he was under arrest, Paul spent a lot of time praying for the different churches he started. One of the churches he prayed for was in Philippi, a city in Macedonia not far from the sea. Did you know Paul hadn't even planned to visit Philippi? He was going in the opposite direction, but the Holy Spirit stopped him and gave Paul a vision of a Macedonian man who was calling out, "Come over to Macedonia and help us" (Acts 16:9). So Paul obeyed God's leading and that is how he got to Philippi. When he arrived Paul told the people about Jesus, and many of them believed. Soon they started the Philippian church.

Now that Paul was in prison, he couldn't visit his friends in Philippi, so he decided to write them a letter. He wanted to encourage them, teach them, and remind them to keep following Jesus. Paul started his letter by writing, "I thank God every time I remember you. Whenever I pray for you, I am filled with joy because from the first day I met you until now, we have worked together for Jesus. I am sure that God who began this good work in you will keep it going. He will finish his work in you when Jesus Christ comes back."

Paul knew that if the Philippian church was going to stay strong, the people would need to live like Jesus lived. He told them, "Don't just think about yourselves. Think about each other. Be humble. Take care of other people as if they are more important than you are." As he wrote, the Holy Spirit reminded Paul that Jesus was the best example of humility the world has ever seen. So Paul pointed the Philippians to Jesus, who gave up all the wonderful things he had in heaven to come and help us. As God, Jesus could have stayed where angels loved and worshiped him, but instead Jesus left his place in heaven to become a little human baby in a manger. Finally, Paul said, he was willing to die on the cross for our sins (Philippians 2:8). The perfect Son of God, who had never done anything wrong, died like a criminal because he wanted to take the punishment we deserved.

Because of his great sacrifice God the Father praised and honored Jesus and gave to him a name above all others, so one day everyone in heaven and on earth and under the earth will bow down when they hear the name "Jesus." And one day every person will honor Jesus Christ as the Lord over all. Paul told his friends, "Think about how Jesus lived for us and live like him. If you do, you will shine like lights in a dark world. I will know my work and prayers for you will not be wasted, even though I can't be with you."

None of us can really understand what it was like for Jesus to become a man and take our punishment. Paul said for Jesus to come from heaven to earth was like making himself nothing. Paul knew that if the Philippians could remember all Jesus gave up to serve them, it would help them love and serve each other. We need to remember that too. Jesus traded his glory in heaven with God the Father for a terrible death on a cross for all of us. Our lives should show how thankful we are for this wonderful gift we don't deserve.

Let's Talk About It!

Where is Jesus now, here on earth or in heaven?

What did Jesus do to humble himself?

What can we do to walk in humility?

Keep Your Eyes on the Prize

ACTS 16:16–40;
PHILIPPIANS 3

When Paul first preached the gospel in Macedonia, one of the very first Philippians to become a Christian was a guard at the prison. It happened this way: Paul and Silas were arrested, beaten, and thrown in prison for the work of the gospel. While the Philippian jailer guarded their cell, Paul and Silas started singing and praising God. Around midnight God sent a great earthquake to shake the prison. The cell doors flew open and the chains fell off the prisoners. When the guard saw what had happened, he thought the prisoners had escaped, and he was going to kill himself. But Paul called out to him to stop and said that none of the prisoners had left. The jailer was stunned and called out to Paul and asked, "What must I do to be saved?" (Acts 16:30). Paul told him to believe in Jesus, and that is just what he did. That night the jailer and his whole family trusted in Jesus and were baptized.

Later, when Paul was writing his letter to the Philippians as a prisoner in Rome, he made sure to tell them that God was using his imprisonment in Rome to spread the gospel too. Paul wrote, "Everyone in the imperial guard knows I am a prisoner because of my love for Christ. And my Christian brothers aren't afraid because of what has happened to me. God has made them even braver when they talk about Je-

sus!" Just like in Philippi, God was using Paul's time in jail to bring the good news about Jesus to more and more people. God taught Paul that even a hard thing like being in jail could be part of God's wonderful plan to spread the gospel.

For Paul, the most important things in life were to know and trust Jesus. Paul said that compared to Jesus everything else was rubbish! He meant that it was worthless compared to knowing Jesus. That's why Paul

tried harder to live like Jesus and become more and more like him every day. Paul knew he wasn't perfect, but he said, "One thing I do: forgetting what lies behind and straining forward to what lies ahead, I press on toward the goal for the prize of the upward call of God in Christ Jesus" (Philippians 3:13–14). Paul couldn't wait to get to heaven and see Jesus, and Paul wanted that for the Philippians too. Instead of getting excited about the things of this world, Paul said, "Remember, your real home is in heaven. Someday Jesus will come back for us, and when he does, he will change our earthly bodies to be like his glorious body." Won't that be amazing! The world promises to make us happy if we run after earthly treasures like money, or becoming famous, or gaining a lot of things. With all that tempting us, it's easy to forget about the real treasure we have in Jesus. Even though he had been very successful before he became a Christian, Paul knew that Jesus was the most important treasure of all. You see, Paul was born a Jew and grew up to be an important Pharisee. But when God saved him he gave it all up to follow Jesus. Like the Philippians who first read his letter, we can imitate Paul's life and follow the example he left for us.

Let's Talk About It!

Who are the men in the picture?

How did the chains come off Paul and Silas?

What happened to the guard?

Let's Talk About It!

What is the pastor, the tall man, doing?

What are his children doing?

Why do you think this man makes a good pastor?

Character Counts

ACTS 16:1—5; PHILIPPIANS 2:19—22;
1 TIMOTHY

Before Paul's imprisonment in Rome, he took time to visit a few of the cities where he had first preached the gospel. During one of his stops, some Christians in Lystra introduced him to a young Christian man named Timothy. Timothy loved the Lord. His mother had taught him from the Bible since he was a child. Paul was so impressed that he invited Timothy to travel with him. Timothy agreed and as they worked together, the two men became close friends. Paul taught Timothy how to care for God's people, and Timothy helped Paul with the work of ministry. Paul came to love Timothy so much he called him his son. After Timothy's time of training was over, Paul sent him on his own visits to the churches Paul started, where Timothy would help train the leaders and care for the people.

One church Timothy visited was the church in Philippi. Paul wrote ahead to them in his letter saying, "I hope God allows me to send Timothy to you soon. That way I can be cheered up by the good news he sends me about you. I have no one else like him. He really cares about what is best for you. Other people care more about themselves than they do about Jesus. But Timothy has worked with me like a son with a father and has proven to be someone who wants to serve the Lord."

Even after Timothy left, Paul continued teaching and encouraging Timothy by letter. He gave Timothy special instructions to help him recognize what to look for in a man called to be a pastor.

"Those who want to become a leader of God's people," Paul wrote, "must be able to teach and have a heart and life that honors God. It is important to God that pastors lead their people by their example, not just their words." Paul gave Timothy a list of character qualities Timothy could use to decide if men were ready to be pastors. Paul said a pastor should have only one wife. He should be a man who knows self-control. He should be a careful thinker whom people respect. He should enjoy opening his home to people. He should be gentle, not someone who likes to argue. He should not be a violent person or a lover of money. Paul also wrote that a pastor must lead his own family well, because if someone does not know how to take care of his own family, "how will he care for God's church?" (1 Timothy 3:4–5).

Paul gave Timothy a similar list for deacons and their wives. Paul knew how important it was for leaders to have godly character. That way, people would not be led into sin by leaders they trusted.

Did you know that the way we live as Christians affects what others think about Jesus? That's why it's so important for pastors to live lives that honor God. Pastors lead by example. If the pastors of a church are sinning and don't repent, they can lead the people who follow them into sin. Unbelievers who are watching might think the gospel isn't true. But when pastors are changed by Jesus and live in a way that honors him, the whole church learns how to trust and obey God. Others who are looking on see that Christians are different. Soon they want to know Jesus too.

God Breathed the Scriptures

2 TIMOTHY 3:1—17

After Paul had lived under house arrest for a while, the Romans let him go. Right away, Paul started traveling again to tell people about Jesus. But before long Paul was arrested again and put back into jail in Rome. This time Paul didn't think the Romans would let him go. He believed they would put him to death. Paul's friend, Luke, who wrote the Gospel of Luke and the book of Acts, visited Paul and spent time with him. Paul also really wanted to see Timothy, the man he called his dearly loved son in the faith. He wrote Timothy a letter and asked him twice to come to Rome. Paul was hoping to see Timothy before he died.

This must have been a hard time for Paul. Although Paul knew he would soon pass away, he knew God's Word and the gospel would carry on. The good news he shared with people was not just the words and ideas of men. It was the inspired Word of God—God's thoughts and words given by the Holy Spirit to men who wrote them down. That is why Paul wrote about the importance of God's Word in his last letter to Timothy: "Do not be ashamed of the story of Jesus, and don't be ashamed that I am in prison. God's power can help you through your challenges too. Remember that God called us to spread the gospel—a plan he thought of before the world was

even created." Paul told Timothy to pass on the teaching he'd heard from Paul to faithful men. After that, Paul wanted those men to teach others, so God's message would be passed on forever. The Romans might be able to put Paul in chains, but nothing could stop God's Word from advancing.

Paul also told Timothy to teach patiently and carefully so his message would always be true to God's Word. "Remember how important the Bible has been in your life," Paul reminded Timothy. "Ever since you were a child, your mother Eunice and grandmother Lois taught you the Word of God. This is what opened your mind to faith in Jesus." Paul wrote, "All Scripture is breathed out by God" (2 Timothy 3:16). And Paul said all Scripture is useful for teaching us the truth, for showing us when we are wrong, for showing us how to put things right, and for learning how to be holy and righteous as God wants us to be.

God's Word is so valuable that Timothy should be ready to preach it whenever he could—"in season and out of season," Paul said. But he warned Timothy that not everyone would listen. Some would turn away from the truth to follow false teachers. Finally, Paul asked Timothy to do his best to come before winter and to bring his books and a cloak he'd left behind. Most of all Paul wanted Timothy to bring his parchments, which were probably Paul's copies of the Scripture.

Did you know what Paul meant when he said that the Bible was "breathed out by God"? Paul wanted us to know that even though God used men to write down his Word, God was at work through the Holy Spirit, directing what they wrote. His Holy Spirit was working in their hearts to tell them what to say and help them remember what Jesus said, so that their words were God's words. Jesus said that "every word" comes from the "mouth of God" (Matthew 4:4). That's why even though it was written by the hands of men, we call it the Word of God.

Let's Talk About It!

Who is helping Paul write?
What is he writing?
Why is that important for us?

Let's Talk About It!

What did James say starts our quarrels and fights?

What are the girls fighting over in the picture?

Why do you think they love this more than God?

The Heart's Desires

JAMES 4:1–10

Did you know that Jesus was not the only child in Mary and Joseph's family? The Bible mentions four brothers: James, Joseph, Simeon, and Judas. At first Jesus' brothers did not believe he was the Messiah. But after his resurrection Jesus appeared to James, and by the time the Holy Spirit came down at Pentecost, Jesus' brothers believed and were present praying with the other disciples in the upper room. Of all the brothers, James played the most important role. He became the leader of the church in Jerusalem. Paul went to see James after he became a Christian. And later, when Paul brought the gift of money to the church in Jerusalem, he delivered it to James.

God used James to help the church at a time of confusion. When the Gentiles first started becoming Christians, the leaders in the Jerusalem church didn't know what to think about it. But James, who led the council, spoke up to welcome the new Gentile Christians into God's family. James decided that the church leaders should write a letter to help the Gentile Christians understand how to live the Christian life. That short letter was the first letter the apostles sent to guide the new churches. Many other letters followed. James himself wrote a letter to teach Jewish believers who were scattered in different churches. God preserved his letter, and it became a part of our Bible so we could benefit from his teaching too.

In his letter James asked his readers a question: "What causes you to quarrel and fight with each other?" That was an important question since everyone has a quarrel or a fight now and then. We usually like to blame others when we get angry, but James knew our anger and sin come from inside our hearts. He said, "The reason you fight is because you don't get what you want." Instead of loving God more, we love our things more. When someone tries to take away what we want or keep us from getting what we desire, we become angry. It happens with little children, and it happens with adults.

James also said, "You don't have the things you want because you don't ask God for them. Or, when you do ask, God doesn't give it to you because you want it all for yourself." James knew that we are supposed to love God more than the things of this world. If we love God most we won't become angry when we lose something or have it taken away. The next time you get angry think about what James said. Ask yourself this important question: what did I want that I did not get?

James wanted to help Christians know when they were drifting away from loving God to loving the things of this world. He wanted them to remember that Jesus is the greatest treasure we can ever have. Our salvation should bring us a greater joy and peace than any earthly treasure. Jesus said the things of this world will all pass away, but heavenly treasure will never pass away! If we remember what Jesus did for us on the cross, which is the greatest gift and treasure of all, the things of this world won't seem so important to us.

Born Again!

1 PETER 1:1–12

James and Paul were not the only men the Holy Spirit inspired to write letters to believers around the world. The apostle Peter also wrote letters, and two of them are in our Bibles today. He wrote to encourage Christians in a place called Asia Minor, who were being persecuted for their faith. They were being treated poorly, insulted, and even beaten for believing in Jesus.

Peter knew that the best way to encourage Christians is to remind them of what Jesus has already done for them. He began his first letter this way: "Blessed be the God and Father of our Lord Jesus Christ! According to his great mercy, he has caused us to be born again to a living hope through the resurrection of Jesus Christ from the dead" (1 Peter 1:3). Peter knew that suffering Christians needed to remember that Jesus had already won our greatest battle. Jesus won the victory over sin and death, and prepared a place for us in heaven where there will be no more suffering. Peter also explained that God was in control of their lives. He allowed the hard things so their faith could get stronger.

Peter had seen Jesus heal the sick and raise the dead. He heard Jesus teach and watched as Jesus was arrested and crucified. Most exciting of all, Peter spent time talking to Jesus after he rose from the dead. But most of the Christians he was writing to had never seen Jesus. They had only heard about him, yet they had put their trust in him. Peter wanted them to know that because of their faith, God would give them a reward in heaven that would never run out, spoil, or fade away.

Peter ended his first letter by encouraging them to live humble lives and to trust in God's mighty power to take care of them. He warned them that the devil prowls around like a roaring lion, looking for someone to attack. But Peter knew the devil was not as strong as God so he told them, "Stand up to him and be strong in your faith, because Christians around the world are going through the same kinds of sufferings. After you have suffered a little while, God will strengthen you and help you to stand."

Did you ever think that God is the one who sends trials—hard things—into your life? At first that doesn't seem like something God would do. But God knows that difficulty and hard times can help us grow in our faith. People often pray more when they are going through a trial. They know they have to depend on God when times are hard, but that's easy to forget when life is easy. God uses trials to help our trust in him to grow. Trials also help us to look forward to heaven, when we will be with Jesus and all our trials will end. Knowing that God is in control of our difficult days and they are for our good can help us trust in him to make it through.

Let's Talk About It!

Who did Peter compare to a lion in this story?

What weapon do we have to fight against him?

What hard thing has God sent into your life?

Let's Talk About It!

What is the sword doing to the heart in the picture?

What is coming out of the heart?

Why does God want us to see the sin in our hearts?

God's Word Is Living

HEBREWS 4:12—16

There is a mystery about the book of Hebrews—we don't know who wrote it! Some people think it must have been the apostle Paul, but others disagree because Paul began all his other letters by mentioning his name. Other people think it might have been a teacher named Apollos. Luke said Apollos was a man who spoke wisely and understood the Scriptures (Acts 18:24). When he taught in public he was able to prove that the Jews' arguments against Jesus were wrong, using the Scriptures to show that Jesus was the Messiah (Acts 18:28).

Although we don't know if it was Apollos, whoever wrote the book of Hebrews used the Old Testament to prove that Jesus was the promised Messiah the same way Apollos did. For example, the Holy Spirit inspired him to explain how all the Old Testament sacrifices pointed to Jesus' death on the cross. He also compared the high priests of Israel to Jesus, who is our high priest. The high priests of old sacrificed thousands of lambs for the sins of Israel, but Jesus, the Lamb of God, gave up his life for our sins as the last sacrifice for all time (Hebrews 7:27).

The writer of Hebrews reminded his readers that in Moses' day the people hardened their hearts against God's Word. Because of that they were not allowed to go into the Promised Land. "Don't follow their bad example," he warned. "Today, if you hear his voice, do not harden your hearts as [the Israelites did] in the rebellion" (Hebrews 3:15).

To help his readers understand just how powerful God's Word is the writer of Hebrews wrote, "The word of God is living and active, sharper than any two-edged sword" (Hebrews 4:12). God's Word can cut deep into our hearts to show us what we really want and desire. We can say we love God, but deep inside our hearts we might really love something else more. The Holy Spirit can use the sharp sword of God's Word to open our hearts and show us our sin.

Did you know that the Bible is the only book that is living and active? The gospel is more than the words of a story written on a piece of paper. The Holy Spirit touches our hearts as we read it. He helps us understand what we read, and he helps us want to do what it says. That's why the Bible is living and active—God works through it to change our lives. The Bible tells us that Jesus is the Word of God who became a man to live among us. God uses Jesus' words and the gospel story of his life to bring us salvation. No other book can do that!

STORY 153

By Faith

HEBREWS 11

The person who wrote the book of Hebrews wanted his readers to understand something very important: everyone in the Old Testament and the New Testament became a part of God's family the same way—by their faith in God. The writer of Hebrews described faith this way: "Faith is being sure of what we hope for and believing things we do not see." When you believe God created the world by the words he spoke, you trust him by faith. You didn't see him do it, but you believe it is true. The book of Hebrews has a long list of people who believed God for great things they could not see. Here are some of the people who had faith.

Abel offered God a sacrifice because he had faith. By faith Enoch pleased God with his life and was taken up to heaven without dying. By faith Noah built an ark. Even though he didn't see any rain, he trusted God's word. By faith Abraham obeyed God's call to leave his home, even though he did not know where God was sending him. Abraham lived in tents, following God, looking forward

to the heavenly city God was preparing for him, even though he couldn't see it. By faith his wife Sarah had a baby who fulfilled God's promise, even though she was very old. By faith she and Abraham believed God's promise to make Abraham's descendants as many as the stars in the sky and as uncountable as the grains of sand on the seashore.

The list in Hebrews keeps going. By faith Abraham offered Isaac as a sacrifice because he believed God could raise him from the dead. Moses was hidden by his mother because of her faith in God. Moses refused to stay with the Egyptians but joined the people of God because he had faith in their God. He trusted God as he led the people out of Egypt. He kept the Passover and put the blood of the lamb on the doorpost because he believed what God told him. By faith the people of God marched through the Red Sea on dry ground. Because she believed in Israel's God, Rahab hid Israel's spies from the rulers of Jericho. If the writer of Hebrews had wanted to, he could have talked about many other people who walked with God by faith, like Gideon, Samson, David, Samuel and others.

Did you know that faith is still the way we please and follow God today? By faith we believe that Jesus died on the cross for our sins. By faith we believe he rose from the dead. By faith we believe that Jesus has gone back to heaven to prepare a place for every believer. By faith, like Abraham, we look forward to the heavenly city built by God, where we will live forever. One day everyone who believes in Jesus will join the great heroes of the faith, like Abraham, Moses, Sarah, and Rahab, worshiping the Lord together. In fact, the writer of Hebrews tells us that "without faith it is impossible to please [God]" (Hebrews 11:6).

Let's Talk About It!

What does the blindfold on the man have to do with faith?
Name some of the people in the Old Testament who lived by faith.
What does God want you to believe by faith?

Let's Talk About It!

What is the boy doing with the little girl in the picture?

Why is there a cross behind him?

How do you think his sharing makes the girl feel?

Loving One Another

1 JOHN 3:1—4:19

When Jesus talked about the laws in the Old Testament, he said you could sum them up with just two commands: "You shall love the Lord your God with all your heart and with all your soul and with all your mind….And…you shall love your neighbor as yourself" (Matthew 22:37, 39). Matthew, Mark, and Luke included these words in their Gospels, and Paul and James put them in their letters too. But no one wrote about God's love more than the apostle John. John was the one who wrote down the new command Jesus gave his disciples the night before he died (John 13:34–35). Jesus said, "I am giving you a new commandment: love one another. You should love one another just as I have loved you. That is how people will know you are my disciples, by your love for one another."

John was still thinking about love when he later wrote a letter to the churches Paul began in Asia. He told them that loving one another was the message they had heard from the very beginning. He warned them not to be like Cain, who killed his brother. Instead, they should be like Jesus, who showed us how to love. John wrote, "By this we know love, that [Jesus] laid down his life for us, and we ought to lay down our lives for the brothers" (1 John 3:16). John knew it is easy to say "I love you" but then not do anything about it. He said, "Little children, let us not love in word or talk but in deed and in truth" (1 John 3:18). How can we say we have God's love if we don't share what we have with someone in need? It's good to say we love someone but even better to show our love by what we do. That is how God loved us when he gave up his only Son Jesus to die on the cross for our sins.

Did you know the Holy Spirit inspired John to use the word "love" twenty-four times in his short letter? God wanted the early church, and all of us who can read John's letter in our Bible to know that love is at the center of all we do, and that the reason we should love others is because of the love Jesus showed us on the cross. John wrote, "We love because he first loved us" (1 John 4:19). Before God changes our hearts, we only think of ourselves. But when God opens our eyes to believe and see how Jesus loved us when he died for us, we want to show that same love to others. If you are struggling to love someone, remember the gospel and how God demonstrated his love for you by giving Jesus to die on the cross. Then ask God to change your heart so you can show that kind of love toward others too.

Worthy Is the Lamb

GENESIS 49; REVELATION 5

When Jacob was on his deathbed, he called his twelve sons and said, "Gather yourselves together so I can tell you what will happen to you in days to come." Then, starting with his oldest son Reuben, Jacob gave each son a prophecy about his future. When he came to Judah, Jacob said, "Judah is a lion's cub," and "the scepter [of leadership] shall not depart from Judah" (Genesis 49:9–10). This meant that the leaders of Israel would come from Judah's family. We know that Judah died, but a ruler did come from his family who fulfilled Jacob's word about his son. Jesus came from the tribe of Judah and was crucified as "King of the Jews." But Jesus didn't stay in the tomb like the other kings of Judah; he rose again and went back to his Father in heaven, to hold the scepter of leadership forever.

Years later when the apostle John was very old, the Roman emperor sent him to the island of Patmos as a punishment for his faith. While he was on that island God sent an angel to John in a vision. He told John how the prophecy God first gave Jacob would be fulfilled by Jesus. John wrote down the vision in what we now call the book of Revelation. In John's vision God held a scroll sealed with seven seals. John wrote,

"I saw a strong angel proclaiming with a loud voice, 'Who is worthy to open the scroll and break its seals?' And no one in heaven or on earth or under the earth was able to open the scroll or to look into it" (Revelation 5:2–3). John began to cry because no one was able to open God's scroll. The scroll represented God's plan to bring an end to sin once and for all, and to bring all his children into heaven. Only someone God the Father approved could even try to open it. Then, suddenly, one of the elders told John to stop crying. There was one person who could break the seals and open the scroll—"the Lion of the tribe of Judah." But when John looked for the Lion, he saw a Lamb who looked as though he had been sacrificed.

The Lamb and the Lion both represent Jesus Christ. Jesus was sacrificed like a lamb for our sins, but he conquered sin and death like a mighty lion. Jesus the Lamb reached for the scroll, and God the Father allowed him to take it. Then the four living creatures and the twenty-four elders began singing a new song that never had been sung before. They sang to Jesus, "You are worthy to take the scroll and to open its seals, because you were slain, and your blood has saved 'people for God from every tribe and language and people and nation.'" (Revelation 5:9). Then everyone in heaven joined in saying, "Worthy is the Lamb who was slain, to receive power and wealth and wisdom and might and honor and glory and blessing!" (Revelation 5:12). Jacob's far-off great-grandson Jesus, the Lion of the Tribe of Judah, was able to open the scroll!

Isn't it amazing to know that God planned to bring us his salvation through Jesus thousands of years before Jesus was ever born? Way back then, God gave Jacob a prophetic word for his son Judah that looked ahead to Jesus' first coming. Today, in the book of Revelation, God gives us a look ahead to Jesus' second coming. When we read John's revelation, we look ahead to the day when Jesus will come again to take the scroll of God's plan of salvation, break open its seal, and complete God's saving plan.

Let's Talk About It!

Why are all the people so excited?
Why did John call Jesus the Lamb?
Why is Jesus also called a Lion?

At the Throne Worshiping

REVELATION 7:9—17

Have you ever read the last chapter of a book first so you would know ahead of time how it ended? When God gave John the vision of Revelation to write down for all of us, he was letting us see what happened at the end of his story. Revelation gives us a peek at the last days. We might still have hard times here on earth, but we can be sure that Jesus has won the battle against sin and death. The book of Revelation tells us that one day all his children will join him in heaven. Jesus, the Lamb of God, will bring an end to the curse of sin that ruined his wonderful creation.

In his vision on the island of Patmos, John got to see how all of God's plan of salvation works out in the end. He wrote, "After this I looked and saw people in a group so big that no one could count them, from every nation, from all tribes and peoples and languages. They all stood in front of the throne of Jesus, wearing white robes, with palm branches in their hands. They cried out with a loud voice, 'Salvation belongs to our God who sits on the throne, and to the Lamb!'" (Revelation 7:10).

Then more people than John could count fell on their faces to worship God. God had once promised Abraham that his descendants would be like the sand of the seashore, and now it had all come true. When John was asked if he knew who the people in the white robes were, he didn't know the answer. But then he was told they were all the people who believed in Jesus, whose robes were washed white, cleansed of their sin by the blood of Jesus.

You and I still sin every day, but in John's vision no one was sinning anymore! Everyone who stood in front of God's throne was worshiping and serving him day and night in his temple. In heaven our sin is gone and so is our suffering. John writes, "No one will be hungry or thirsty ever again. The sun and scorching heat won't burn them. The Lamb of God who sits on the throne will be their shepherd. They will live forever and 'God will wipe away every tear from their eyes'" (Revelation 7:16–17).

Do you remember how this wonderful story began? Adam and Eve enjoyed living with God in the garden, but after they sinned they had to leave it all behind. People became more and more wicked until the days of Noah, when God destroyed the earth with a flood. After they left the ark people sinned just as much as before, so God confused their language at Babel. From then on people went their own way, hating God and each other—until Jesus came. Jesus conquered death and broke the power of sin so we could love and obey God. One day Jesus will come back to destroy the power of sin forever and to welcome people from every nation into heaven.

The book of Revelation gives us a sneak peek at how everything in God's plan will finally happen. God's promise to step on the head of the serpent and bring people together from every nation will one day come true. Until Jesus comes back our faith can get stronger by reading the end of the story. If you put your trust in Jesus and what he did on the cross, one day you will be there with millions of others, worshiping at the throne of God. You will join all the believers who ever lived and take your place in the last chapter of God's gospel story. What a great day that will be!

Come back soon, Lord Jesus!

Let's Talk About It!

Why are all the people wearing white robes?

Who is at the center of the picture?

How is this a picture of the way we should live?

the Gospel Story for Kids

Marty Machowski

A Unique Program Connecting Children to the Gospel Story from Genesis to Revelation

An interactive program for home and classroom that grounds children in gospel-centered, biblical truth. Children who begin this program at age three and continue through age twelve will have absorbed the gospel story from Genesis to Revelation three times. At each age level children are taught the gospel through age-appropriate illustrations, activities, coloring pages, object lessons, and memorization.

Three-year 156 story, Sunday school curriculum for preschool through upper elementary.

(NT available January 2013)

Two companion family devotionals, *Long Story Short* (OT) and *Old Story New* (NT) that follow the same 156 stories as the Sunday school curriculum and reinforce the gospel story at home.

An illustrated Bible storybook, *The Gospel Story Bible*, highlights the same 156 stories for churches and families.